THE I TATTI
RENAISSANCE LIBRARY

James Hankins, General Editor

HUMANIST TRAGEDIES

ITRL 45

HUMANIST TRAGEDIES

TRANSLATED BY

GARY R. GRUND

THE I TATTI RENAISSANCE LIBRARY

HARVARD UNIVERSITY PRESS

CAMBRIDGE, MASSACHUSETTS

LONDON, ENGLAND

2011

Printed in the United States of America

Series design by Dean Bornstein

Library of Congress Cataloging-in-Publication Data

Humanist tragedies / translated by Gary R. Grund.
p. cm.—(The I Tatti Renaissance library ; 45)
In Latin, with English translations.
Includes bibliographical references and index.
ISBN 978-0-674-05725-8 (alk. paper)
1. Latin drama, Medieval and modern—Translations into English. 2. Latin drama (Tragedy)—Translations into English. 3. Latin drama, Medieval and modern. 4. Latin drama (Tragedy) 5. Humanism—Drama. I. Grund, Gary R. (Gary Robert), 1946– II. Mussato, Albertino, 1261–1329. Ecerinis. English & Latin. III. Loschi, Antonio, d. 1441. Achilles. English & Latin. IV. Corraro, Gregorio, 1411–1464. Progne. English & Latin. V. Dati, Leonardo, 1408–1472. Hyempsal. English & Latin. VI. Verardus, Marcellinus. Fernandus servatus. English & Latin.
PA8165.H87 2011
872′.0308—dc22 2010040617

Contents

Introduction

The Idea of Tragedy

As it developed during the Italian Renaissance, humanist tragedy proved to be a much less popular and stable literary form than its sister genre, humanist comedy. Ancient comedy—Latin New Comedy in particular—was more broadly attractive to Latin humanists of the quattrocento (and to later vernacular writers as well) because, unlike ancient tragedy, it presented narratives drawn from ordinary life. Comedy turned on human imperfections, and its events were unheroic; it drew its inspiration from the ageless commonplaces of love, money, sex, and manners. Tragedy was always about great ones, powerful men and women trapped in situations demanding impossible choices, so it was perhaps natural that it would have a more limited appeal. It may very well be that although humanist tragedy began much earlier than comedy—Albertino Mussato's *Ecerinis* was written in 1314—it turned out to have a much shorter shelf life precisely because, as always, the chamber pots of comedy were more easily adaptable to daily life than the ill-starred misfortunes of kings.

The plays of Plautus (third century BCE) and especially of Terence (second century BCE), moreover, on which Italian humanists based their Latin comedies, continued to enrich the culture of the West long after the performing traditions of Latin New Comedy had died out. Their twenty-seven surviving plays were adapted, redacted, and easily absorbed into the academic milieus of the Middle Ages and early Renaissance, especially as pedagogical models of Latin style and a source of moral maxims. Sources for ancient tragedy were less readily available. Ancient Greek models for tragedy did not become widely available until the cinquecento, when the plays of Sophocles and Euripides were first translated into Latin and then the vernacular.[1] The nine Latin tragedies the

Renaissance attributed to Seneca (first century CE) — on whose plays the humanist tragedies included in this volume were all modeled to one degree or another — were the only surviving sources for Roman tragedy. They were little known before the late thirteenth century. With their recovery by early Paduan humanists, the Renaissance tradition of Senecan tragedy was launched. The five humanist tragedies in this volume — Albertino Mussato's *Ecerinis* (1314), Antonio Loschi's *Achilles* (ca. 1390), Gregorio Correr's *Procne* (ca. 1427/30), Leonardo Dati's *Hiempsal* (ca. 1440/42), and Marcellino Verardi's *Ferdinand Preserved* (1493) — constitute a representative sampling of Latin tragedies written during the trecento and quattrocento. In addition to tracking the gradual mastery of Senecan verse achieved by Italian humanists, they reflect the wider changes in the literary and cultural conventions that occurred during the period. Mussato's crude attempt to out-Seneca Seneca in the presentation of bloody sensationalism, the rhetorical flourishes of set speeches, and the terror of Fortune's unruly wheel culminates, at the end of the period, in a problematizing of the tragic genre itself, exemplified by Verardi's *tragicomedia*. Here was a work that pioneered the cross-fertilization of genres in a development that would prove significant for the future of drama.

Yet from its very beginnings, tragedy as a literary genre had been interpreted in a variety of conflicting ways.[2] In the *Theaetetus* Socrates (surprisingly for us) identifies the greatest masters in the two kinds of poetry as Epicharmus in comedy and Homer in tragedy. And since Plato had Socrates quote a line from the *Iliad*, it is clear that he believed his epic poetry best exemplified the genre (152e). Later in the *Laws* Plato's Athenian deemed the "dramatization (*mimesis*) of a noble and perfect life . . . the most real of tragedies . . . the finest of all dramas" (7.817b). Aristotle's *Poetics*, surely following Plato, defined tragedy broadly so as to include narrative and dramatic works, and Aristotle explicitly identified the *Odyssey* as well as the *Iliad* as tragic creations (1448b–1449a). Although he would distinguish between the Homeric epics—commending the *Iliad* for its pathetic ending and the *Odyssey* for its ethical resolution, whereby the protagonist received his just deserts (1459a)—Aristotle's ambiguities may be explained by the dramatic practice of the Greek tragedians themselves. For example, Aristotle praised Euripides' *Iphigenia in Tauris* as the best kind of tragic drama (1452b), despite its fortunate outcome: Iphigenia, about to sacrifice Orestes, recognizes him as her brother at the last moment and spares him. In the plays too that feature Medea as the protagonist, although she moves from one unspeakable crime to another, she also moves from adversity to triumph. Our own loose understanding of what constitutes tragedy—that any sad story is a "tragedy"—could certainly be accommodated by Aristotle's. Indeed, he proposed an even broader definition that put any serious story at all within the realm of tragedy.

Aristotle's famous definition of tragedy is "an imitation of an action that is serious, complete, and of a certain magnitude" and that employs heightened language. This definition privileged the serious nature of the representation, and he was careful to refine his understanding of the imitated action to refer to the critical fortunes of heroic figures (*spoudaioi*). Tragedy was thus a subject matter shared by both the genres of drama and epic, epic being an unactable form of tragedy (1449b24–25). Since Aristotle also said that the best tragedies drew on the histories of a few families—such as those of Alcmaeon, Oedipus, Orestes, and Thyestes—we may further take it to mean that traditional myths were the source of tragic subject matter.[3] And in his catalogue of possible plots for tragedy (1452b), Aristotle noted that a plot showing a bad man achieving good fortune is the most untragic of all (*atragodotatos*), the implication being that the movement from good to bad fortune is to be preferred. At 1453a he characterized the best tragedy as the story of a man who is not preeminently virtuous but who, through some flaw (*hamartia*) in him, falls from his high station and good fortune to adversity, arousing in the spectators the requisite emotions of pity and fear. As stated earlier in the *Poetics,* the purpose of tragedy is to bring about a relief (*katharsis*) of these passions (1449b), an emotional process peculiar to this form of art. Although his concept of catharsis has been used directly or indirectly in post-Renaissance discussions as the single, most defining characteristic of Aristotelian poetic, Aristotle never mentioned it again in his treatise, and the concept is not to be found in later classical theories of tragedy and only rarely in medieval and early Renaissance commentary. Most later discussions, however, insisted on the inclusion of pitiable, dreadful, and pathetic events, particularly in the resolution of the tragedy, even more than Aristotle himself did.

When Theophrastus succeeded Aristotle as head of the Lyceum after 322 BCE, he continued to teach Aristotelian theory, sometimes with interesting elaborations of his own, but rarely departing from or contradicting his master. One such variation, however, is of importance in the evolution of the literary genre of tragedy, a variation that became known in the Latin world via Theophrastus' followers, the grammarians Diomedes and Donatus (both fourth century CE). According to Diomedes, Theophrastus said that "tragedy is concerned with the crisis of a hero's fortune in adverse circumstances."[4] Theophrastus appeared here to have captured the essence of Aristotle's doctrines concerning characterization and plotting in tragedy, but Diomedes extracted certain elements that influenced the experiments in tragic drama during the trecento and quattrocento. First of all, he emphasized the crisis that tragic characters undergo in adversity, thereby recalling the Aristotelian notion that tragedy produces pity and fear. Somewhat later in his *Ars grammatica,* in assessing the differences between comedy and tragedy, Diomedes also said that "in tragedy heroes, leaders, and kings are introduced; in comedy, humble and private persons. . . . Tragedy frequently and almost always has sad outcomes to happy affairs, and the recognition that one's children and one's former good fortunes have taken a turn for the worse."[5] Diomedes thus expanded characterization in tragedy to include leaders and kings as well as heroes. The social distinction of its main characters became a critical standard by which tragedy was defined. Furthermore, he underscored the unhappy ending as a recurring component of the genre.

During the same era in which Diomedes flourished, Theophrastian and other post-Aristotelian elaborations of tragedy were also transmitted to the Middle Ages and Renaissance via the commentary of Donatus on the comedies of Terence. In explaining the nature of comedy, Donatus naturally felt called upon to deal with tragedy as well, and handed on doctrines in many ways similar to those of Diomedes:

> Between tragedy and comedy, however, there are many things that distinguish the two, since comedy involves the everyday fortunes of men, dangers of small moment, and actions with happy endings; but in tragedy everything is different: imposing men, great fears, and disastrous endings are dealt with. . . . Tragedy presents the sort of life that one seeks to escape from . . . and tragedy is often derived from historical truth.[6]

Here there is an even greater stress on the unhappy ending as a distinctive trait of tragedy, almost to the exclusion of other kinds of tragic resolutions. Crucially, Donatus points to history as a reservoir of tragic stories, a source that would prove extremely useful to humanist practitioners of the form. Donatus' notes on dramatic structure in comedy were soon combined with those of other commentators in the extant scholia on Terence. Manuscripts of Donatus' commentary were sporadically available in the Middle Ages, became well known to Italian humanists after 1433, and reached print in Venice in 1472.[7]

Although Diomedes and Donatus never suggested a clear purpose for comedy or tragedy, there can be no doubt that Aristotle's goal for tragedy—affecting the emotions for moral and aesthetic purposes—was implicit in their approaches to the tragic climax. The Romanized version of tragedy, then, emphasized Aristotle's preference for the unhappy ending, expanded the possibilities of the *dramatis personae,* underscored the necessity of employing a heightened, poetic style, and broadened the nature of potential subject matter available to the genre. These were the central concerns that passed from the later Latin world into the Middle Ages through the agency of many intermediate theorists.

It should be noted, however, that the text of Aristotle's *Poetics* was largely ignored in antiquity; he exercised greater influence with regard to literary subjects through his *Rhetoric.* This pattern was even more pronounced during the Middle Ages and early Renaissance.[8] The *Poetics* was not translated from the Greek until the Latin version of William of Moerbeke appeared in 1278. It was almost completely ignored, and only two manuscripts of the work survive, both of them copied in Italy. The redaction of Aristotle's original that did appeal to at least a few medieval thinkers was Averroës' *Middle Commentary on Aristotle's Poetics* as translated from the Arabic by Hermanus Alemannus in 1256. The work's relative popularity is attested by its survival in twenty-four manuscripts; it reached print in 1481. Averroës interpreted and recast Aristotle's celebrated definition of tragedy as an "imitation of an action that is serious, complete, and of a certain magnitude," as a genre devoted to praising, that is, to inciting virtue, as comedy was interpreted as a genre of blame, one that castigated vice. The effect was further to transform Aristotle's poetics into a rhetorical and moral program. Averroës' commentary was printed in 1498 with Giorgio Valla's new Latin translation of Aristotle's *Poetics* (the first to be published) and was included with the 1508 Aldine printing of the Greek original as part of an anthology of *Rhetores graeci*.

Thanks to the steady reacquisition of Greek by Italian humanists during the quattrocento, dependence on medieval versions of Aristotle lessened. Around 1480 Angelo Poliziano (1454–1494) was referring to the *Poetics* in his lectures at the University of Florence, as Ermolao Barbaro (1454–1493) had done before him at Padua. Carlo Verardi, uncle and mentor of the Marcellino Verardi whose *Ferdinand Preserved* is published in this volume, cited the *Poetics* (1451b ff.) in his *Historia Baetica* of 1493.[9] Still, it is important to note that Giorgio Valla's short treatise on poetry, the *De poetica* (written 1492/94, published in his *De expetendis et fugiendis rebus opus* of 1501), was in the end much more indebted to Diomedes' *Ars grammatica* and to Horace than to Aristotle. Despite the publication of Aristotle's Greek text by Aldus Manutius in 1508 noted above, the *Poetics* had little immediate impact on the theory and practice of tragedy. It was only during the second half of the cinquecento that Aristotle's text became more intelligible and influential as a result of the many new translations, commentaries, and studies. The surge of interest was stimulated by Francesco Robortello's commentary of 1548 and the first Italian translation by Bernardo Segni in 1549. It was hardly accidental that the full assimilation of Aristotle's theories took place at the same time that the works of the ancient Greek tragedians were also being made accessible. Alessandro de' Pazzi (1483–1530), the first writer to provide a truly reliable Latin translation of the *Poetics* (published in 1536), also prepared the first Latin and then vernacular translations of Sophocles and Euripides.

It is impossible to list in detail the many definitions of tragedy formulated by grammarians and rhetoricians during the late classical world and the Middle Ages; the genre, if it can be called a genre, was in a continuing state of flux, realignment, and adaptation. The writings of Lactantius (fourth century CE), Boethius (sixth century), Isidore of Seville (seventh century), and Remigius (tenth century), among many others, all contributed to the ongoing discourse that seemed to put the theory of tragedy into a permanently unsettled state. In late antiquity Christian applications of the term "tragedy," for example, became even more vague. Such disparate events or stories as Nero's murder of his mother, Agrippina, the Biblical story of Herod and his wife and children, the martyrdom of saints, and even the incarnation of Christ were all somehow considered "tragedies." Dante's early *De vulgari eloquentia* (ca. 1305) defined tragedy as a genre that used heightened diction and syntax in dealing with elevated subjects, yet cited lyric poems, including some of his own, as examples of tragedy (2.4.7). In his *Inferno* he also had Vergil refer to his *Aeneid* as "my high tragedy" (XX, 113). The celebrated and seemingly contrary passage in Dante's *Epistle to Cangrande* (if it is by Dante), wherein the poet defined tragedy as a work that ends in misery, owed more to medieval intermediaries than to classical sources. Even though many of Aristotle's writings were being introduced into the Latin world of the twelfth and thirteenth centuries directly from the Greek and through Arabic intermediaries, the *Poetics,* as we have seen, was not one of them.

The Recovery of Seneca

A real turning point was reached and a direction established, however, with the rediscovery of the eleventh-century Codex Etruscus of the tragedies of Lucius Annaeus Seneca (first century CE) at the Benedictine abbey of Pomposa during the trecento. In fact, the history of Latin humanist tragedy during the trecento and quattrocento is largely the story of the imitation and adaptation of Seneca. Seneca's popularity, however, was largely a phenomenon of the late Middle Ages. Although nearly four hundred manuscripts of his tragedies survive today, most of them are from the quattrocento; for many centuries the tragedies had a remarkably limited circulation. Citations and direct references in late antiquity and the early Middle Ages are rare.[10] The Carolingian and twelfth-century renaissances for the most part took no notice of the Roman dramatist. After the *Codex Etruscus* (E) was discovered by the Paduan scholar-poet Lovato dei Lovati (1240/41–1309), Padua would become the chief center of Senecan influence during the late Middle Ages.[11] The E codex represented the earliest complete manuscript of Seneca's nine tragedies—*Hercules Furens, Troades, Phoenissae, Medea, Phaedra, Oedipus, Agamemnon, Thyestes,* and *Hercules Oetaeus.* This collection of plays was prefaced by two excerpts from Isidore of Seville's *Etymologiae,* one of which (Book 18) stated that tragedians sang of the crimes of wicked kings before an audience. True, Lovati's interest in Seneca was chiefly metrical: the *Nota domini Lovati* discriminated between the iambic trimeter used by Seneca to describe the ruin and fall of great kings and princes, and the heroic dactylic hexameter used by Ennius, Vergil, and Statius to describe triumphant victories. Yet Lovato and the most significant of his pupils, Albertino Mussato, whose *Ecerinis* appears in this volume, showed a deeper understanding of Senecan dramatic form than had been achieved for centuries.[12]

As a result of the work of the Paduan scholars, the popularity of Seneca's tragedies grew in the course of the trecento. A commentary on the plays has been attributed to Dionigi de' Roberti (ca. 1300–1342), Petrarch's confessor, and by the 1380s Antonio Pievano da Vado and Domenico Bandini of Arezzo were lecturing on Seneca in Florence. Petrarch too prized Seneca not only as a moralist but also as a poet, saying of his plays that "*apud poetas profecto vel primum vel primo proximum locum tenent* (among poets they surely hold either first or second place)."[13] An interest manifested itself, especially at the papal court at Avignon in the early years of the trecento, in making the difficult and unfamiliar text of

Seneca's plays accessible; thus a Dominican of Blackfriars, Oxford, Nicholas Trevet (1257/65–in or after 1334), was commissioned by another Dominican, Niccolò Albertini da Prato, cardinal of Ostia and a member of the papal curia, to prepare a commentary. Trevet's commentary was based on a manuscript possibly of English origin, the C codex. (A different manuscript from the same family contains Petrarch's handwriting in the margins.) Before Trevet completed his work on Seneca (*Expositio super tragedias Senece*) about 1314, he had written an influential commentary on Boethius' *Consolation of Philosophy* (*Expositio super librum Boecii de consolatione*); this was perhaps Trevet's first work, written as early as 1304. The work is important because Trevet's research on Boethius provided him with a knowledge of tragedy from nonclassical traditions which he would bring to his analysis of Senecan tragedy. Of particular interest to Trevet (and to scholars interested in following the development of the tragic genre) was Boethius' second book. Here, within the context of Boethius' dialogue with Philosophy, in which he portrays himself as a man driven to despair by adverse fortune, Philosophy asks him to listen to Fortune explaining her own nature. In the course of her monologue, Fortune cites Herodotus' account of Croesus, king of the Lydians, as an example of a great man coming to misery (1.87) and Livy's treatment of the calamities of King Perses as a prisoner of Aemilius Paulus (45.8), two instances of Fortune's wheel capriciously turning things upside down. She asks Boethius: "What other thing does the clamor of tragedies bewail but Fortune overthrowing happy kingdoms with an unexpected blow?" (2.Pr 2, 38–40).[14] The emphasis is on the disasters and misfortunes that are undeserved and unforeseen.

Trevet was careful to explicate this passage and in doing so relied on earlier medieval definitions of tragedy, especially Isidore's, as a poetic expression dealing with great iniquities and moving from prosperity to adversity:

> When she says, "What does the clamoring of tragedies," she demonstrates that the mutability of Fortune is commonly discovered in daily clamorings, for the clamorings of poets reciting their tragedies every day in the theater contained nothing other than the mutability of Fortune . . . Hence tragedy is a poem about great crimes or iniquities beginning in prosperity and ending in adversity. . . . Fortune says, therefore, "What else does the clamoring of tragedies bewail except Fortune overturning happy kingdoms with an unforeseen blow," that is, with an uncertain outcome, as if to say [in answer to her rhetorical question] "Nothing." (2.Pr 2, 29)[15]

There is no causal relationship in either Boethius' original or Trevet's commentary between the *casus regum* and their wickedness, no sense of retributive justice. Their actions may be mournful to the audience, but missing is any reference to the Averroës/Alemannus interpretation of tragedy as a genre devoted to inciting virtue, as comedy is to castigating vice. When Trevet wrote his commentary on Seneca's tragedies—doubtless he had not yet known of Seneca's plays when he composed his commentary on Boethius—he revised his notions about tragedy.

Seneca's plays, of course, reinforced the idea that tragedy dealt with great crimes, but Trevet discovered in them a purpose, namely, the presentation of praiseworthy matters as well as matters deserving of condemnation. Although such ideas do seem to reflect the Averroës/Alemannus commentary on Aristotle's *Poetics*, as has been suggested, the same terms may be found in Cicero's rhetorical theories and in Thomas Aquinas' ethical doctrines. In his prefatory letter to Cardinal Albertini, Trevet speculated more fully about Seneca's motives in writing his tragedies:

> I believe that his schooled maturity, hovering at the arduous peak of virtue, was inclined to write tragedies so that, like

> prudent physicians who cover bitter antidotes with honeyed sweetness and administer them for the purging of humors and the fostering of health with no offensive taste, he could enjoin ethical teachings on infirm minds in a delightful manner, by clothing them in the appealing guise of fables, in order that by teaching the nature of vice and sowing the seeds of virtue, he might produce a fruitful harvest.[16]

He implies here that Seneca had earlier composed other works of moral instruction that could be admired. It may be useful to recall that during the trecento and quattrocento the moral essays and letters of Seneca, which inspired many writers in the Middle Ages, continued to find receptive audiences among Renaissance readers and Renaissance schools, like Guarino da Verona's at Ferrara, mined Seneca's plays for their *sententiae*.[17]

Reinforcing the increasingly moral view of drama was the vital tradition of devotional representation within the Church that produced the great mystery cycles of the Middle Ages. In Renaissance Italy religious dramas were called *sacre rappresentazioni*. They belonged to a popular genre created by clerics for the instruction of lay people and were, therefore, written in the vernacular. Their origins may be traced to the *laude* of thirteenth-century Umbria, religious poems based on the liturgy and on the songs of praise in the morning Office, and to its later form, the *devozioni*. The *sacre rappresentazioni* used biblical and allegorical characters in their depiction of the endless struggle between the forces of good and evil. Allegory, whether it was the overt personification of Ambition, Envy, and Discord in Dati's *Hiempsal* or the figural symbolism of Satan in Mussato's *Ecerinis* and St. James in Verardi's *Ferdinand Preserved*, continued to be ubiquitous in humanist tragedy.

Seneca's tragedies, for example, abound in moral ideas, and his dramatic preoccupation with emotional pathology and with the destructive consequences of passion, especially anger, is deeply indebted to the Stoic tradition. The world of Senecan tragedy was built largely on the world Euripides established in Greek tragedy. Seneca's interest—that is, in sexual themes and revenge motives, his highly rhetorical characters (especially that of the Messenger), his choral episodes, often dissociated from the plot, his pointed use of stichomythia—was primarily Euripidean. Periclean Athens, however, was different from the Rome of Nero in which Seneca moved. While Euripides' plays often inspired terror, as Aristotle noted, they were controlled by an all-embracing sense of divine dispensation meted out to the doers of terrible deeds. Seneca's plays not only generated terror but also emphasized the unmitigated horror at work in this world; and the theme of personal vengeance often supplemented or superseded that of divine retribution.

Classical scholars do not agree on whether Seneca's tragedies were performed on stage during his lifetime, but it is plain that the ancient practice of *recitatio* affected the form of Seneca's plays. Whether the terms "closet drama" or "recitation drama" are appropriate for Senecan drama in its ancient context, rhetoric surely dominates theatricality in its Renaissance revival.[18] The appeal of Seneca's tragedies to a period that Marc Fumaroli has styled *L'age de l'eloquence* is obvious, for his plays are largely constituted by a succession of long speeches, declamatory or narrative accounts of action, detailed, almost compulsive, verbal depictions of horrid deeds, and reflective soliloquies that employ finely phrased examples of Stoic wisdom in a highly rhetorical mode. "Senecan rhetoric," however, "is no mere verbal ornament; bombast, *suasoriae*, stichomythic exchanges, word-play and *sententiae* are used in the creation of tragic character and the revelation of states of mind." Seneca wrote tragedy that focused "on the inner workings of the human mind, on the mind as *locus* of emotional conflict, incalculable suffering, insatiable appetite, manic joy, cognitive vulnerability, self-deception, irrational guilt."[19] Above all, Senecan tragedy is centrally concerned with *infanda*, shocking acts of unspeakable iniquity and horror, and the dramatic action often turns on the moral and religious reactions of individuals and groups to such *infanda*.

Albertino Mussato's Ecerinis

The tragedy *Ecerinis* was the first tragic drama to emerge in the immediate aftermath of Lovato dei Lovati's discovery of Seneca's plays at Pomposa, and it was natural that it should be written by Lovato's disciple, Albertino Mussato (1261–1329), statesman, poet, and historian. Composed in 1314, the play did not deal with the mythological characters typical of true Senecan tragedy, but dramatized historical events in northern Italy during the previous century. In particular, the play depicted episodes in the terrifying career of Ezzelino III da Romano (1194–1259), the "tyrant of Padua," one of the emperor Frederick II's lieutenants in battles between Guelf and Ghibelline that characterized that epoch. Mussato's depiction of Ezzelino's cruelty, however, was a thinly veiled portrait of a contemporary Veronese tyrant, Cangrande della Scala, who threatened Padua's independence during the second and third decades of the trecento. The *Ecerinis* was thus written in part to warn his fellow Paduans of the dangers of tyranny. Mussato played an active role as diplomat and soldier in the wars between Padua and Verona from 1312 to 1328, and his Paduan patriotism was nourished in his youth by the *Cronica in factis et circa facta Marchie Trivixane* (ca. 1262) of Rolandino of Padua (1200–1276). This work was Mussato's main source for the historical information in his play. In addition, Rolandino's defense of civic liberty served as a model for the two large-scale historical works Mussato composed on the history of his own time that dealt with the loss of his city's independence: the *Historia Augusta de gestis Henrici VII* and the possibly unfinished *De gestis italicorum post Henricum VII Caesarem*.

As models for his *Ecerinis,* Mussato himself utilized a number of Senecan plays, particularly the *Thyestes,* as well as the pseudo-Senecan tragedy *Octavia,* a *fabula praetexta.*[20] Although it is generally agreed today that *Octavia* is not by Seneca, it does have the distinction of being the only surviving play from Roman antiquity written about a historical subject: the murder of Octavia, Nero's first wife, on the orders of her ex-husband. There were surely other *praetextae* composed between 200 BCE and 100 CE, but the records are scanty; it is clear that such plays (the term *praetexta* was taken from the *toga praetexta* worn by leading Roman citizens) dealt with Roman identity and nationhood. *Octavia* was as much a tragedy of the Roman people as one of Octavia herself, and the depiction of Nero as an aberration, a monster destined by Fortune to fall, was the connecting link between the two. Ezzelino played the same role in Mussato's tragedy. In the pseudo-Senecan play, too, the citizens were greatly involved in the plot; the community was a witnessing, reacting, participating character that represented a moral anchor and a reminder of traditional values. Its very presence was a reminder that right order could conceivably restore itself. In Mussato's hands, the Chorus was made up of the Paduan *populus* and had a similarly leading role. So successful was Mussato's play that its author was crowned with the poetic laurel on December 3, 1315—at his own laureation in Rome on April 8, 1341, Petrarch recalled this Paduan precedent—and a statute was passed that the play should be recited every Christmas season to strengthen the patriotism of the citizenry. The readings took place in Mussato's presence in the town hall of Padua.

While the pseudo-Senecan *Octavia* provided Mussato with a model for refracting Paduan history in dramatic form, his reliance on the authentic corpus of Seneca's plays is no less striking. Mussato said that he chose Ezzelino's deeds because they reminded him of Seneca's Medea and Thyestes. As noted earlier, Lovato's interest in Seneca's plays was chiefly focused on his prosody, and he left no evidence of his opinions regarding matters of genre or theory. But Mussato did. None of the Paduan circle of prehumanists knew of Trevet's commentary on the *Octavia* and the genuine plays of Seneca, but Mussato was well aware of a number of post-classical writers on tragic theory. In a verse epistle written after his *Ecerinis* was composed, Mussato provided a purpose for tragedy: "The voice of the tragic poet makes minds strong when confronted by adversities, so that cowardly fear evaporates."[21] Like Trevet, Mussato was concerned with the salutary effects of tragedy, its ability to "sow the seeds of virtue." Later in the same epistle he stressed the genre's other lessons: that only mutability is constant, that glory is fleeting, and that death is not only inevitable but also omnipresent. Secular tragedy thus dramatized the most fearful kinds of cruelty found in a life of uncertainty. It was this kind of moral that *Ecerinis* calls to mind, but it was clearly meant to be interpreted as a Christian moral. After Ezzelino's death is reported in gruesome detail by the Messenger, the Chorus sums up the lesson: "Young men, together let us pay thanks befitting the giver of such great blessings. . . . May God, born of a Virgin, show his approval to the vows that we have addressed to Him." (ll. 521–22, 535–36). Echoes of the *sacre rappresentazioni* continued to be heard in Mussato's *Ecerinis*. Even though the Chorus earlier in the play had expressed a more pagan sentiment by saying "the wheel [of Fortune] turns round and round forever" (ll. 146–47), the shocking scene of the immolation of Alberico's wife and five daughters (ll. 570 and ff.) surely functioned as powerfully as the fires of hell did in sacred drama. Mussato's protagonist certainly confronts adversity, but he was begotten by the devil and was monstrous in his unmitigated cruelty He is not a prehumanist version of the Miltonic Satan; he is a villain who, in fact, boasts that "contrary fortune strengthens powerful men and crushes the worthless" (459–60), a villain much blacker than Seneca's Thyestes.

In his *Evidentia tragediarum Senece,* written also after *Ecerinis* in the form of an imaginary dialogue between himself and Lovato, Mussato attempted to define the nature of tragedy. Mussato had Lovato characterize tragedy as a "lamenting description of an overthrown kingdom," and when he is asked for the source of his definition, Lovato cites Fortune's rhetorical question to Boethius: "What else does the clamor of tragedy bewail. . . ? *(Quid tragoediarum clamor aliud deflet. . . ?)*"[22] Again, in his *Life of Seneca* Mussato quoted from the last chapter of William of Moerbeke's translation of Aristotle's *Poetics* from 1278. Mussato was the only known user of Moerbeke's translation during the Middle Ages, and it may very well be Mussato's hand as glossator in one of the codices of Moerbeke's work.[23] The reference Mussato makes is to Fortune's mocking question again, adding that Seneca chose the iambic meter to narrate "the downfall and death of kings and leaders as Boethius says in his *Consolation*."[24] We have seen, especially in antiquity, that tragedy could also include the epic narration of the triumphs of kings, for which the dactylic hexameter was more appropriate; this was the meter employed by Ennius, Lucan, Vergil, and Statius. It is clear that Mussato tried to give his tragedy some of the qualities of the epic, as is reflected in its title: it is not *Ecerinus* but *Ecerinis*—"the *Ecerinid*" as it might be rendered in English, on the model of "the *Aeneid*"—a designation that emphasized not the heroism of the villain Ezzelino but the heroic struggle of Padua.

By a somewhat roundabout textual route, then, Mussato had returned to the ancient Greek concept of tragedy, which accepted all kinds of outcomes, as long as the subject matter was elevated and the characters persons of consequence. History, myth, and drama collide in *Ecerinis.* In all ten tragedies written by various hands during the trecento and quattrocento,[25] Mussato's championing of Seneca had a role to play. His inclusion of the *tragoedia praetexta* of *Octavia* had more immediate consequences in the varied treatments of Italian history in at least four later plays: *On the Misfortune of Cesena* (*De casu Cesene*, 1377) by Ludovico Romani da Fabriano; an unfinished tragedy (fifty-eight verses of the Chorus have survived) by Giovanni Manzini della Motta (1387) on the fall of Verona and of Antonio della Scala; the *Tragedy on the Captivity of Duke Giacomo* (*De captivitate ducis Iacobi tragoedia*, 1465) by Laudivio Zacchia da Vezzano; and the *Tragedy of Italian Affairs and the Triumph of Louis XII, King of France* (*De rebus italicis deque triumpho Ludovici XII regis Francorum tragoedia*, 1499–1500) by Giovanni Armonio Manso. It was only just that, writing eighty years after the composition of *Ecerinis*, Coluccio Salutati (1331–1406), the Florentine humanist and chancellor, in recognition of Mussato's work of poetry and patriotism, placed him among the forebears of Petrarch in his survey of the restorers of learning.[26]

Antonio Loschi's Achilles

Antonio Loschi (1369–1441) was an important humanist and diplomat of Leonardo Bruni's generation. He was born at Vicenza, studied in Padua, Pavia, and (briefly) Florence (where he met Coluccio Salutati), worked first in the chancery of Giangaleazzo Visconti, the duke of Milan, and later found employment as a secretary in the papal curia under popes from Gregory XII to Eugene IV. He acquired a wide reputation thanks to the rhetorical commentary he wrote during the 1390s on eleven of Cicero's orations. However, Loschi is best remembered today for his exchange of Latin invectives with Salutati during and after the three wars between Florence and Milan that raged between 1390 and 1402.[27] Despite this literary conflict, Loschi remained on good terms with Salutati and Salutati's disciple Leonardo Bruni, later his colleague in the papal curia; Bruni's translation of Plato's *Phaedrus* was dedicated to Loschi.[28]

Despite his connections with Florence, Loschi's intellectual roots were in the soil of early Paduan and Lombard humanism, so it is not surprising, especially given his interest in rhetoric, that Loschi would follow in Mussato's footsteps by writing a Senecan tragedy of his own.[29] Loschi's subject was the death of Achilles, which looked to the same world of Homeric heroes, filtered through the Greek tragedians, whence Seneca had drawn his inspiration. Loschi's main source was not Homer himself or the Greek tragedians, however, but the *De excidio Troiae historia* by pseudo-Dares the Phrygian, one of the sources by which the Homeric legends were transmitted to the Middle Ages.[30] The play is divided into five acts, but the titular hero appears onstage only in the second act; the catastrophe of the drama, the death of Achilles, occurs before Act III begins. There is no personal grief expressed for the fall of the Greek hero, not even by the Greek messenger who describes his death in Act IV, nor by Agamemnon in Act V, who simply muses about the fickleness of Fortune. *Achilles* is a drama written alternately from the Trojan and Greek point of view. There are two competing choruses, one Greek and the other Trojan, and two tragic heroes. Paris is the man of peace, who is persuaded by shame to become a treacherous murderer; Achilles is the warrior whose love for Polyxena leads to folly and whose invincibility leads to hubris.

It is worth noting that there is a striking similarity between the openings of *Ecerinis* and *Achilles*. In Mussato's play Adelheita recalled a horrifying nocturnal visit from her demonic lover, and it is her narration of the event that precipitates the action that follows. Loschi also placed center stage another Medean mother, Hecuba, who is visited in her dreams by the ghost of Troilus, who along with Hector is one of her two sons slain by Achilles. The revenge, the retribution, the operation of the *lex talionis* that was at the core of Senecan tragedy is set in motion as Paris is persuaded by his mother to ambush Achilles in Apollo's temple. He is lured there by his promised marriage to Polyxena, a daughter of Priam and Hecuba. The power of love will be not only the instrument of vengeance but also the possible antidote to the evils of war. This idea is neither Homeric nor Senecan.[31] Polyxena never appears in Homer, and even though the first choral ode in Seneca's *Hippolytus* (ll. 274 and ff.) does recognize the power of Cupid, romantic love played a very small role in Seneca's tragedies. Loschi, however, was at some pains to romanticize love in his tragedy. Achilles' soliloquy addressed to Cupid in Loschi's second act is balanced by the second choral ode at the end of the act, which echoed Seneca's chorus. Both had important purposes: Achilles' paean exposes the titular hero as overconfident and foolhardy, the very qualities that will bring about his victimization in Paris' love-intrigue, and the concluding choral ode in the act establishes the connection between love and fortune that will dominate the remaining choral songs in the play.

In fact, fortune—pagan fortune—played a much more pervasive role in Loschi's tragedy than in Mussato's, so that in this regard *Achilles* is a decidedly more Senecan play. "All our acts depend on the turning stars, and the course of the heavens rules all things on earth. Not even a god himself can alter whatever is woven by the Fates on high" (ll. 937–40). As we have seen, the very nature of tragedy typically included a belief in an overarching fate, and Loschi consciously avoided any inclusion of a divine providence at work in his dramatic world. The plot functioned merely as a scaffold upon which the inevitability of fate is constructed. The anticlimactic fifth act simply establishes the perpetual cycle of fortune and violence, as Calchas calls upon the son of Achilles to avenge his father's murder. Hecuba's vengeance begets Pyrrhus' vengeance. No peace lies in prospect to bring resolution to the tragic passions.

Of the two plays created during the trecento, both *Ecerinis* and *Achilles* display a reliance on Senecan dramatic conventions, but they also represent a divergence from their model. Both plays were meant to be read in private or recited to an audience, so we can understand why such closet dramas neglected stagecraft in favor of a heightened narrative presentation of incidents. Adherence to any Senecan principles of time and setting was easily suspended as well—events described in the *Ecerinis* covered more than half a century and the play tolerated large gaps of time between its acts, while *Achilles* freely changed the scene of the action. The emphasis in these early plays was on melodrama, the stylizing of behavior and emotion. Mussato's observation that Ezzelino reminded him of Seneca's *Medea* and *Thyestes* privileged the presentation of gruesome deeds, in Mussato's case reflecting equally horrible deeds that were occurring during his own lifetime. In both Mussato's play and Loschi's the delirium of a wronged woman like Medea provided the inciting force of the drama. Their obsessive emphasis on and fascination with cruelty, particularly the vengeful cruelty of maternal love in Loschi, will be reenacted in the best Latin tragedy of the quattrocento, Correr's *Procne,* a story of sexual lust and unspeakable horror written by a teenager.

Gregorio Correr's Procne

Gregorio Correr was born in 1409 into a patrician family in Venice that had acquired distinction in part through its close relationship with the papacy. The last pope of the Roman obedience during the Great Schism was Antonio Correr, Gregory XII, and two later popes of the quattrocento, Eugenius IV and Paul II, were Correr's relatives. In addition, two of the most important cardinals of the quattrocento, Antonio Correr and Angelo Barbarigo, were closely connected with his family. When he died in 1464, having been appointed patriarch of Venice only months before his death, he had been living since 1448 in Verona at S. Zenone, where he devoted himself as abbot to the monastic community and to the embellishment of the church. (Correr commissioned Andrea Mantegna in 1450 to erect its famous altarpiece.) Earlier, in the 1430s, Correr had functioned as his uncle Cardinal Antonio's secretary, attending the Council of Basel (1433–1434), and had lived with him until his uncle's death in 1445. Correr's life and literary production fall into two distinct periods that depended upon his uncle's influence and his relationship to the Church.

Correr's early literary works were composed between 1426 and 1431 and included not only *Procne* but also a number of songs written in hexameters, satires, an eclogue, a prose collection of sixty apologues or fables in the manner of Aesop, and a pedagogical treatise. The satires were dedicated to Vittorino da Feltre (1373/79–1446), perhaps the most famous of humanist educators with whom Correr had studied for five years, and the educational work expressly invoked the pedagogical principles of Vittorino. (Correr wrote in this work about the pleasure he felt when he learned that his former teacher had wept upon reading the *Procne*.) This first phase of Correr's life was marked by his commitment to the Renaissance movement for the revival of classical antiquity. After about 1433 he wrote only in prose, his tone became more moralistic and religious, and he openly condemned the corruption of the papacy. In these years he wrote orations, soliloquies, and epistles. Typical of his later period was his letter in 1443 to Cecilia Gonzaga—Vittorino da Feltre was tutor to the Gonzaga family—as she prepared to enter a nunnery: "So you must put aside your beloved Virgil, with Vittorino's pardon. Take up instead the psalter and instead of Cicero, the Gospel. Believe me, I speak from experience: even if secular literature causes no harm beyond this, it leads the mind away from divine reading. You have in ecclesiastical writers, if you require it, the highest eloquence."[32]

Despite this transformation, Correr's major work, *Procne*, continued to be well received by influential figures. Enea Silvio Piccolomini (Aeneas Sylvius), who would be elected Pope Pius II in

1458, wrote in his own treatise on teaching the young, *De liberorum educatione* (1450), that the plays of Seneca were very efficacious and profitable, "but we have no Latin tragedian besides Seneca, except Gregorio Correr of Venice, who, when I was a youth, turned the story of Tereus, which comes from Ovid, into a tragedy."[33] Piccolomini's admiration for Correr's tragedy suggests two things: first, Seneca's plays were by then in circulation as models of the tragic form and, second, there was an increasing emphasis on Seneca's Latinity, his gravity and elegance. When at age eighteen Correr wrote his tragedy, he prefaced his play with a synopsis of the plot and an acknowledgement that he had imitated Seneca's *Thyestes* (Argument, 6)—a play, as we have seen, that also greatly influenced both Mussato and Loschi. Correr's model and inspiration may have been Senecan, but his subject matter was Ovidian. Although *Procne* adhered to the traditional meter of ancient Roman tragedy, Correr also prefaced his work with a rather didactic introductory section on metrics, in which he itemized the numerous metrical forms he had employed. These innovations allowed the tragedy to attain greater emotional complexity than its predecessors, especially in terms of characterization and dramatic intensity.[34]

The lurid sensationalism of earlier humanist tragedy was maintained by Correr and, indeed, was enhanced by his choice of Ovid's *Metamorphoses* (6.424–674) as his source, where the narrative of Tereus, Procne, and Philomela is, perhaps, the most horrific and disgusting of all the tales Ovid tells. Correr took full advantage of the story's horror. He did not follow Seneca's *Thyestes* in naming his play after the victim of revenge; rather, he follows the *Medea* in designating the avenger as his protagonist. He also compressed the Ovidian narrative, which occupies years, into a matter of a few days and created the illusion for the reader/audience of the action transpiring over a few hours. According to Ovid, too, Tereus raped Philomela again, and repeatedly, before Procne exacted her revenge (ll. 561–62). Correr eliminated this part of the story in order to augment the image of Procne's courage; her ferocity and lack of repentance were similarly intensified. She ordered the guards of Philomena's place of imprisonment to be killed, and the final preparation for the act of vengeance occupied the long third act of the play, as the Messenger recounted the unspeakable horror of it all in the fourth act. An Ovidian narrative year was condensed into one dramatic day. The final act is the banquet scene, which takes place onstage rather than being reported, as decorum might seem to require; in fact, there are no messengers and no chorus in the last act. All that was not essential in the bloody feast was stripped away. Procne's rescued sister is brought onstage at the same time that the severed head of Itys is presented to Tereus, who sips his son's blood in his wine. The dialogue in this final episode of the tragedy was carefully abbreviated by Correr, with spondees heightening the grief and brutal rage of husband and wife. Correr also chose, therefore, to exclude the moment of transformation when, as Ovid related, Tereus raises his sword to slay the two sisters, only to be changed into a hoopoe, as Procne is metamorphosed into a swallow and Philomela into a nightingale. Correr was not interested in the etiological value of the story or in the Christian allegorizing of the finale that Ovid's story generated in such works as the fourteenth-century *Ovide moralisé*. Correr understood the difference between narrative and theater very well.

Leonardo Dati's Hiempsal

If Correr's *Procne* demonstrated the theatrical possibilities of Senecanizing Ovid, *Hiempsal*, by Leonardo Dati (1407–1472) exhibited the adaptability of the theatrical form to the presentation of Roman history and humanist ideals. The origins and intentions of his tragedy are far more interesting than its effectiveness as Senecan drama. His play was not just a literary curiosity but an innovative blending of old and new, ancient and modern.

Dati was born in Florence, and during the 1440s he was an official of the papal curia of Eugenius IV, which at the time was resident in Florence. Later, as bishop of Massa, he served as papal secretary to Callixtus III, Pius II, Paul II, and Sixtus IV. A distinguished Latinist, Dati took his subject matter, not from Greek myth, but from Roman history—in fact, from an African episode from Roman history. In his *Bellum Iurguthinum*, a work valuable in its time as a political polemic as well as a sober historical account, Sallust (first century BCE) dealt with the war in Numidia that arose in 112 BCE when the kingdom was divided. History was used by Sallust as a vehicle to express his own fear of the decline in Roman moral virtue. In Dati's hands the story was completely simple and straightforward, the plot flaccid, and the dramatic interest minimal. On his death, Micipsa, king of Numidia, leaves his kingdom to his two sons, Adherbal and Hiempsal, as well as to their illegitimate half brother, Jugurtha, much to Hiempsal's resentment. Envious of Jugurtha's inheritance and his military prowess, Hiempsal insults him, whereupon Jugurtha plots and carries out his revenge by murdering the titular hero and his retinue. After Jugurtha's departure in the final act, one of the mourning matrons extracts the appropriate moral: "Learn from these events how wicked and pestilent an evil Envy can be" (ll. 738–39). In his preface Dati had already prepared his audience for the lesson: "Ambition begot Envy. Envy begot Discord. Discord begot Treachery, from which follow Poverty, Thievery, and Plunder."

Despite the fact that Dati employed many of the conventional devices of Senecan tragedy—the chorus, messengers, the wise counselor, five acts all salted with *sententiae*—and verbally and metrically echoed Seneca's plays, there were many elements in Dati's model that are absent, such as the obsession with mythological detail and the macabre fascination with bloody events. Most striking of all was Dati's reliance on allegory, part of the legacy of the *sacre rappresentazioni.* Not only did the subject of envy frame the play, every act of the tragedy emphasized it. For example, the opening of the drama finds Ambition and Modesty discussing the violent nature of Envy, who is pursuing her own mother, Ambition; two real characters, Asper and Polymites, then do the same, and the succeeding Chorus completes the dramatic symmetry. Another allegorical tableau occurs duly in the final act (ll. 631ff.), where Envy's daughter Discord discusses the ruin she has brought about with the aid of her accomplice, Perfidy. It has often been convenient to regard Dati's work as a sort of morality play *manqué,* costumed as a Senecan adaptation. However, Dati's tragedy may be better understood by considering the contemporary Florentine background.

On October 22, 1441, a literary contest, the *certame coronario,* modeled on ancient literary competitions, was organized by Leon Battista Alberti (1404–1472), one of the great humanists of the age, at the cathedral of Santa Maria del Fiore in Florence under the sponsorship of Piero de' Medici. The goal was to promote poetic compositions in the vernacular. A number of writers were invited to submit their works on the ancient theme of friendship. Among the submissions were works by Benedetto Accolti (1415–1464), Cyriac of Ancona (1399–ca. 1455), and Leonardo Dati. Dati's work, a dramatic poem called *Scaena,* written in the Tuscan dialect, was one of the first attempts to adapt Latin quantitative meter to Italian verse. The panel of judges included some of the most prominent humanists of the day: Poggio Bracciolini (1380–1459), Flavio Biondo (1392–1463), Carlo Marsuppini (1398–1453), and probably Leonardo Bruni (1370–1444), among others. A silver crown was to be awarded to the winning author. Dati was recognized by most observers as the winner of the poetic competition, although no one was awarded the prize, which, instead, was placed on the altar of the Virgin Mary as a gift. The judges said of Dati that "his poem had not spoken fully of friendship and that, although it was quite rich, well structured, and agreeably ornamented, it was outclassed by several others in *sententiae*."[35] Alberti was disappointed and complained in his *Protesta* that the indecision of the judges was the result not of the poor quality of the submissions but of their envy. He therefore proposed, rather mischievously, a second *certame* for the following year, the theme of which would be *invidia*, envy.

Dati mentioned in his argument to *Hiempsal* that his play was intended for this second contest about *invidia*. Alberti, too, in his vernacular dialogue *Profugiorum ab aerumna libri* (1441–1442) confirmed that Dati had composed his play for this contest.[36] When Bruni asserted that it was *stultitia*, folly, not envy that led to the judges' indecision in 1441, an exchange of letters between Bruni (who also mentioned Dati's *Hiempsal*) and Alberti ensued; Alberti had taken the charge personally, believing with Dati that envy was, in fact, the real cause and that Bruni was being vindictive in his defense. Although Bruni offered an apology to Alberti, in which he said he had not intended to malign either Dati or Alberti, the second *certame coronario* never took place.[37]

Given this politically charged context, *Hiempsal* may, at least in part, be read almost as an allegorical roman à clef. If his earlier submission lacked sufficient moral precepts, he filled his next entry with a number of useful *sententiae*. If the vernacular *Scaena* was not really worthy of the prize because it said too little about friendship, every act of the Latin *Hiempsal* emphasized the malevolence of envy. It is important to recall that Dati's play was in circulation before the contest was to be held, and its currency may well have contributed to the cancellation of the event. Within the play Dati frequently echoed the pseudo-Senecan *Octavia*, the *tragoedia praetexta* that Mussato found so useful in his response to contemporary history; perhaps this ancient dramatic model provided a similar way of contextualizing recent Florentine history. If Sallust's *Jugurthine War,* Dati's source, dealt with the struggles of republican power against the arrogance and insolence of the nobles in ancient Rome, Florence, the heir of *respublica Romana,* would become in his hands the literary battleground on which a contemporary struggle was to be fought. At the end of *Hiempsal* Dati's second messenger exclaims, "O tempora, O mores!" (l. 725). This quotation from the most famous of Cicero's Catilinarian orations certainly had a special relevance to quattrocento Florence. Even more salient is the line from Micipsa's speech to his three sons that became the most famous of all quotations from Sallust in the Renaissance: "Harmony makes small states great, while discord undermines the mightiest empires" (10.6) — a line done in mosaic on the wall of the Florentine Signoria's private chapel in the Palazzo Vecchio. This line too found an echo in *Hiempsal* (l. 474). Dati's tragedy was an innovative experiment within the tragic form, but in terms of its message, it might also be seen as a kind of extended commentary on that famous *sententia.*

Marcellino Verardi's Ferdinand Preserved

The final and much the latest of the plays included in this volume is Marcellino Verardi's *Ferdinand Preserved,* a play probably written early in 1493, and one which further problematized the genre of tragedy. As we have seen, the writers of Latin tragedy during the trecento and quattrocento drew their subject matter from Seneca's tragedies, from Ovid's myths, from the histories of Greece and Rome, from Italian history, and from the *sacre rappresentazioni.* During the cinquecento, when Latin humanist tragedy had lost most of its appeal to lay society, vernacular tragedy continued to rely on the same sources as well as on the Italian *novelle* (which also nourished the plots and characters of earlier Latin comedy). While its varied components might suggest that Verardi's play would be a culmination of the many dramatic forces at work since the time of Mussato's *Ecerinis, Ferdinand Preserved* was a vehicle of propaganda couched in the trappings of Senecan drama, a religious allegory, a court entertainment, and a contemporary history—in other words, a kind of dramatic hybrid, which nevertheless seems to have exerted very little influence on later drama.

The play deals with an unsuccessful assassination attempt on Ferdinand II of Aragon, the king of Spain, which occurred at Barcelona in early December 1492. The attempt was made by one Juan de Cañamares, called "Ruffus," described as a madman by royalist sources. It was an incident described by many contemporary writers, some of whom witnessed the attack. Earlier in 1492, Marcellino's uncle, Carlo Verardi (1440–1500), had written another play in which Ferdinand was the protagonist, his *Historia baetica*, which concerned the king's conquest of Granada and the expulsion of the Moors in the same year. The popularity of the Spanish king as a subject of Latin drama in Italy may be partly explained by the recent election on August 11, 1492, of the latest Borgia pope, Alexander VI, who was born in Valencia (his uncle was Pope Callixtus III). Even before the election of the Spanish pope, the Spanish monarch had been a popular figure: the celebrations of the conquest of Granada and the expulsion of the Moors from Spain were among the most elaborate public spectacles in Rome during the pontificate of Innocent VIII (1484–1492).[38] On the first Sunday after the news from Granada had reached the city, all the clergy and religious congregations gathered at St. Peter's Basilica, where the pope celebrated Mass. Afterward, a *tauromachia*, a bullfight, was organized in the streets by Rodrigo Borgia, soon to be the next pope, a mock battle of Granada took place in the Piazza

Navona, and a *mascherata* was staged, in which the figures of Ferdinand and Isabella rode in a *carro trionfale* with a defeated Moor at their feet. The occasion, in other words, was designed to integrate the solemn Christian ritual typically found in *sacre rappresentazioni* with pagan blood sport, allegorical battles, and a classicizing *trionfo*—a Christian revival of ancient Roman glory.

In addition to the public demonstrations, the carnival festivities of 1492 also involved the private, aristocratic performance of a play. The organizer of both the public and private celebrations was Cardinal Raffaele Riario. Under Riario's patronage the humanist Accademia Romana, originally presided over by Pomponio Leto (1425–1498)—who also had encouraged the first performances of Latin New Comedy—had become enthusiastic about the recovery of ancient theater. In this context it is worth noting that Riario was the dedicatee of the first printed edition (1486) of the *De architectura* by Vitruvius, in the prefatory letter of which the editor, Giovanni Sulpizio da Veroli, had urged Riario to construct a theater. It was in the Palazzo Riario that a performance of Seneca's *Phaedra* (with the famous humanist Tommaso "Fedra" Inghirami in the title role) was given in 1486, and Riario also arranged performances of the play at the Castel S. Angelo and the Forum. It was in Riario's palace, too, that, some years later, in April 1492, the victory over the Moors was celebrated by a specially commissioned Latin drama in a temporary theater constructed for the occasion. The play was Carlo Verardi's *Historia baetica*. The text of the first edition printed at Rome in 1493 included an elegy by Carlo's nephew Marcellino and the music of the instrumental work, "Viva el gran re Don Fernando," composed by Carlo.

As he recorded in the preface to his nephew Marcellino's *Ferdinand Preserved*, Carlo later that same year worked up in prose a dramatic sketch of Ferdinand's deliverance from the assassin's sword, then handed it over to his nephew for versification. Like Carlo's *Historia baetica*, *Ferdinand Preserved* was duly presented before the new pope and members of the papal court, once again at the Palazzo Riario; the close connection between the two works is shown by the early editions, where the two plays were often bound together. The topicality of the subject matter of both plays, of course, clearly made an impression on the Borgia court, and, given the contemporary appetite for performing Latin plays, both comedies and tragedies, in courtly venues, the Verardis were quick to emphasize and illustrate the novelty of both works. Carlo's prologue to his work boasted that "I come bearing not comedies of Plautus or Naevius, which you know are all fictitious stories (*fictas fabulas*), but I bring you a new and true history (*historia*)."[39] The remark alluded to a similar distinction made by Isidore of Seville among *historiae*, *argumenta*, and *fabulae* (*Etymologies* 1.44.5): "Histories are true and have happened; arguments are things that could have happened even if they didn't; fables [*fabula*, the usual Latin word for 'play'] are things that did not happen and are impossible because unnatural." According to this distinction, Verardi's work is history, not fiction; thus by dramatizing real events that had recently occurred, the two Verardi plays made a claim to novelty.

There is another claim to novelty in the same preface. Marcellino's *Ferdinand Preserved* is there called a *tragicocomoedia*, "because the rank of the characters and the impious attack on His Majesty point to tragedy, while the happy ending belongs to comedy." The term "tragicomedy" was drawn explicitly from Plautus' prologue to his *Amphitruo*, where it was hardly more than a bit of comic bargaining between the god Mercury and the audience; it did not lead in antiquity to the creation of a new genre. But that is precisely what happens in the sixteenth century. If Verardi's view of tragicomedy reminds one of Aristotle's definition of one kind of tragedy — a serious action with a happy ending — later Renaissance drama would follow out the implications of Plautus' prologue and create a kind of tragicomedy, in which the comic and the tragic were mixed in innovative patterns. Hence *Ferdinand Preserved* can be regarded as a first experiment with the new form of tragicomedy so characteristic of the sixteenth century, with its love of generic ambiguity—a first step toward the better-known innovations of Giovanni Battista Giraldi Cinthio and Giovanni Battista Guarini.

In his *Ferdinand Preserved,* Verardi attempted to position Spanish Catholic propaganda derived from recent events within the context of court theater, a literary mode that is also public, and thus to heighten as much as possible—literally, to dramatize—the triumph of the ideal Christian king. Theater has become part of the technology of royal government. Ferdinand's characterization is one-dimensional, wooden, and crude; he is simply allegorized as the divine instrument of universal goodness, piety, and honesty who laid waste to the kingdoms of Pluto. Ruffus, his assailant, is an evil madman goaded into action by the Furies: Alecto, Megaera, and Tisiphone; their plan to avenge Pluto's defeat and their seduction of Ruffus occupy two of the three scenes in the play. In the final scene—the attack occurs offstage before the last scene commences—before she meets her recovering husband, Isabella is comforted by St. James, the patron saint of Spain, who balances the pagan Senecan characters seen earlier. And as she prays she invokes a god at once Christian and pagan who, through divine intervention, has saved her husband: "O pater omnipotens, o summi rector Olympi" (l. 470). As befitted his royal protagonist, Verardi employed hexameters in *Ferdinand Preserved,* the meter of Homer and Vergil, as history merged with epic myth. At the same time, pagan drama has yielded to Christian history, Moorish evil to Catholic virtue, and drama has given way to the spectacle of a miracle.

The research for this volume was carried out at a number of libraries and collections: the Widener and Houghton Libraries of

Harvard University, the John Hay and John D. Rockefeller, Jr. Libraries of Brown University, the Biblioteca Apostolica Vaticana and the Biblioteca Nazionale Centrale in Rome, the Biblioteca Riccardiana and the Biblioteca Nazionale Centrale in Florence, the Biblioteca Nazionale Marciana and the Museo Civico Correr in Venice, the Bibliothèque Nationale de France, the British Museum Library, the Bodleian Library of Oxford University, the Hispanic Society of New York, the University of Rhode Island Library, and the James P. Adams Library of Rhode Island College. I wish to express my appreciation to the research staffs at these institutions and, especially, to Myra Blank of Rhode Island College for her unstinting labors on my behalf. I am also grateful to Professor Joseph Carroll, who suggested a good many improvements, and to Professor Emeritus Robert E. Hogan, a former colleague, who once again aided and abetted my work with a scholar's careful eye and a friend's thoughtful suggestions. All of the errors that remain are, surely, my own. The Faculty Research Fund and the Faculty Development Fund at Rhode Island College provided me with the financial support to conduct my research. Finally, I have been most fortunate to have Carrie Mitzel as my wife, who has always offered me the broadest support and sustained generosity of spirit at those inevitable moments of self-doubt and uncertainty. To our children — Bill, Jon, and Laura — as always, I wish only the best.

NOTES

1. It should be noted, however, that there was some early interest in Greek tragedy in Florence, and Leonzio Pilato had translated about four hundred lines of Euripides' *Hecuba* for Boccaccio around 1360. This remained in manuscript, however. In 1493 we hear of Alessandra Scala reciting Sophocles' *Electra* in Greek in her home in Florence, a performance that won the admiration of Poliziano.

2. This account of the history of the tragic genre is drawn primarily from Kelly, *Ideas and Forms of Tragedy*, and Charlton, *The Senecan Tradition in Renaissance Tragedy*, esp. xxix–li. (Full citations of items in this Introduction may be found in the Bibliography.)

3. Kelly, *Ideas and Forms of Tragedy*, 9.

4. Ibid., 9–10.

5. Ibid., 10.

6. Ibid., 12 (but my trans.).

7. L. D. Reynolds, et al., *Texts and Transmission: A Survey of the Latin Classics* (Oxford: Clarendon Press, 1983), 153–56 (by Michael D. Reeve).

8. E. N. Tigerstedt, "Observations on the Reception of Aristotelian *Poetics* in the Latin West," *Studies in the Renaissance* 15 (1968): 7–24.

9. Julius Ebner, *Beitrag zu einer Geschichte der dramatischen Einheiten in Italien* (Leipzig, 1898), 56, 161ff., cited by Tigerstedt, "Observations," 20–21n.

10. Kelly, *Ideas and Forms of Tragedy*, 134–35; Reynolds, *Texts and Transmission*, 378.

11. On early Paduan humanism see Witt, *In the Footsteps of the Ancients*, chaps. 3 and 4.

12. Kelly, *Ideas and Forms of Tragedy*, 135.

13. V. Rossi and U. Bosco, eds., *Le familiari* [*Familiarium rerum libri*], 4 vols. (Florence: G. C. Sansoni, 1933–1942), 1:195.

14. Cited by Kelly, *Ideas and Forms of Tragedy*, 33 (Kelly's translation).

15. Ibid., 128 (Kelly's translation).

16. Ibid., 133 (Kelly's translation).

17. Paul Grendler, *Schooling in Renaissance Italy* (Baltimore: Johns Hopkins University Press, 1989), esp. 250–60.

18. A. J. Boyle, *Tragic Seneca: An Essay in the Theatrical Tradition* (London: Routledge, 1997), 11. Boyle by contrast emphasizes Seneca's "theatrical mastery in the shaping of dramatic action, the structural unfolding of dramatic language and imagery, the blocking of scenes and acts" and other theatrical skills.

19. Ibid., 24–25.

20. On the textual and structural connections between Mussato's *Ecerinis* and the pseudo-Senecan *Octavia*, see the introduction by Silvia Locati to her edition (2006) of Mussato's play, especially 148–56. Witt, *In the Footsteps of the Ancients*, 126–28, emphasizes the debts to Seneca's *Thyestes*, while the recent critical edition of Chevalier (2000) discloses debts to other plays of Seneca, such as *Oedipus, Phaedra, Troades, Medea,* and *Hercules*, as well as to Boethius' *Consolation of Philosophy*.

21. *Albertini Mussati Historia Augusta Henrici VII Caesaris et alia quae extant omnia*, Epistle I, 39–42.

22. Albertino Mussato, *Argumenta tragediarum Senecae, Commentarii in L. A. Senecae tragoedias, Fragmenta nuper reperta cum praefatione, apparatu critico, scholiis edidit*, ed. A. Megas (Thessalonica: Aristoteleion Panepistemion Thessalonikes, 1969), 125.

23. Kelly, *Ideas and Forms of Tragedy*, 117; but as Kelly remarks, "Aristotle's work had no effect whatsoever upon Mussato's ideas of tragedy."

24. Albertino Mussato, *Lucii Annei Senece Cordubensis vita et mores [Vita Senece]*, ed. A. Megas (Thessalonica: Aristoteleion Panepistemion Thessalonikes, 1967), 159.

25. Staüble, "L'idea di tragedia nell'umanesimo," 205–6.

26. Cloetta, *Beiträge zur Literaturgeschichte des Mittelalters und der Renaissance*, 90. Salutati also had a copy of Mussato's play bound with Seneca's.

27. The invectives are printed in *Prosatori latini del Quattrocento*, ed. E. Garin (Milan: R. Ricciardi, 1952; [repr. Turin, 1977]), 8–22.

28. On Loschi see the important article of Dieter Girgensohn, "Antonio Loschi und Baldassare Cossa vor dem Pisaner Konzil von 1409," *Italia medioevale e umanistica* 30 (1987): 1–94.

29. Joseph R. Berrigan, "Early Neo-Latin Tragedy in Italy," *Acta Conventus Neolatini Lovaniensis*, ed. Jozef IJsewijn and Eckhard Kessler (Munich: Fink, 1973), 89. But for the possible influence on Loschi of Pilato's partial version, made for Boccaccio, of Euripides' *Hecuba*, see note 39 to the translation of Loschi's *Achilles* in this volume.

30. The work is found online in English at http://www.theoi.com/Text/DaresPhrygius.html. See esp. chaps. 27, 30, 34. In pseudo-Dares, the part assigned to Paris by Loschi is played by "Alexander"; this is only one of several mythological details in Dares that Loschi, drawing on his knowledge of Greek mythology, adapts or corrects.

31. Marvin T. Herrick, *Italian Tragedy in the Renaissance* (Urbana: The University of Illinois Press, 1965), 13.

32. Margaret L. King and Albert Rabil, Jr., eds., *Her Immaculate Hand: Selected Works by and about the Women Humanists of Quattrocento Italy* (Binghamton: MRTS, 1983), 103.

33. Aeneas Silvius Piccolomini, "The Education of Boys," in *Humanist Educational Treatises*, ed. and trans. Craig W. Kallendorf (Cambridge: Harvard University Press, 2002), 223.

34. For an extensive discussion of Correr's prosody, see Casarsa's edition (1981), 107–9.

35. Guglielmo Gorni, "Storia del Certame Coronario," *Rinascimento* n.s. 12 (1972): 135–81.

36. Leon Battista Alberti, *Opere volgari*, ed. Cecil Grayson, 3 vols. (Bari: Laterza, 1960–1973), 3: 144.

37. Leonardo Bruni, *Epistolarum libri VIII*, recensente Laurentio Mehus (1741), ed. James Hankins, 2 vols. (Rome: Edizioni di Storia e Letteratura, 2007), 2: 157–58 (Ep. IX,10). See also J. R. Berrigan's treatment of the contest in his edition of Dati (1976), esp. 86–89.

38. Stefano La Via, Pierluigi Petrobelli, and Roger Parker, eds., *Pensieri per un maestro: studio in onore di Pierluigi Petrobelli* (Turin: EDT, 2002),

7–10. Descriptions of similar festivities can be found in a contemporary source, Joannes Burchard's *Diarium sive rerum urbanarum commentarii 1483–1506*, ed. L. Thuasne, 3 vols. (Paris: Ernest Leroux, 1885), esp. 1: 440ff.

39. *Caroli Verardi Caesenatis cubicularii pontificii in historiam Baeticam ad reverendissimum patrem Raphaelem Riarium S. Georgii diaconum cardinalem* (Rome: Eucharius Silber, 1493), A4–A4v.

HUMANIST TRAGEDIES

ALBERTINI MUSSATI

ECERINIS

Adelheita, Ecerinus, Albricus

Ad. Quodnam cruentum sidus Arcthoo potens
regnavit orbe, pestilens tantum michi,
gnati, nefando flebiles cum vos thoro
genui? Patris iam detegam falsi dolos
infausta mater. Non diu tellus nefas
latere patitur; durat occultum nichil.
Audite nullo tempore negandum genus,
devota proles. Arx in excelso sedet
antiqua colle, longa Romanum vocat
aetas: in altum porrigunt tectum trabes,
premitque turrim contigua ad austrum domus,
ventorum et omnis cladis aëreae capax.
Hoc accubans ipso Monachus olim loco
parens eburno vester Ecerinus thoro est

ALBERTINO MUSSATO

ECERINIS

CHARACTERS

Adeleita,[1] *mother of Ezzelino*
Ezzelino, *her son*
Alberico, *her son, brother of Ezzelino*
Ziramonte, *half brother of Ezzelino*
Friar Luca[2]
Ansedisio,[3] *nephew of Ezzelino*
Soldiers
Messenger
Chorus

: ACT I :

Scene I

Adeleita, Ezzelino, Alberico

Adeleita. What bloody star, destructive to me alone, ruled mighty in the northern sky, my sons, when on that unspeakable bed I gave birth to you, crying? I, your unfortunate mother, shall now lay bare the deceits of your lying father. Not for long can the earth conceal a wicked deed; nothing stays hidden. My loving[4] children, hear of that lineage of yours that can never be denied. On an ancient hill sits a citadel on high; long age calls it Romano.[5] Its beams lift the roof to the sky, and on its southern face the house abuts a tower, which is open to the winds and every airborne calamity. Long ago in this very place your father,

dormire visus, cuius ad laevum latus
supina iacui. Iam eloqui factum pudet,
pavet animus, advenit horror et membra occupat.

Ec. Effare, genetrix: grande quodcumque et ferum est
audire iuvat.

Ad. Heu me nefandi criminis
stupenda qualitas! Quasi ad vultum redit
imago facti. Frigore solutum cadit
exangue corpus.

Ec. Erige labantem cito,
Albrice, matrem: illusit amentem timor.
Resperge faciem, sincopim limphis leva.
Facile resurget.

Al. Pristinas vires habet.

Ec. Recolis?

Ad. Recolo, primogenite, primum tui
natalis.

Ec. O mea mater, id pande ocius.

Ad. Cum prima noctis hora, communis quies,
omni teneret ab opere abstractum genus,
et ecce ab imo terra mugitum dedit,
crepuisset ut centrum et foret apertum chaos,
altumque versa resonuit caelum vice:
faciem aëris sulphureus invasit vapor,
nubemque fecit. Tunc subito fulgur domum
lustravit ingens, fulminis ad instar, tono
sequente: oletum sparsa per thalamum tulit
fumosa nubes. Occupor tunc et premor,
et ecce pudor, adulterum ignotum ferens.

Ec. Qualis is adulter, mater?

Ad. Haud tauro minor.
Hirsuta aduncis cornibus cervix riget,
setis coronant hispidis illum iubae:

Ezzelino the Monk,[6] was lying on an ivory bed, apparently sound asleep, and I lay on my back to his left. It shames me to speak of it now. My spirit trembles as the horror of the deed rises and invades my limbs.

Ezzelino. Speak out, mother. It's a fine thing to hear about something great and monstrous.

Adeleita. Woe is me, the nature of that unspeakable crime strikes me dumb. It is as if the image of the deed appears before me again. My bloodless body . . . weakened by a chill . . . faints away.

Ezzelino. Quick, Alberico, hold up our fainting mother. Her fear has taken away her senses. Splash her face and relieve her swoon with water. She'll get up again easily.

Alberico. She has her strength back.

Ezzelino. Do you remember?

Adeleita. I do remember, my firstborn, the beginning of your birth.

Ezzelino. O my mother, explain it to us quickly.

Adeleita. When the first hour of the night, the common time for rest, released folk from all work, behold the earth from its very depths gave out a moan so that its center cracked open and chaos was unleashed. Heaven on high echoed in response, and a sulfurous fog fell upon the air and formed a cloud. Then, suddenly, a great flash, like lightning, illuminated the house, followed by thunder. The smoky cloud spread through the bedroom and carried its stench with it. At that moment, I am seized and raped. Behold my shame, not even knowing who violated me.

Ezzelino. What kind of a man was the adulterer, mother?

Adeleita. As big as a bull.[7] His hairy neck is erect with curved horns and a mane of shaggy hair covers his crown. A bloody

sanguinea binis orbibus manat lues,
ignemque nares flatibus crebris vomunt:
favilla, patulis auribus surgens, salit
ab ore; spirans os quoque eructat levem
flammam, perennis lambit et barbam focus.
Votis potitus talis ut adulter suis
implevit uterum Venere letali meum,
cum strage cessit victor e thalamo, petens
telluris ima; cessit et tellus sibi.
Sed heu recepta pertinax nimium Venus
incaluit intus viscera exagitans statim;
onusque sensit terribile venter tui,
Ecerine, digna veraque propago patris.
Testor supernum numen adversum michi:
quos egi abinde tunc gravida menses decem,
lacrimae fuere angustiae gemitus dolor;
interna gessit bella visceribus furor.
Nec monstruoso, nate, sine partu venis.
Ec. Qualis?
Ad. Necis pronosticus ventrem levas
cruentus infans, fronte crudeli minax,
terribile visu atroxque portentum indicans.
Tu, care fili Albrice, iam video, tuos
attendis ortus: nosce. Si quicquam scio,
tu quoque scies: penitus dubia semper fui,
quis te huic nefando corpori inseruit pater.
A tempore quidem, nate, dicti criminis
semper medullas ussit Aethnaeus calor,
viscera malignus abinde torsit spiritus,
nec nostra curis pectora absolvit sopor.
Cum me vigilia vana seu somni quies
incerta tenuit, — vera ne prorsus negem

liquid drips from both eyes, and snorting rapidly, his nostrils spew flame. Hot cinders, rising up to his wide ears, burst from his mouth which belches a thin flame too when he breathes, and a perpetual fire licks upon his beard. Having satisfied his lust, the adulterer filled my womb with the deadly seed of Venus, then left the bedroom victorious, wreaking havoc as he went, seeking the depths of the earth, and the earth yielded to him. But, alas, the seed I had received held fast and burned within my vitals, tormenting them all at once; my womb felt the dreadful weight of you, Ezzelino, the fitting and true offspring of your father. I call upon the divinity above, no friend to me, to bear witness:[8] for the next nine months I suffered through a pregnancy of tears, pain, grief, anguish. Inside me, madness made intestine warfare against me. It was not without a monstrous birth, my son, that you came into the world.

Ezzelino. Of what kind?

Adeleita. A presage of death, you relieved my womb as an infant, covered in blood, menacing with your cruel brow, pointing to a dire portent, terrible to behold. My dear son Alberico, I see you now waiting to learn of your birth. If I know anything, you will know it too. I always had deep doubts what father it was who seeded you in this accursed body of mine. Ever since the aforesaid crime, my son, a heat like Etna's ever burned my marrow, and an evil spirit continued to twist in my vitals, nor did sleep free my heart from care. While sleepless vigils and rest troubled by dreams took hold of me—I would not entirely deny the

aut falsa fatear—utitur eodem stupro
adulter idem verus Ecerini pater.
Ec. Quid poscis ultra, frater? An tanti pudet,
vesane, patris? Abnegas divum genus?
Diis gignimur. Nec stirpe tanta Romulus
Remusque quondam Marte tolluntur suo.
Hic maior est, latissimi regni deus,
rex ultionum, cuius imperio luunt
poenas potentes principes reges duces.
Erimus paterno iudices digni foro,
si vindicemus operibus regnum patris,
cui bella mortes exitia fraudes doli
perditio et omnis generis humani placent.

Sic fatus ima parte secessit domus
petens latebras, luce et exclusa caput
tellure pronus sternit in faciem cadens
tunditque solidam dentibus frendens humum
patremque saeva voce Luciferum ciet.

Depulse ab astris, mane iam lucens polis,
pater superbe, triste qui regnum tenes
chaos profundi, cuius imperio luunt
delicta manes, excipe ex imo specu,
Vulcane, dignas supplicis gnati preces:
te certa et indubitata progenies vocat.
Potiare me; experiare, si quicquam potest
insita voluntas pectori flagrans meo.
Paludis atrae lividam testor Stigem,
Christum negavi semper exosum michi
odique semper nomen inimicum Crucis.
Assint ministrae facinorum comites michi:

truth nor would I confess what is false—the same adulterer, the true father of Ezzelino, raped me again.

Ezzelino. What more do you want, my brother? Or are you ashamed, crazy fellow, of so great a father? Do you deny your divine origin? We are born of gods. Mars did not exalt Romulus and Remus, once upon a time, by so great a lineage. This god is greater by far, a god of the widest realm, a king of vengeance, at whose command mighty princes, kings and leaders suffer punishment. We shall be judges worthy of our paternal tribunal if by our actions we lay claim to the kingdom of our father, who delights in wars, death, ruin, deceit, fraud and the perdition of the whole human race.

Scene II

Thus he spoke and withdrew into the innermost part of the palace, seeking the shadows; and shut away from the light, flat on the ground, falling on his face and touching his head to the ground, he pounds on the hard earth while gnashing his teeth, and with a bestial cry summons his father Lucifer.

Ezzelino

Expelled from the stars, now shining bright from the heavens each morning,[9] proud father, you who rule over the sad kingdom of deep Chaos, by whose command the shades of the dead atone for their crimes, accept from the deepest cavern, o Vulcan, the worthy prayers of your suppliant son; your true and unquestioned offspring calls upon you. Make me yours; test what the innate resolve burning in my breast can do. I summon the livid Styx of the black swamp as witness: I have always denied Christ as one hateful to me and have always despised as something hostile the name of the Cross. Let the ministers of

suadeat Alecto scelera, Thesiphone explicet,
Megaera in actus saeva prorumpat truces,
faveatque coeptis diva Persephone meis.
Ingenia praedae quisque sollicitus paret,
nec inferorum spiritus quisquam vacet;
animos ad iras odia et invidias citent.
Ensis cruenti detur officium michi:
ipse executor finiam lites merus:
nullis tremescet sceleribus fidens manus.
Annue, Sathan, et filium talem proba.

Chorus

Quis vos exagitat furor,
o mortale hominum genus?
Quo vos ambitio vehit?
Quonam scandere pergitis?
Nescitis cupidi nimis
quo discrimine quaeritis
regni culmina lubrici:
diros expetitis metus,
mortis continuas minas:
mors est mixta tyrannidi,
non est morte minor metus.
Ast haec dicere quid valet?
Sic est: sic animus volat;
tunc, cum grandia possidet,
illis non penitus satur;
cor maiora recogitat.
Vos in iurgia, nobiles,
atrox invidiae scelus
ardens elicit, inficit:

crimes be present as my companions: let Alecto inspire in me evil deeds, let Tisiphone give them shape, let fierce Megaera force ferocity into action, and may the goddess Persephone favor my undertakings.[10] Let each one of them sedulously turn their minds to plunder; let not one of the infernal spirits sit idly by; let them whip their spirits up to wrath, hatred and scorn. Let the tasks of the sword be given me, dripping with blood; I myself, as absolute executor, shall prescribe lines of dispute; my trusty hand will tremble at no crime. Grant my prayer, Satan, and give your approval to such a son.

Scene III

Chorus

[*In Padua*]

What frenzy drives you on, O mortal race of men? Where does ambition carry you? What heights do you strive to climb, pray? In your excess of desire you know not the danger that besets your quest for the slippery heights of power. It is dreadful fears you chase after and unending threats of death. Death is inseparable from tyranny, nor is fear something less than death. But what does it avail to tell you these things? It is thus, thus that the spirit takes wing; then, when it comes to possess greatness, it is not satisfied, but the heart imagines even greater things. The deadly, burning sin of envy entices you into quarrels, no-

numquam quis patitur parem.
O quam multa potentium
nos et scandala cordibus
plebs vilissima iungimus!
Illos tollimus altius,
hos deponimus infimos:
leges iuraque condimus,
post haec condita scindimus.
Nobis retia tendimus,
mortale auxilium damus,
falsum praesidium sumus.
Haec demum iugulis luunt:
nos secum miseri trahunt,
nos secum cadimus; cadunt.
Sic semper rota volvitur,
durat perpetuum nichil.
En, cur Marchia nobilis
haec Tarvisia sic fremit,
signis undique classicis
clamor bellicus obstrepit,
exardet furor excitus,
gentes e requie trahit,
cives otia deserunt?
Dirum pax peperit nefas.
Bullit sanguinis impetus
et certamina postulat,
partes crimina detegunt,
ferrum poscitur urbibus,
turbat iustitiae forum.
Verona venit anxius,
qui iam fert nova, nuntius.

blemen, and tinges you;[11] never does one of you endure an equal. O how many scandalous acts of the powerful do we and the vilest rabble clasp to our hearts! The powerful we raise still higher; the rabble we push down to the bottom. We establish laws and statutes, and then, after establishing them, tear them down. We spread nets for ourselves, give deadly help, and are but an illusory source of protection. In the end they pay for this with cut throats, and the wretches drag us down along with them; they fall and we fall with them. So the wheel[12] turns round and round forever; nothing endures. Tell me, why is the noble March of Treviso[13] so filled with uproar, why does the clamor of war with its trumpet calls resound everywhere, why do frenzy and excitement burn so hot, dragging people from their rest and citizens from their leisure? Peace has begotten dreadful crime. The lust for blood boils and demands strife. Factions reveal their crimes, cities look to the sword, the courts of justice are thrown into confusion. Even now a messenger, filled with anxiety, comes from Verona bearing news.

Nuntius, Chorus

Nu. Excelse mundi rector, omnipotens Deus,
altos abhinc tu forsitan caelos colis
nostro remotos aethere, et Marti sinis
soli regendas climatis nostri plagas?
O dira nobilium odia, o populi furor!
Finis petitus litibus vestris adest;
adest tyrannus, vestra quem rabies dedit.
Nefanda vidi.
Ch. Pande, quod series habet,
flatu remisso; siste, dum cedat frequens
anhelitus.
Nu. Dicam aliquid ex gestis prius,
dedere quae praesentibus causas malis.
O, semper huius Marchiae clades vetus,
Verona, limen hostium et bellis iter,
sedes tyranni, sive sit terrae situs
belli capacis sive tale hominum genus
natura ab ipsa tale producat solum.
Intrinseca odia civium peperit nefas
in Marchia tunc, cum regimen urbis gerens
Estensis Azo marchio eiectus fuit:
favore falso fulta; non notus sagax
Ecerinus erat, in ambitum flagrans suum.
Hic coepta lis, hic Marchiae exitium fuit.
Nam pulsus inde marchio iusta furens
exarsit ira, cuius in partem comes
Bonifacius haerens iunxit ultrices manus.

: ACT II :

Scene I

Messenger, Chorus

Messenger. Exalted ruler of the world, Almighty God, do you dwell, perhaps, in the high heavens, far removed from our clime, and allow Mars alone to rule our region of earth? O dreadful feuds of the nobles! O madness of the people! The end of struggles you sought is at hand; the tyrant is at hand whom your rage created. I have seen unspeakable things.

Chorus. When you have caught your breath, explain what has happened; wait until your breath returns to normal.

Messenger. First let me say something about the deeds that caused the present evils.[14] O Verona, always the ancient ruin of this March, gateway of enemies and route for wars, seat of tyrants! Is it the situation of your land that makes you prone to war or is it the very nature of your soil that begets a bellicose race of men? Sin gave life to the intestine hatreds of the citizens in the March at the time when the marquess, Azzo d'Este, the governor of the city, was expelled. These hatreds were propped up with hidden partisanship; Ezzelino, unnoticed, was crafty and on fire with ambition. Here is where the strife began, here was the destruction of the March. For the marquess, driven from his fief, was ablaze with justified anger; Count Bonifacio, who belonged to the marquess' party, added his troops to the ven-

Braida cruentae sustulit caedis nefas,
litem diremit sanguine effuso prius
campestre bellum, fusus et campis cruor.
Dedere victi terga Monticuli fugae
turpi recessu, scelere seducti suo,
quos arce tuta sustulit Gardae lacus.
Non ullus inde litibus finis fuit:
fortuna varios partibus casus dedit.
Exertus hinc Ecerinus, et vires agens
in iurgia Salinguerra Monticulis favens,
exinde comes et marchio, iuncti simul,
traxere saeva ad bella populorum manus
facile paratas. O, labans hominum genus,
vulgus, et ad omne facinus in clades ruens,
voces secutum et negligens facti fidem!

Ch. Procede: redeas unde coepisti prius.
Sermone cur nos anxios dudum tenes?
Quae nova?

Nu. Nova audietis et finem statim.
Iam iam peregi exordia et causas cito
saevae tyrannidis. Ita ut ancipites vices
facileque verti Marchiae vidit statum,
tunc fovit odia Ecerinus, exacuens dolo
partes amicas, litis et causas movet
sedatque motas arbiter dirus latens.
Sic sic repente, ut maior, augmentat statum,
sicque eminentes clanculum calcat viros,
dum restat ipse, magna qui solus potest.
Quidnam revolvo? Taliter serpens fera
subiit tyrannis, sicque Veronam iugo
dolis et astu traxit Ecerinus suo.
Quid plura? Coepti colligo formam novi.
Eversa terra nobilis pretio iacet

detta. Braida[15] endured unspeakably bloody slaughter, and after blood was spilt, the quarrel was settled on the battlefield, and gore was poured out in the fields. The conquered Montecchi turned tail and fled in shameful retreat, withdrawing from the scene of their wickedness and taking refuge in a citadel on the Lago di Garda. There was no end to the fighting thereafter; fortune gave the factions victory and defeat by turns. On one side, Ezzelino rose up and Salinguerra, favoring the Montecchi, drove his forces into the quarrel. On the other side, the count and the marquess joined forces and dragged into the cruel wars throngs of the common people whom they easily assembled. O the rabble, that fickle race of men, ready for every outrageous act, ever rushing headlong toward disaster, following voices but neglecting reality.

Chorus. Continue. Return to the point where you began. Why do you leave us hanging on your words? What news do you have?

Messenger. You'll hear the news and the end of the story at once. Just now I ran quickly through the origins and causes of the cruel tyranny. When Ezzelino[16] saw that the situation was in doubt and the stability of the March easily subverted, at that moment he nourished hatreds, aggravating partisanship through deceit; he sets in motion legal quarrels and then quells them, hiding the cruel judge inside. Thus in an instant, growing great, he augments his power and in this way secretly tramples down eminent men, while he himself remains the only one capable of achieving greatness. Why do I brood over this? A brutal regime has insinuated itself like a serpent, and thus Ezzelino through treachery and cunning forced Verona under his yoke. What more is there to say? I'll summarize the shape of

parens tyranno Padua: iam sceptrum tenet,
agens superbas dirus imperii vices
Ecerinus. Ah quot exitia, populis minax,
promittit atrox! carceres ignes cruces
tormenta mortes exilia diras fames.
Sed, o maleficis digna permittens Deus
supplicia, meriti nobiles primi luunt;
qui vendidere, scelera iam expendunt sua.

Chorus

Christe, qui caelis resides in altis
patris a dextris solio sedentis,
totus an summi illecebris Olympi
gaudiis tantum frueris supernis,
negligis quicquid geritur sub astris?
Non tuas affert fremitus ad aures
rumor humani generis per auras?
Sanguis Abel ad Dominum querelas
pertulit, fratrem perhibens cruentum.
Foeda Gomorrae Sodomaeque labes
imbre divinam satiavit iram.
Cur modo non sic, moderator aequi,
cernis errores hominum modernos?
Praepotens nostro dominatur aevo
saeva tyrannis,
nulla quam mundo memoravit aetas.
Bistonis cedit stabuli vetustas
nota seu torvi rabies Procustis,
cedit et pravi feritas Neronis.
Carceres edunt tenebris opacis

the new enterprise. Padua, a noble land, has been ruined, sold out, and lies prostrate, obedient to a tyrant; already, merciless Ezzelino holds the scepter, acting as the proud vicar of the Empire. Ah, with how many forms of ruin does the cruel tyrant menace his peoples: dungeons, flames, crosses, torture, death, exile, deadly famine! But, O God who permits fitting punishments to evildoers, the nobles deserve to expiate their crimes first: those who sold out their city are already paying for their crimes.

Scene II

Chorus

O Christ, who dwells in heaven on high, at the right hand of his Father who sits upon his throne, can it really be that you are charmed completely by the allurements of high Olympus, delighting only in supernal joys, while neglecting what goes on beneath the stars? Doesn't the clamor of the human race send its cries through the air to your ears? The blood of Abel raised its laments all the way to the Lord, indicting his bloodstained brother. The foul corruption of Sodom and Gomorrah satiated the divine wrath in a rain of fire. Dispenser of justice, why do you not see men's sins of the present day in this way? A cruel, overpowering tyranny dominates our age, a tyranny such as no age of the world can recall. The ancient stables of Thrace, the infamous rage of grim Procrustes,[17] even the brutality of the depraved Nero falls short. From the dark shadows of his dun-

morte vivaci gemitus iacentum;
mors famis vinctis sitis et nefandae
donat extremum miseranda finem
saepe petitum.
Plebe cum tota populus subegit
colla, devoti veluti iuvenci
victimis sacras veniunt ad aras.
Invenit causas dominus patrandae
caedis in cives sceleratus omnes:
pervigil semper timet, et timetur.
Iura naturae vitiis laborant,
exulat nostris pietas ab oris,
regnat Herinis.
Frater, ut saevo placeat tyranno,
fratris incumbit iugulo cruentus:
proh dolor! patrem rogitat cremandum
natus, ardentes subicitque flammas.
Ille tantorum scelerum superstes
asperans saevas Ecerinus iras,
prolis ut semen pereat futurae,
censet infantum genital recidi,
feminas sectis ululare mammis.
Stratus in cunis chorus innocentum
luget indocto mutilatus ore;
lumen in caecis tenebris requirit
lumine cassus.
Quid Deus tantos pateris furores,
quos soles et non iacularis ignes?
Terra cur non sub pedibus dehiscit,
hic ut infernas subeat tenebras
anguis, humani generis peremptor?
Te Patrem caeli populus redemptus
invocat supplex, iterum relapsus.

geons there issue the groans of those lying helplessly in living death. Pitiful death gives to those in chains their final release, long desired, from starvation and unspeakable thirst. Together with the whole plebs the people[18] bend their necks, like doomed oxen who come as victims to the sacred altars. Their wicked master invents pretexts for slaughtering all the citizens; sleepless all night long, he fears, and is feared. The laws of nature are burdened with vice, piety is banished from our shores, the Erinyes[19] reign. A bloodstained brother, to please a cruel tyrant, falls on the throat of his own brother. O misery! A son demands that his father be burnt to ashes and applies the blazing torch himself! Ezzelino, witness to a thousand crimes, further exasperates cruelty and rage by ordering that babies have their genitalia mutilated, so that the seed of their future offspring may perish, and that screaming women should have their breasts cut off. Lying in their cradles a chorus of maimed innocents laments, though they have not yet learned to speak; devoid of light, they seek for light in the blind darkness. God, why do you allow such cruel madness, why do you not hurl down lightning as is your wont? Why does the earth not yawn beneath his feet so that this snake, destroyer of the human race, may go down to the darkness of hell? Your redeemed people, fallen once again, call upon you in supplication, Heavenly Father!

Ecerinus, Albricus

Ec. Matris relatu, vera quem prodit fides,
Ditis cruenti semine egressi sumus,
hoc digni patre; tale nos decuit genus.
Sic fata forsan expetunt, quae non Deus
prohibere curans, esse sic ultro sinit;
nam quisque liber arbiter in actus suos.
Delicta poscunt gentium ultrices manus:
ergo, ministri scismatis mundo dati,
quid plus inanes ducimus frustra moras?
Capiamus urbes undique et late loca.
Verona Vicentia Padua nutu meo
iam subiacent: progrediar ulterius cito.
Promissa Lombardia me dominum vocat:
habere puto. Meos nec ibi sistam gradus.
Italia michi debetur. Haud equidem satis
nec illa. Ad ortus signa referantur mea,
meus unde cecidit Lucifer quondam pater,
ubi vindicabo forsitan caelum potens.
Numquam Typheus aut Encheladus olim Jovi
tantum intulere proelium aut ullus gigas.
Convertam ad austrum signa, qua medius dies
flagrat tepenti sidere.
Al. Infernus annuat pater.
Ec. Propere annuet.
Et tu quid audes, frater?
Al. Edissero statim.

: ACT III :

Scene I

Ezzelino. Alberico

[At the palace in Verona]

Ezzelino. According to our mother's trustworthy account, we were born from the cruel seed of Dis,[20] and are worthy of this father; such a lineage befits us. Perhaps the Fates were aiming at things which God, not caring to thwart them, voluntarily permitted to exist; for each man is a free judge of his own actions. The sins of nations demand avenging hands; thus, since we have been given to the world as ministers of schism, why do we wait any longer in vain? Let us seize cities and territories wide and far. Verona, Vicenza, and Padua already lie subject to my will; I shall soon advance even further. Lombardy is promised me and calls me master; already I count it mine. Nor will my steps halt there. Italy ought to be mine. Not even that is enough. Let my banners be carried back to the east whence my father Lucifer once fell,[21] where perhaps I shall in power lay claim to heaven. Never did Typhoeus or Enceladus or any giant in the past wage so mighty a battle against Jupiter.[22] I shall then turn my banners to the south where midday blazes under the hot star.

Alberico. May our infernal father give his consent.

Ezzelino. He will do so speedily. And you, brother, what act of daring will you do?

Tarvisium tyrannidi paret meae:
Feltro subacto, ad Julii pergam Forum
subigamque totas Arcthici gentes poli.
Hoc quoque parum est. Non desinam. Restat michi
vicenda triplex Gallia et sero videns
pars occidentis usque quo oceanus diem
absorbet.
Ec. O mi frater, o magno sate.
Plutone, tantis ausibus vires ferat,
tellure rupta spiritus nocuos pater
nobis faventes commodet; functi quibus
corpora trahamus et animas Orcho simul.
I, dire frater, infimi proles dei,
et bella mecum, pace sublata, move
sub fraudis astu; finge te iratum michi:
dolosa species haec ad interitum trahet
hinc inde multos transfugas. Absit fides
pietasque nostris actibus semper procul.

Ecerinus, Ziramons, Frater Lucas

Ec. Ziramons?
Zi. Domine.
Ec. Dic age, quid est? Propere indica.
Iacet Monaldi corpore abscisum caput,
nullo tuente?
Zi. Publico squalet foro
putata cervix; nullus et caesum movet.
Ec. Quicquam rebelle constat?
Zi. Omnino nichil.
Ec. Hem vicimus! Iamque omne fas licet et nefas.
Ferro tuenda civitas nostro vacat.
Cum plebe pereat omne nobilium genus;

Alberico. I shall tell you immediately. Treviso obeys my tyranny; Feltre has been subdued. I shall move into Friuli and subdue all the peoples of the northern regions. Even this is too little. I shall not stop. It remains for me to conquer triple Gaul[23] and at last the land of the setting sun, up to where Ocean devours the day.

Ezzelino. O my brother, seed of great Pluto, may our father give his strength to our great enterprises, rend open the earth, and supply us with evil spirits who will favor us. Our work done, let us bring both our bodies and souls together down to Orcus. Go, dread brother, offspring of the god of the abyss, and putting an end to peace, make war with me, using cunning deceits: pretend you are angry with me. This stratagem will drag to destruction many deserters on both sides. May loyalty and religion be forever far distant from our actions!

Scene II

Ezzelino, Ziramonte, Friar Luca

[*Under the ramparts at Mantua*]

Ezzelino. Ziramonte?

Ziramonte. Master.

Ezzelino. Speak up, what is it? Tell me immediately. Does the head of Monaldo, severed from his body, lie unguarded?[24]

Ziramonte. His bodiless head lies caked with dirt in the public square, and no one takes the slaughtered man away.

Ezzelino. Is there any sign of rebellion?

Ziramonte. None at all.

Ezzelino. Ha! We have won. And now everything, whether right or wrong, is allowed. The city is devoid of protection against my sword. Let all the lineages of the nobility perish with the

non sexus aetas ordo non ullus gradus
a caede nostra liber aut expers eat.
Vagetur ensis undique et largus cruor
abundet atra tabe perfusus foro:
hinc inde patulae corpora ostentent cruces;
subdantur ignes, illa qui flammis crement,
stilletque sanies: fumus ad summos polos
a me litatas victimas tales ferat.

Fr. Inclite Ecerine, parce, da fandi locum;
annue parumper, obsecro, ut tutus loquar.
Ec. Contexe.
Fr. Mira res. Quid est quod te movet,
o homo? Homo es, nec est ut hoc unum neges.
Mortalis ergo; nam omne, quod oritur, occidit.
Servare seriem cuncta, si pensas, vides.
Terra mare caelum et illa, quae substant eis,
gerunt statutas legibus certis vices.
Quae pallet hieme, tempore aestatis viret,
certasque certis mensibus fruges alit
tellus. Procellis aestuat vastis mare,
turbine remisso quod patitur ultro rates.
Caelum intueris orbibus motum suis;
stabiles perennis sustinet cardo polos;
disposita sidera peragunt cursus vagos
sub lege certa. Sed quis haec praepotens movet?
Excelsus horum motor omnipotens Deus:
hic aequus aequa lance dispensat sua,
quae fecit, opera: dictus hic ordo sacer
iustitia. Iustus hanc coli voluit Deus

rabble; let not sex, age, rank, nor any status of person escape or be exempt from our slaughter. Let the sword roam at will, hither and yon, let oceans of gore flow, soaking everywhere in the forum, reeking and grisly; let crosses, boasting of bodies, be erected everywhere; let fires be lit beneath to consume them in flames, and let the filthy discharge from their wounds drip down; let smoke bear up to the heights of heaven the victims I have offered in sacrifice.

Scene III

Friar Luca and Ezzelino

Friar. Noble Ezzelino, pardon me, give me leave to speak; I beg you, allow me to speak in safety for a little while.

Ezzelino. Go on, weave your web.

Friar. What an astonishing thing! What is it that drives you so, O man? You are a man, and this is one thing you can't deny. Therefore, you are mortal, for everything that is born dies. If you think about it, you see that everything follows this process. The earth, sea, heavens and that which lies beneath them go through their ordained cycles according to immutable laws. That which pales in winter grows green in summer, and the earth nourishes the same fruits in fixed seasons. The sea rages with great storms, but the windstorm subsides so as to invite ships to sail. You gaze upon the heavens moving each in its orbit; an everlasting axis sustains the poles; the stars are set in order to go through their wandering courses according to fixed law. But who is so prepotent as to set all this in motion? Almighty God on high is the mover of these things. He distributes fairly the works he has created using fair scales. And this

a se creatis hominibus mortalibus.
Hos esse tales edocent primo insitae
natura ab ipsa Caritas Spes et Fides.
Has, crede, quisque pectori innatas habet,
traducat error devius quemquam licet.
Converte, quaeso, igitur ad has species boni,
ut Caritas pia proximo parcat tuo,
speresque gratiam misericordis Dei;
quae consequi omnia sancta te faciet Fides.
Ec. Videtne celsus ista quae facio Deus?
Fr. Videt.
Ec. Retundet ipse cum prorsus volet?
Fr. Quidni? Retundet.
Ec. Ergo quid segnis facit?
Fr. Expectat humilis, pertinax cedat furor
et ipse retrahas caedibus tantis manum.
Ec. Unius igitur interit multos salus.
Quis hic Deus, cui carior multis fui?
Fr. Ecerine, crede, carior Saulus fuit,
peccare postquam desiit. Mitis Deus
redemptor animas ipse venatur suas
errore falso devias pastor bonus;
errore lapsos adiuvans vitam suis
ad abluenda crimina elongat pius.
Ec. Me credo mundo, scelera ut ulciscar, datum,
illo iubente. Plurimas quondam dedit
vindex iniquis gentibus clades Deus,
ceteraque meritis debita exitia suis.
Diluvia culices grandines ignes fames,
ne mentiar, Scriptura testatur Vetus.
Dedit et tyrannos urbibus, licuit quibus
sine ordine, sine fine, strictis ensibus
saevire largo sanguine in gentes vage.

sacred order is called justice. The just God ordained that justice be practiced by the mortal men he has created. Faith, hope, and charity, implanted in us by Nature herself, teach us that these things are so. Believe me, each man has these virtues innate within his breast, but error can lead anyone from the right path. I beg you, therefore, convert yourselves to these species of the good, so that holy charity may spare your neighbor, so that you may hope for the grace of a merciful God, all of which a devout faith will cause you to follow.

Ezzelino. Does God on high watch what I do?

Friar. He does.

Ezzelino. Will he himself restrain me when he so desires?

Friar. Without a doubt he will.

Ezzelino. Then why is he so slow in doing so?

Friar. He waits humbly for your stubborn rage to cease and for you yourself to withdraw your own hand from endless slaughter.

Ezzelino. So the salvation of one man destroys many men. Who is this God to whom I am dearer than many?

Friar. Ezzelino, believe me, Saul was dearer after he stopped sinning.[25] Gentle God himself, our Redeemer, the good shepherd, seeks out his souls wandering about in misguided error, helping those who have fallen in error and out of love lengthening their lives to wash away their sins.

Ezzelino. I believe I have been given to the world on his orders to punish sins. In the past an avenging God gave countless calamities to sinful peoples as well as other disasters that their deeds merited. If you don't believe me, the Old Testament gives testimony to floods, vermin, hail, fire, and famine. He also gave cities tyrants and allowed the latter to roam far and wide, raging with drawn swords through oceans of blood, without restraint,

Nabuchodonosor, Aegyptius Pharao, Saul,
proles Philippi gloriosa Macedonis,
hi pervetustae memoriae, nostrae quoque
praelata mundo Caesarum egregia domus,
felicis unde memoriae exortus Nero,
polluere caedibus quot hi mundum suis?
Quantis cruoribus rubuit altum mare,
illis iubentibus? Nec inspector Deus
prohibere voluit, esse sic ultro sinens.

Nuntius, Ecerinus, Ansedisius, Commilitones

Nu. Audi negandum, teste nisi certo, novum:
en, ipse vidi. Parce, dum verum loquar.
Ec. Evelle nugas, vane iactator, tuas.
Nu. Progressa Venetis exulum fervens aquis
invasit agros magna Patavorum cohors
Ferrariensiumque, quot plenae rates
deferre poterant, totus et Venetus favor,
cruce praevia Papaeque legato duce.
Districtualium subito victis locis,
venere ad urbem. Currit ad pontem pedes;
subiectus altas incremat portas focus
undante fumo. Desuper nullus stetit,
omnisque cessit victa custodum manus.
Capta Padua est, et exules illam tenent.
Ec. Abscede, mendax serve: mulctatus pede
praemium relatu tolle condignum tuo.

Ec. Ast Ansedisius ecce venit hac. Hem, quid est?
An. Amissa Paduae civitas: hostes habent.

without limit: Nebuchadnezzar, the Egyptian Pharaoh, Saul, and the glorious offspring of Philip of Macedon,[26] all in remotest times; and in our own times the noble house of the Caesars was exalted over the world, the house from which Nero of happy memory arose. With how many murders did these men defile the world? With how much blood did the deep sea redden on their orders? And your watchful God didn't want to stop them! He let it all happen willingly!

Scene IV

Messenger, Ezzelino

Messenger. Listen to the news, impossible to believe except it comes from a reliable witness. I myself actually saw it. Don't condemn me as I speak the truth.

Ezzelino. Out with your nonsense, you empty braggart.

Messenger. Advancing over Venetian waters, a huge seething throng of exiles from Padua and Ferrara, as many as fully loaded boats could carry, invaded the fields with the complete support of Venice, with the Holy Cross at the front and led by a papal legate. With the outlying districts quickly conquered, they came to the city. A foot soldier ran to the drawbridge, and throwing torches underneath, he burned their lofty gates, smoke billowing. No one resisted from above. The entire defending force yielded and Padua was taken. The exiles occupy the city.

Ezzelino. Get out, you lying slave! You've been fined with the loss of a foot—take that as the reward your report deserves.

Scene V

Ezzelino, Ansedisio, Soldiers, Chorus

Ezzelino. But, look, Ansedisio approaches. Well, what is it?

Ansedisio. The city of Padua is lost; the enemy controls it.

Ec. Amissa vi?
An. Vi amissa.
Ec. Qua?
An. Ferro fuga
et ignibus, vinci quibus et urbes solent.
Ec. At te superstite, sola quem facies notat
illaesa noxium, sceleris index tui?
Secede, cui non poena sufficiat necis.
Commilitones, nostra quid virtus petit?
Animos viriles casus infestus probat.
Co. Magnanime princeps, tolle consilium tuis
salubre votis. Subito Paduanos cape,
Verona vinctos teneat et carcer tuus:
mortes minare rigidus et Paduam celer
accede; muros milites cingant tui.
Invade trepidos, tolle pendentes moras;
terror suorum, noster et magnus vigor
sternent rebelles: victor optatum feres.
Fortuna vires ausibus nostris dabit.
Ch. O fallax hominum praemeditatio
eventus dubii sortis et inscia
venturae! Instabiles nam variat vices
motus perpetuae continuus rotae.
En atrox Ecerinus citus advolat.
Assuetam Paduam colla iugo dare
infestam reperit, iussaque spernere
vallatam aspiciens, agmine circuit;
ad ripas acies fluminis admovet.
Stat contra series ordine militum
inspectans oculis ora tyrannica;
infandas rabies ausibus exprobrat.
Postquam nulla virum spes Paduae manet,
retro vertit equum castraque summovet;

Ezzelino. Lost by force?

Ansedisio. Lost by force.

Ezzelino. Of what kind?

Ansedisio. By the sword, by flight, by fires—the usual way cities are conquered.

Ezzelino. Yet you survived? Your unharmed face alone shows that you are guilty; it's a telltale sign of your villainous behavior. Get out! The death penalty isn't enough for you. [*Ansedisio leaves.*] Fellow soldiers, what does our valor demand? Misfortunes test manly courage.

Soldiers. Valiant prince, take whatever counsel advances your desires. Take the Paduans at once, let your dungeon at Verona hold the captives in chains. Sternly threatening them with death, march swiftly on Padua; let your soldiers surround its walls. Attack the fearful. Stop this uncertainty and delay. The fear for their own people and our great vigor will strike the rebels down; with victory you will have what you desire. Fortune will give strength to our daring.

Chorus

[*Padua*]

O the deceptive foresight of men, ignorant of uncertain outcomes and of our future lot! For the constant turning of the never-ending wheel changes with each changing circumstance. Look, the brutal Ezzelino advances quickly. Padua, used to bending its neck under the yoke, he finds hostile, and seeing the entrenched city spurn his orders, he surrounds it with his troops. He advances his line of battle to the banks of the river. Opposite stands a line of troops in strict order, staring in the face of the tyrant, reproaching his unspeakable fury with their daring. Having lost all hope of taking Padua, Ezzelino turns his

Veronam redit iram exacuens suam.
Ad caedes properat concitus impias,
captivos Patavos innocuos fame
caecis carceribus conficit et siti,
et vitas adimit milibus undecim.
Nullis plaustra vehunt agnita corpora:
non natum genetrix, non mulier virum
agnovere suos certave funera:
communes lacrimae desuper omnibus.
Desunt praedia tot busta recondere,
corrumpit sanies aethera desuper.
Spectator queritur iudicii parum,
dum restat Patavum quod reparet genus.

Ec. Adversa vires fortibus praebet viris
fortuna, viles opprimit: pugnat vigor
adversus eius impetum. Restat suo
vincenda Padua tempore. Abscedite retro.
Lombarda signis appetit subdi meis
gens tota ab infra Gallicis degens iugis.

Nuntius, Chorus

Nu. Huc huc venite quisquis optatum velit
finem malorum scire et e summo datam
caelo quietem, thure placetis Deum;
iuvenes senes viduae, colite festum diem:

horse about and breaks camp. He returns to Verona, his anger razor sharp. He rushes headlong to unholy slaughter and murders innocent Paduan prisoners by starvation and thirst in his gloomy dungeons. He takes the lives of 11,000 of them. Carts carry off the bodies, identified by no one; mother does not claim son, nor wife husband, nor are there funeral rites for individuals; common tears are shed over all. There isn't enough land to bury so many bodies, and the smell of corruption poisons the air over them. Surveying the carnage, Ezzelino complains that the just vengeance he has taken is too little, so long as there remains a Padua to restore its race.

: ACT IV :

Scene I

Ezzelino

Ill fortune gives strength to brave men while it crushes cowards; vigorous action fights Fortune's onrushing force. Padua remains to be conquered in its own time. Withdraw. The entire Lombard nation dwelling south of the Alpine ridges longs to be subdued by my banners.

Scene II

Messenger, Chorus

[Padua]

Messenger. Here, come here, whoever wishes to learn of the longed-for end of evils and the peace granted by highest heaven. Seek God's favor with incense. Young men, old men, widows — cele-

in vos ab alto iustus inspexit Deus.
Ch. Tanta ergo nova iam breviter expedias, bone.
Nu. Iam iam occupata Brixia, Ecerinus ferox,
favore Cremonensium, rupta fide
exclusit illos: Pellavicino quoque
iam dudum amico mortis insidias tulit.
Spe ductus alta deinde nobilium, celer
movit iter et fraude Mediolanum petit.
Sed spe tyrannus ipse delusus sua
in se paratas hostium sensit manus;
sensit Cremonae Mantuae Ferrariae
unaque Bosi et Pellavicini fides
in eius omnes sponte iuratas necem.
Collata ad Aduae signa fixerunt vadum,
a quo reverti constat Ecerinum loco.
Nec segnis alia parte Martinus gradum
distulit, et armis, plebe stipatus sua—
a Turris alto sanguine educens genus
Martinus audax—egit ancipitem retro
senem tyrannum. Dumque convertens iter
ad flumen Aduam signa, quae ad pontem, videt
infesta, quid agat anxius dudum stetit.
Ch. Quid ille tantis viribus septus facit?
Quis vultus aut actus?
Nu. Facit, ut alvo lupus
pleno repulsus, dentibus frendens, canes
circumlatrantes conspicit, multam ferox
ex ore spumam mittit et orbes rotat.
Ch. Progredere et ultra.
Nu. Hinc inde seclusus, furens,
miscere in hostes impares horret manus.
Pons occupatus transitum prorsus negat;
hinc inde et hostes parte conflictum parant

brate this festive day! From on high a just God has looked upon you with favor.

Chorus. Now, my good man, explain briefly this great news.

Messenger. With Brescia recently occupied thanks to the men of Cremona, brutal Ezzelino broke faith and shut out the Cremonese; he plotted to kill Pellavicino[27] also, long his ally. Then, induced by high hopes for an insurrection of nobles, he makes a forced march and attacks Milan by stealth. But the tyrant is himself deluded in his hope, having realized that the enemy's troops were ready for him; he realizes that there is a sworn pact among them all—Cremona, Mantua, Ferrara, together with Buoso[28] and Pellavicino—deliberately committed to his destruction. They planted their banners, all united, at Adda's ford where Ezzelino would make his retreat. Nor was Martino slow in marching from another direction, and supported by the plebs in arms, this daring Martino della Torre,[29] who traces his lineage from noblest blood, pressed the irresolute old tyrant from the rear. As Ezzelino was changing direction, he saw the hostile banners placed at the bridge[30] by the river Adda, and for a long time stood there, uncertain what to do.

Chorus. What did he do, hedged in by such powerful forces? How did he look? How did he act?

Messenger. He acted like a wolf with a full belly being driven back, gnashing his teeth, glaring at dogs barking on all sides, ferocious, foaming at the mouth, rolling his eyes.

Chorus. Go on. And then?

Messenger. Trapped on both sides, enraged, he shrinks from committing his inferior forces to battle against the enemy. The bridge is occupied, he is denied all passage. From both direc-

utraque; dignis concitant illum probris.
Tragula sinistrum missa traiecit pedem
cunctantis, a qua parte nitatur fugae.
Commilitones expetit nomen loci.
'Hic Adua fluvius hocque Caxani vadum.'
'Heu Caxan Axan Baxan! Hoc letum michi
fatale dixti, mater; hic finem fore.
Quis fata revocet sensibus fidens suis?'
Tunc concitatum calcaribus urgens equum
viam per undas aperit et ripam occupat,
idem inchoatum ceteris pandens iter.
Tunc ordo militum impiger contra stetit;
caedit ruentes, terga quoque dantes viros,
illum sequentes. Capitur Ecerinus statim
frustra resistens: unus allidit caput,
fracto cerebro; quisquis is, dubio vacat.
Abductus inde spernit oblatas dapes
curas salutis atque vitales cibos
acerque moritur fronte crudeli minax
et patris umbras sponte Tartareas subit.
Positum cadaver tumba Suncini tenet.

Ch. Vota solvamus pariter datori
digna tantorum, iuvenes, bonorum:
vos senes, vos et trepidae puellae,
solvite vota.
Venit a summo pietas Olympo,
quae malis finem posuit patratis;
occidit saevi rabies tyranni
paxque revixit.
Pace nunc omnes pariter fruamur,
omnis et tutus revocetur exul,
ad lares possit proprios reverti
pace potitus.

tions the enemy prepares for battle on two fronts and taunts him with the insults he deserves. An arrow pierces his left foot as he is hesitating whither he should try to escape. He asks his soldiers the name of the place: "This is the Adda River and this the ford of Cassano." "Alas, Cassano, Assano, Bassano![31] Mother, you told me this was where I was destined to die, that here would be my end. What man who trusts his own instincts may cancel his destiny?" Then, spurring his horse, he opens a path through the waters and seizes a bank of the river, showing the way for the rest to follow. Then a formation of troops opposes him energetically; they slaughter those charging and also those running away; they follow Ezzelino. Ezzelino is captured at once, resisting in vain. One soldier struck him on the head, fracturing his skull; who the man was is in doubt. Led away, Ezzelino spurns offers of refreshment, medical assistance, even the sustenance needed to keep him alive. Fierce, menacing and with an expression of cruelty he dies and willingly passes below to the Tartarean shadows of his father. A tomb in Soncino holds his corpse.

Chorus. Young men, together let us pay thanks befitting the giver of such great blessings! You, old men, and you, timid maidens, give thanks! From highest Olympus comes a devotion which has put an end to the evils that have been committed. The madness of a cruel tyrant has been cut down, and peace has come to life again. Now let us all alike rejoice in peace, and let every exile be summoned home in safety. To his own hearth

Supplices renes feriant habenis,
ictibus crebris domitent reatus.
Annuat votis Deus, ut petitis,
virgine natus.

Nuntius, Chorus

Nu. A parte nulla tutus Albricus sui,
iam derelictis rebus—ut fuerat parum
credendus ulli, et creditus nullis fuit—
Zenonis arcem profugus in tutam fugit,
consorte sociaque et sobolis omnis grege.
Posuere castra circiter montem secus
urbs ultiones expetens dignas triplex,
Tarvisium Vicentia Padua: paribus
adiere votis altus Azo marchio
reliquique secum Marchiae illustres viri.
At spes ut illi nulla praesidii fuit
serperet et intro seditio et urgens fames
mortisque metus instans, capitur ultro locus.
O fulmini par hostis irati furor!
Irrumpit agmen tecta sublimis domus.
Hic rapti ab ubere matris infantis pedes
carpit, tenellum robori allidens caput:
fuso cerebro sparsus inscribit cruor
genetricis ora. Ecerinus occurrit novus
gladium tenenti, quem puer patruum vocat
triennis. Ille 'Patruus edocuit tuus

may each man return in full possession of peace. Let suppliants flagellate themselves with lashes, with frequent blows let them tame their guilty acts. May God, born of a Virgin, show his approval to the vows that we have addressed to Him.

: ACT V :

Single Scene

Messenger, Chorus

Messenger. Alberico too, being insecure on all sides, and now neglecting affairs of state—he was little trusted by anyone, and himself trusted no one—fled, a fugitive, to the safety of the citadel of San Zeno with his wife, his retinue and all his children.[32] A league of three cities, seeking rightful vengeance—Treviso, Vicenza, and Padua—pitched camp around the mountain. With the same intentions the noble marchese Azzo[33] approached, and with him the illustrious men of the March. But for Alberico there was no hope of protection; inside the citadel rebellion was creeping in, along with sharpening hunger and the ever-present fear of death. The stronghold fell on its own. O how like a thunderbolt is the rage of an angry enemy! The troops burst into the buildings of the lofty citadel. One soldier seized an infant by the feet, tearing it from its mother's breast, and dashed its tender head against an oak beam; the gore splattering from the baby's brains marked his mother's face. A baby Ezzelino came upon a soldier holding a sword, whom the three-year-old child called his uncle. The soldier

tradere nepotibus simile munus suis'
ait, et patentes gutturis venas secat.
Utque patulo immane populis constet scelus,
affigit hastae squalidum longae caput:
corrugat ora repens rigor et orbes rotat,
manum ferentis sanguinis replet lues:
aliusque tremulum dentibus mandit iecur.
Haec masculinae prolis Albrici horrida,
sic dira et atrox triplicis strages fuit.
Utque arce summa Albricus in populi manus
venit, paranti falsa iam vulgo loqui
ponitur apertae subditum frenum gulae,
ducto, ut suorum vivus inspectet neces.
Et ecce, thalamo rapta de summo, feris
abstracta turbis, uxor Albrici venit,
caelo refusis lumina intendens comis:
strictus revinctas funis arcebat manus.
Abinde quinque virgines tractae simul
ante ora patrum crinibus fusis erant,
devota proles ignibus. Circumstetit
hos vulgus omnis exprobrans actus truces.
Ut, ad cubile belluis pressis, stetit
circum rapaces turba venatrix lupos,
patrata memorans damna et adducens canes,
a caede gratas sponte subducens moras.
Ch. Procede, nobis pande supplicii modos.
Nu. Ardebat alta roboris magni strues.
Odore piceo subditae exudant faces
pinguisque stipites alit olivae liquor,
atramque nubem fumus ad caelum facit;
fulgur superni murmurat ad instar toni,
dabantque gemitus antra, ne quisquam neget
intro subesse numen inferni Jovis;

said, "Your uncle taught us to give gifts like these to his nephews," and slit the boy's throat. And to make a show of his monstrous crime to the people, he affixed the bloody head to a long pike. The sudden stiffness of death had wrinkled his face and made his eyes roll. The putrescent blood filled the hand of the one carrying the head as another chewed the quivering liver with his teeth. Such was the horrid death of Alberico's three male offspring; it was a dreadful and inhuman slaughter.[34] And at the top of the citadel Alberico falls into the hands of the populace; as he prepares to tell lies to the mob, a gag is stuffed into his open mouth. Still alive, he is led forth to watch the murder of his family. And, look! Snatched from her lofty chamber, dragged down by the wild mob, Alberico's wife comes, her hair loose and her eyes turned toward heaven, her hands bound tightly behind her back. Next their five virgin daughters, their hair loose, are dragged at the same time before their parents' eyes, offspring destined for the flames. Around them all the mob stands, reproaching them for their brutal acts. It was like a band of hunters surrounding ravenous wolves, trapped in their lair, who were describing the losses they had suffered, bringing up their dogs, but deliberately delaying the slaughter for their pleasure.

Chorus. Go on: describe for us the manner of their punishment.

Messenger. A high pyre built of great oaks was burning. The torches placed beneath it gave off the stench of pitch. Thick oil from olive trees fed the logs, and smoke in a black cloud rose to heaven. The sparkling fire crackled like a sound from heaven, and groans came from inside the pyre, so that no one could doubt that the spirit of the infernal Jove was present within;

erant caminis ora, quae flammas vomunt.
O misera sors parentibus spectabilis!
Ordo innocentum imponitur in ignem prius.
Incendit urens ut puellares sinus
tetigitque flavas ardor infestus comas,
retro resiliunt cassa quaerentes patrum
praesidia: nocuis his sed amplexus negant.
Ut vana spes per ambitus illas vage
egit furentes, subito violentas manus
iniecit ardens lictor, et matrem trahens
una patenti subdit et gnatas rogo.

Ch. Quo filiarum et coniugis vultu necem
Albricus, etsi non loqui poterat, tulit?

Nu. Volvebat atrox, sicuti alludens, caput,
ut parvi pendat, nutibus pandens suis.

Ch. Quis finis eius, fare, supremus fuit?

Nu. Tum plura stantem tela certatim virum
petiere: pressit unus in dextrum latus
gladium, sinistra parte qui fixus patet;
per utrumque vulnus largus effluxit cruor:
effulminat spatulas alius ensem tenus.
Cervice caesa, murmurat labens caput,
stetitque titubans truncus ad casum diu,
donec minutim membra dispersit frequens
vulgus, per avidos illa distribuens canes.

Ch. Haec perpetuo durat in aevo
regula iuris. Fidite, iusti:
nec, si quando forsitan ullum
quemquam nocuum sors extollat,
regula fallit. Consors operum
meritum sequitur quisque suorum.
Stat iudicii conscius aequi
iudex rigidus, iudex placidus;

there were faces in the furnace that vomited flames. O what a wretched lot to be made a spectacle for parents! First, the innocent children were put in a row on the fire. As the burning fire set the maidens' gowns ablaze and the hostile flame touched their golden tresses, they leapt back vainly, seeking their parents' protection, but embraces were denied to the criminals. As vain hope drove the girls to run about like lunatics, suddenly an angry guard laid violent hands on the mother and, dragging her up, threw her onto the open pyre together with her children.

Chorus. He couldn't speak, but how did he look when he saw his wife and children killed?

Messenger. The abominable brute rolled his head, nodding as though in mockery, to show he didn't care.

Chorus. Tell us, what was his final end?

Messenger. At that point, many weapons were competing to reach the man where he stood. One soldier plunged a sword into Alberico's right side which, skewering him, came out on his left. Blood poured from both wounds. Another soldier brought his sword down like a thunderbolt as far as his shoulder blades. With his neck severed, his head fell with a thud, and for a long time the trunk of his body stood reeling, ready to drop, until the mob tore it apart, limb from limb, throwing the pieces to greedy dogs.

Chorus. This rule of justice endures forever. Just men, trust in it! If one day fortune should happen to raise up some criminal, still the rule does not fail. Responsible for his works, each man gets what he deserves. The stern Judge, the mild Judge, is mindful of fair judgment; he rewards the just and punishes the un-

donat iustos, damnat iniquos.
Haud hic stabilis desinit ordo:
petit illecebras virtus superas,
crimen tenebras expetit imas.
Dum licet ergo moniti stabilem
discite legem.

just. This stable order never ends: virtue seeks the delights of heaven; misdeeds seek the darkness of hell. Therefore, be warned, and pay heed while you may to the unchanging law.

ANTHONII DE LUSCHIS DE VINCENCIA

ACHILES

: I :

Hecuba, Paris, Chorus Troianorum

He. O coniugales horridas Troie faces,
quas profuga coniunx numine infausto tulit,
thalamos secutas regius puppes cruor
cuius pelasgas solvit! Immites deos
placare potuit cede virginea cohors
argiva? Ratibus mille suffecit caput?
Nunc Xantus, alto sanguine immixto fluens,
yliaca pulsat maria; purpureas vehit
Simois procellas cede nec dudum labat
fortuna belli. Victor Atrides premit
menia deorum clara, que Phebus cheli
struxit canora. Sevit armigera potens
Europa classe; quelibet nostram lues
affligit Asiam. Vincimur bello Friges.
Sed maior Hecubam torquet infaustam dolor;

ANTONIO LOSCHI OF VICENZA

ACHILLES

CHARACTERS

Hecuba, *Queen of Troy*
Paris, *her son*
Trojan Chorus
Achilles
Paris' Follower
Greek Chorus
Priam, *King of Troy*
Cassandra, *his daughter, a prophetess*
Agamemnon, *Greek commander*
Menelaus, *his brother*
Calchas, *a Greek seer*

: I :

Hecuba, Paris, Trojan Chorus

[Inside the city of Troy]

Hecuba. [*To herself*] O the grim marriage torches of Troy which the fugitive wife[1] brought with ill-starred omen! Royal bloodshed[2] unfurled the sails of the Greek ships sent in pursuit of that marriage bed! Could the Argive host appease the merciless gods with the sacrifice of a virgin? Did her lone life suffice for a thousand ships? Now Xanthus, flowing and mixed deep with blood, throbs into Ilium's seas; Simois carries its stormy waves dyed dark red with blood from slaughter, and the fortune of war does not falter for long.[3] Victorious Agamemnon presses in on our famous, god-built walls, which divine Apollo constructed with the music of his lyre.[4] Powerful Europa rages with her well-armed fleet; every kind of pestilence afflicts our Troy; we Phrygians are defeated. But a greater sorrow tortures unhappy Hecuba; I find rest and comfort neither by night nor

nocturna non me nec fovet lucis quies.
Hinc fortis Hector, mille quem metuunt rates
adhuc iacentem, graia qui solus fugans
tot regna curru celsus aurato stetit;
auspicia Troylus Hectoris bello gerens
Achilis ense cesus: hinc matris dolor.
Astus Ulixis Thetidis et claras fleo
nimium latebras. Ylios periit decus.
Hectorea traxit membra thesalici ducis
extincta currus, pondere excelso rote
tremuere. Laceras vidimus gnati comas
emptumque Priamo corpus. En Hector sat est,
millena cuius classis extimuit facem.
Sed sobolis alte Troylus clarum genus,
Achilis ira iacuit. O dirum nefas!
Adeste, adeste, summe dominator poli,
trisulca cuius tela iaculatur manus
numenque Phebi tuque qui pelagus regis,
Neptune, quorum Troia munitu viret.
Quid, misera, luctu questibus volvis diem?
Non damna fletus reparat; extincti iacent.
O segnis Hecuba, pateris ultrici manu
carere natos? Sceptra dum Priamus gerit
inimica Danais, perage quod natus iubet.
Pa. Quid tacita volvit pectore ardenti parens?
Flamata vultus regiam frontem quatit:
Phebigera virgo qualis inpulsu dei
lacerata crines, qualis aut Menas furens,
percussa Bacho, fronde pampinea comas
impressa fervet, auget atque iras dolor.
Regina, quis te versat amentem furor?
Quisve urget estus? Cohibe vesanum impetum!

by day. There is a mother's grief, on one side, for brave Hector, whom the thousand ships yet fear, though he lies dead, who all alone put numerous kingdoms of Greece to flight, standing high in his burnished chariot; on the other side, for Troilus, wearing the armor of Hector in battle, cut down by the sword of Achilles. I bewail the cunning of Ulysses and the all-too well-known lairs of Thetis' son.[5] The glory of Troy has perished. The chariot of that Thessalian lord dragged the dead body of Hector behind it, the wheels juddering under their heavy load. We saw the mangled head of our son and the body Priam ransomed. Look, enough of Hector, whose fiery torch a thousand ships feared! But Troilus, noble scion of an exalted race, was brought low by the wrath of Achilles. O dreadful crime! O come, come, highest sovereign of the world, whose hand hurls the triple lightning bolt, and you, divine Apollo, and you who rule the seas, Neptune, under whose protection Troy thrives! Why, wretched woman, do you spend the whole day restlessly in reproaches and grief? Weeping doesn't repair what's happened; the dead are dead. O torpid Hecuba, will you suffer the loss of your children to vengeful hands? As long as Priam bears the scepter so hateful to the Danai, do what your son bids you do.

Paris. What is my silent mother turning over in her burning heart? With flushed face she shakes her royal brow; her hair is torn like Cassandra[6] when struck by Apollo or as a raging Maenad, smitten by Bacchus, is roused by her passion, her hair entwined with ivy; and grief swells her wrath. Queen, what frenzy turns you to madness? What passion torments you?

Vicere nundum dorici Troiam duces,
sed sceptra Priamus, munus Alcide, gerit.
He. O summa Iuno, coniugis soror tui
regina celi; tuque quam Friges colunt,
armigera Pallas, prosperum tandem michi
placate fesse numen. Hoc testor deas
quibus negavit munus, ydeas premens
sedes cruentus arbiter, notus sibi.
Phebea nundum sparserat lampas diem,
sed plaustra sicci volverant molem iugi
solusque claro Lucifer stabat polo.
Exigua somni tenuit afflictam quies.
Ecce ima tellus fremuit et cecum chaos
laxavit ora; fulgor invasit domum.
Tunc umbra iuvenis patuit Acherontis vado
emissa: Priami sponte non qualis trahens
dardania secum castra et ultrices manus
gestare cupiens, crine sed sparso iacens
cruore fusus, inquit: 'Ignavi Friges,
iacete segnes. Hecuba tu dormis, parens!
Erramus umbre, spernit ac nostros Caron
gestare manes. Nullus est natis locus.
Vagamur. Hector Paridis ultricem petunt
tuusque dextram Troylus. Dudum negas?
Remeabit ille, cuius Hectoreo graves
sonuere currus pondere? Argolici feret
partem triumphi? Sospes ac victor suum
natum reviset? Orba, quo defles tuos?
I, perage, Achiles decidat fratris manu.'
Tunc horror artus alligat, sanguis gelu
victusque torpet. Misera sed natum sinu
retinere volui. Fugit amplexus celer.

Stop this insanity! The Doric commanders have not yet conquered Troy; Priam still bears the scepter, gift of Hercules.

Hecuba. O highest Juno, sister of Jove, queen of heaven, and you whom the Phrygians worship, Pallas in arms, let your divine nature at last be forgiving and favorable to me in my exhaustion. I call upon you two goddesses as my witnesses, you to whom the prize was denied by that cruel judge[7] on Mount Ida, conscious of his guilt. Not yet had the Phoebean lamp begun to scatter the daylight, but the Wain had rolled its burden up the dry peaks,[8] and only the morning star shone in the clear sky. In my affliction repose held me in a light sleep. Behold! The earth groaned beneath me and blind Chaos gaped wide; a brightness filled the house. Then, from the riverbed of Acheron the shade of a young man[9] appeared. He was not like the man who of his own accord had carried along with him Priam's Trojan camps and had longed to lay avenging hands on the enemy, but rather lay with hair disheveled in a pool of blood, saying, "Base Trojans, you lie prostrate in your sloth![10] Hecuba, my mother, you are asleep! We shades wander aimlessly, and Charon refuses to ferry our ghosts. There is no room for your sons. We wander. Hector and your Troilus seek the hand of Paris to avenge us. Why deny it so long? Will that man whose chariot shuddered heavily under the weight of Hector return home scot free? Will he have his share of the Argive triumph? Will he, safe and victorious, see his son again? Bereaved woman, why do you bewail your sons? Go, take action! Let Achilles be cut down by the hand of our brother!" Then terror bound my limbs; my blood turned to ice; I was overcome and felt weak. But, sick at heart, I wanted to hold my son to my bosom. He

Magnanime, Priami stirpe regali trahens
nomen superbum, cuius ingentes, Paris,
animos Atrides sensit ac luget minor,
te poscit Hector, ripa quos tristis tenet
errante gressu, ac Troylus. Natis quidem
puppis negatur, negligit fratres Caron
adhuc inultos. Vindicem dextram petunt.

Pa. Regina Frigium, mentis est error vagas
umbras putare, dextra si vindex abest.
Mortale quicquid corpus ad letum trahit,
haud parcit anime. Vita cum refugit, nichil
est umbra; miseros ignifer postquam rogus
consumpsit ardens, spiritus moritur simul.
Quid cesa tauri colla ferventi rigant
cruore tumulos? Vana nos movet fides.
Placare nullo credimus vivens loco.
At sola superest fama virtutis; meos
hec ipsa fratres servat; hac vivet diu
animosus Hector, sicca dum fluctu carens
lucebit Ursa, pulcra dum Phebum dies
et nox sororem sentiet, mundi vices
dum volvet annus. Tantali lusor latex
pomigeraque arbor, Sysiphum lapis gravans
celerique cursu raptus Ysion rote
alesque Ticii iecore fecundo furens
et ceca Ditis regio ac pinum manu
furibunda gestans angue mortifero cohors
tricepsque custos Tartari, Caron senex:
inanis iste rumor. Hoc certum puta.
Umbris que vita corpore extincto datur,
aut leta campos querit Elisios statim,
quorum reverti clara prosperitas vetat,
aut Stigia querit protinus tristis loca.

swiftly fled my embrace. Greathearted Paris, you who take your proud name from Priam's royal stock, whose great courage Menelaus knew to his regret, Hector calls for your help as does Troilus, whose wandering steps the sad verge of Acheron restrains. Indeed, the ferry is denied my sons, and Charon passes over your brothers as men still unavenged. They seek the hand of vengeance!

Paris. Queen of the Phrygians, it is a mistake to think souls wander whenever vengeance is absent. Whatever mortal thing drags the body to its death hardly spares the soul. When life departs, its shade is nothing; after the burning pyre consumes the sad wretches, the spirit dies at the same time. Why are the throats of bulls slit and their warm blood used to water burial mounds? It is an empty faith that drives us. We believe we can appease that which has no life anywhere. Only the fame of our virtue survives us; it is only this that preserves my brothers. By virtue courageous Hector will live long, as long as Ursa shall shine dry in heaven, never touching the sea, as long as lovely Day enjoys her Apollo and Night his sister Artemis, as long as the year spins out the seasons of the earth. The illusory pool of Tantalus and the apple-bearing tree, the boulder that burdens Sisyphus, and Ixion hurrying in swift course upon his wheel, and the raging vulture feasting on the fecund liver of Tityus,[11] and the blind realm of Dis and its furious crew, bearing in their hands the pine and deadly snakes,[12] and the triple-headed guardian of Tartarus,[13] and old Charon—all this is empty talk. This alone is sure: the shade to whom life is given on the death of the body either seeks happily the Elysian fields at once, whose glorious bounty forbids it to return, or in gloom seeks the Stygian depths at once. Whoever

Quicunque manes vidit infaustos semel
Ditisque pavido regna tentavit pede,
superna nunquam tetigit. Hoc nulli vacat
exire regno. Generis humani capax
vorago prohibet, demit ac nostri palus
lethea curas. Magna sed fateor, parens,
nati voluntas Troyli visum putat.
Imago somni mentis affectus capit;
compesce diros impetus, temet doma.

He. Ignave miles, cuius est tantum stupro
impensa virtus, raptor alieni thori,
quas Itacus ultra posset aut doli comes
perferre fraudes? Fingis hoc? Magna est quidem
generosa virtus Paridis; haud Hecube satis.
Cum currus ingens thesalus magnum trahens
lustraret arces, inclitas Phebi lira,
Hectora, iacebas coniugis rapte sinu,
pudenda proles Venere tu solum potens
bellum recusas. Dedecus tante domus,
fraterna non te funera aut matris preces
Hecube movebunt? Pateris erranti gradu
fratres vagari? Degener patre inclito,
indigne Priamo, nulla te pietas movet?
Quisnam peremptor Hectoris magni fuit
nisi teda Paridis? Causa Danaidum est bona;
ubi causa iusta deficit, virtus perit.
Ego non aperto bella quod marte ingeras,
sed fraude Achilem perime.

Pa. Qua tantum ducem?

He. Amore claro nobilis Polixenes
furibundus ardet, virginem thoro petit.
Promissa thalami iura fraudabunt virum
fictusque Priami templa continget gener,

has once seen those accursed ghosts and braved with trembling foot the kingdoms of Dis can never touch the upper world again.[14] From this realm there is no return. A chasm deep enough to hold mankind prohibits it, and the pool of Lethe erases the cares of our mortal life. But I do admit, mother, that your powerful will believes it has seen your son Troilus. An image in a dream has taken over your thoughts. Control these dreadful impulses! Get hold of yourself!

Hecuba. Cowardly knight!—you whose virtue is valued only at the price of your adultery, you ravisher of another man's wife, what more by way of trickery could the man from Ithaca or his companion in cunning accomplish? Are you inventing all this? Great indeed is the noble courage of Paris, yet not at all enough for Hecuba. When the mighty Thessalian chariot was dragging great Hector and circling the ramparts, famous thanks to Phoebus' lyre,[15] you were nestling in the bosom of the wife you ravished, shameful offspring that you are, mighty only in love, refusing war. Shame of your great family, do your brothers' deaths and the prayers of your mother Hecuba not move you? Will you allow your brothers to wander aimlessly? Degenerate son of a noble father, unworthy to be Priam's son, does no reverence for your family and the gods move you? What was it that destroyed Hector if not the marriage of Paris? The cause of the Greeks is good; where the cause is unjust, virtue perishes. I do not say you should wage war against Achilles in open battle; kill him by deceit.

Paris. What kind of deceit could kill such a leader?

Hecuba. It is plain that he is madly in love with noble Polyxena and seeks the maiden for his wife. The obligations of marriage that have been promised the man will entrap him, and the pre-

Phebea inermis gente desertus sua.
Cohorte primum cinctus armigera latus,
limen tenebis. Hostis in templo cadet,
cecidere cuius Troylus et Hector manu.

Pa. Licet ira Achilis morte satiari queat
odiumque nostre pestilens domus ruat
Paridis sagita, fine quo cernas tamen.
Fortuna semper impetu primo favet;
extrema virtus cernere est. Video, intuor
quicquid sequetur. Comprime ardentis tue
mentis furores. Bella si iuvant, cadat
patrie ruina dardane gentis cruor.
Salvanda sed si Troia te magis iuvat,
soror est iugali thesalo Polixene
tradenda thalamo; fictus haud templum gener
sed verus intret, sceptra qui potens gerit,
thesalica cuius arva sub regno iacent,
parentis altum sanguine extendit genus
pelagique dive. Magna nos clades premet,
argolica semper bella, divorum furor,
hostilis ardor, fraude si ducem obruas.
Si parcis hosti, sancta si pietas placet,
tibi ipsa parcis, patrie et Priamo simul.
Servare patriam quelibet laudat fides.
Natam pelasge rector Atrides suam
gentis dicavit; crimen extinxit cruor
in sacra missus iura qui sacrum fuit.
Sed nata sospes publicam genti dabit
nostre salutem, sanguinis stringet vias
Troie fluentis. Hostis Alcides tenet
Iunonis Hebem coniugem victor polo.
Parcendo parcis. Talis himeneus potest
firmare Troiam

tended son-in-law of Priam will come to Phoebus' temple, unarmed and bereft of his own kind. Flanked by an armed cohort,[16] you will secure the entrance. The enemy by whose hand Troilus and Hector were felled will himself be felled in the temple.

Paris. Although your wrath can be quenched by Achilles' death, and his pestilent hatred for our house may be destroyed by Paris' arrow, consider, nevertheless, the outcome. Fortune is always favorable to the first assault; virtue consists in seeing the consequences. I see—I know—what will follow. Control the furious passions of your mind. If war is what you want, let the blood of Dardanian race fall with the collapse of its homeland. But if you'd like to see Troy saved, my sister Polyxena should be wed to the Thessalian lord; let him enter the temple as a real, not a counterfeit, son-in-law. He is a mighty man who bears the scepters of power, under whose rule lie the fields of Thessaly. He continues the highborn line of his father and his mother, the goddess of the sea. A great disaster will come down upon us; there will always be Greeks at war with us, the rage of the gods will continue along with the enemy's passion if you destroy this leader by guile. If you spare your enemy, if you favor holy piety, you spare yourself, Troy and Priam, all at the same time. Saving one's fatherland is praiseworthy, whatever one's loyalties. The ruler of the Greek people, Agamemnon, sacrificed his own daughter; since the sacrifice was performed according to the sacred rites, the victim's blood erased the crime. But your daughter, safe and sound, will give public deliverance to our people, will staunch the streams of flowing Trojan blood. Juno's enemy Alcides is a victor in heaven with Hebe,[17] Juno's daughter, as his wife. In sparing you spare. Such a wedding can strengthen Troy . . .

He. coniuge oppressam tua.
Thalamos Achilis patiar impleri meo
inulta fetu? Virgo polutas manus
fratrum cruore sordido tactu feret?
Parentis utero fata volvissent tuos
sine luce fusos, nata, si tales deus
thoros ministrat. Ante sublimes reget
noctivaga currus numinis clari soror
Trivieque Phebus; fervido seges mari
nascetur; Arthos pontus asperget; rates
fessas Caribdis ore placato trahet
et Scilla; mites sentient agne lupos,
tigres iuvenci; flama coniunget mari;
occasus orbi lucidum mittet diem
ortusque merget; Xantus ad fontem retro
labetur unda, sanguinem varium gerens;
fidemque celi Phebus agnoscet; manus
perfracta iunget fila, quam thoro sinam
iungi pelasgo sanguinem clare domus.
I, nate Priami, callidam cedem extrue.
Pa. Sedicio regem non decet.
He. Quicquid licet.
Pa. Servare regis maxima est virtus fidem.
He. Fides ab alto regio distat lare.
Pa. Eruere patriam regis est culpa impii.
He. Tirannus hostem villis haud ultus sinet.
Pa. Hosti salutem denegans, tibi negas.
He. Non dura mors est odia qui secum trahit.
Cur nunc moraris?
Pa. Fraudis occulte pudet.
He. Cedem occupato sola permittit dies.

Hecuba. . . . a Troy crushed by your wife! Shall I allow the marriage bed of Achilles to be filled with my own offspring, while I remain unavenged? Should my virgin daughter endure the touch of a man whose hands are stained with the foul blood of her brothers? If this is the kind of marriage the god provides, O my daughter, the Fates should have planned for you to die lightless in your mother's womb. Sooner will the night-wandering sister of her luminous brother guide the heavenly chariots and Phoebus guide the moon; sooner will crops grow on the frothy sea; the ocean dampen the Great Bear; Scylla and Charybdis draw weary ships to a tranquil shore;[18] sooner will lambs think wolves gentle, and heifers tigers; fire unite with water, the West send out the gleaming day and the East extinguish it; and Xanthus mixed with varied blood return its waves to their source; sooner will Phoebus acknowledge the day's constancy; sooner will the hand of fate rejoin its broken threads than I shall allow the blood of this distinguished house to be joined to that of the Greeks. Go, son of Priam, and contrive a wily murder.

Paris. Betrayal doesn't befit a king.

Hecuba. A king may do anything.

Paris. The greatest virtue of a king is to keep his word.

Hecuba. Trustworthiness stands far from the lofty hearth of a king.

Paris. To destroy one's country is the crime of an impious king.

Hecuba. The tyrant who takes no vengeance on his enemy is contemptible.

Paris. Denying deliverance to your enemy, you deny it to yourself.

Hecuba. Death is not hard when it takes things you hate with it. Why are you delaying now?

Paris. I am ashamed of this hidden treachery.

Hecuba. For someone who spends his time as you do, daytime provides the only opportunity for murder.

Pa. Si tantus dolor pectus inflamat, parens,
peribit hostis, victima ut templis cadet.
Iam iam sateles tale coniugium duci
referat pelasgo.
He. Templa confestim petet.
Ch.T. O magne Tonans, ardua cuius
dextera fulmen quatit, ethereis
viribus actum; genitor superum
hominumque simul, cuius numen
elementa gravi compressa Chaos
solvit proprio iussitque loco
sistere quicquid prius humanum
presserat orbem: se tulit arces
ignis in altas; vicinus ei
stetit angustas aerque vias
subiturus; humum cinxit pelagus.
Nunc dardanias respice gentes
tandem fessas; millena para
fulmina. Puppis troiana premens
ardeat omnis. Concussa manu
mille carinas rutilante Iovis
feriant Danaas fulmina; quicquid
immune fuit facis Hectoree
igne Tonantis maiore cadat.
Tuque o celi regina, fave
inclita Iuno, cuius thalamos
Iupiter intrat. Tu, gorgoneis
armata veni Pallasque minis,
vel mitte tuum nimbo aurifero
fratrem genitum. Sic argolicos
horrore duces pressos retine
semper in arvis qui cede madent.
Et tu nitidum, radiate, diem

Paris. If the grief that burns your heart is that great, mother, our enemy will die, struck down like a sacrificial victim in the temple. A follower of mine will report right away to Achilles that the marriage can take place.

Hecuba. He'll head for the temple at once.

Trojan Chorus. O great Thunderer, whose mighty hand shakes the thunderbolt, driven by the strength of heaven! Father of both gods and men, whose divinity released the elements confined by weighty Chaos and ordered to take its proper place whatever had before weighed down the human globe! Fire betook itself to the lofty heights; next beneath it came the air, settling in narrow channels; the seawater girdled the earth. Cast your eye now on the people of Troy in the extremity of their exhaustion. Prepare thousands of thunderbolts. Let the entire fleet besieging Troy go up in flames. Let thunderbolts, shot from the flashing hand of Jove, strike the thousand Greek ships; let whatever escaped Hector's firebrand be crushed beneath the greater fire of the Thunderer. And you, O queen of heaven, illustrious Juno, you whose bedchamber Jupiter enters, show us your favor. And come, Pallas, armed with Gorgon threats, or send your brother who was born from the golden shower.[19] Hold forever in check the Argive leaders, cowering with dread, in the fields wet with slaughter. And you, radiant one, who bring back the bright day

qui lucifero revehis curru
fessusque diem mergis in undas,
ades, o Titan, defende lire
menia placido structa canore.
Sorte secunda Neptune potens
passus graias per regna rates
mille yliacos quesisse tua
muros? Cur non, infesta petens
menia divum, puppis tumido
ponto iacuit lacerata? Tamen
nos auxilio, quos tua cingit
zonaque Phebi, defende tuo,
licet hoc tarde, Neptune, feras.
Iam iam cecidit robur frigiis
gentibus Hector Troieque decus,
millena facem cuius timuit
argiva ratis. Quid, Troyle, te,
inclite, referam viresque tuas?
Post mala questus verberat auras.
Soror o clare lucisque dei,
insula iacuit firmata quibus
partumque tulit; te virgineus
placare cruor lesam potuit
crimine cerve? Si tota luat
Grecia penas, vix extinguet
scelus exiguo sanguine missum.
O diva fave, menia serva
fratrisque tui veneranda cheli.
Tu dive potens, qui bella regis,
vota yliace suscipe gentis;
rege dardanias marte secundo
aciesque. Tuum Troia precatur
numen: achivas sterne catervas.

in your shining chariot and, when tired, submerge the day in the waves, be here, O Titan, defend the walls built with the tranquil sound of your lyre. Mighty Neptune, you allowed those thousand Greek ships to pass with good fortune through your realms to seek out the walls of Troy. Why didn't that hateful fleet, menacing as it was to the walls built by the gods, lie shattered under the stormy sea? Be that as it may, defend us with your aid, Neptune, late though it may come, we whom your walls and Phoebus' encircle. Now, now Hector has fallen, a bulwark to the Phrygian peoples and the pride of Troy, whose torch a thousand Argive ships feared. Why should I mention you, famed Troilus, and your prowess? After evils, complaints beat upon the air. O sister of the god of clearest light[20]—you for whom Delos stood still at your twin birth—could a virgin's blood appease you, injured as you were by the slaughter of your doe? If all of Greece is meant to suffer punishment, hardly will its guilt be washed away with a small effusion of blood. O kindly goddess, preserve these walls made venerable by your brother's lyre. You mighty deity, who govern wars, accept the prayers of the Trojan people; guide the Trojan ranks in successful battle; all Troy beseeches your divinity: de-

Sed nunc sacris placanda deum
numina nostris superumque colat
quelibet aras troiana cohors.

: II :

Achiles, Sateles Paridis, Chorus Grecorum

Ac. Regem deorum maximum quisquis putat
celi Tonantem, fulmine et sceptro manus
armata cuius orbe concusso furit,
errore mentis fallitur quidem invio.
Est namque maior, falsa quem mundi fides
vocat minorem, tela qui gestat puer
virtute varia. Celsus hic alis volat
quacunque Titan lucido curru nitet.
Quam sepe novit Iuppiter vires dei!
Vicere fulmen tela puerili manu
librata, quamvis impetu tanto furens
descendat, urat contulit quicquid Parens.
Hic tela mittit, vulnus inclusum latet
tectusque membra pestilens ignis vorat.
Dominatur orbi pariter et celo potens
testorque Achiles numinis tanti fidem
viresque teli, cuius auratum gerit
arundo pondus. Ecce victorem diu
me Troia sentit, labitur Xantus meo
mutatus ense; gentis argolice pavor
excelsus Hector, fratre permixto, iacet.
Obscura cede Menonis fulsit parens;
pietate liber Telephus nostram tulit
iram, negando Misie nobis iter.

stroy the Greek troops. But now the power of the gods must be appeased by our holy rites, and let each Trojan cohort honor the altars of the gods.

: II :

Achilles, a follower of Paris, Greek Chorus

[*In the Greek camp*]

Achilles. Whoever thinks the greatest king of the gods is the Thunderer of heaven, whose hand is armed with scepter and lightning bolt and who rages as the earth shakes, is truly deceived by an impenetrable error of the mind. That god is greater whom the false opinion of the world deems the lesser, a boy who carries weapons various in their power. On his wings he flies high aloft wherever the titan Helios gleams in his bright chariot. How often has Jupiter felt the power of that god! The arrows fired from his boyish hand overwhelmed Jove's lightning, even though it descends with furious force and burns whatever the Creator aims at. But when the boy shoots his arrows, the wound lies hidden inside and, concealed as a pestilential fire, devours our limbs. His power commands equally on earth and in heaven, and I, Achilles, bear witness to my faith in his great divinity and the power of his dart, its shaft tipped with weighty gold. Behold how long Troy has acknowledged me as its conqueror. The Xanthus flows, its channel choked with corpses by my sword;[21] the terror of the Argive race, noble Hector, lies dead along with his brother. The mother of Memnon[22] blushed at his inglorious death. Lacking in piety,[23] Telephus felt my wrath when he denied me passage through Mysia.[24] All the

Tamen Cupido superat. O quantum meo
amoris iste pectori affigit puer!
O nata Priami, causa bellorum tibi
iam cedet Helena, vultibus claris nitens.
O spes Achilis quando te nurum ciet
Thetis, iugali thesalo iunctam thoro
vocabit, una gentibus pacem dabis.
Uterque voto supplici divos rogat
hoc populus. At nunc propius advexit gradum
Paridis sateles, nostra qui signa appetit
Himenea letum voce sublimi canens.

Sa. O clara proles Thetidis, o Frigum timor
utrasque fama cuius invasit domos
generosa Phebi, classis argive decus,
tibi Troia supplex nobiles tendit manus,
ensis cruore cuius irrubuit tuus
humilique pacem queritat voto ducem
ut seva cedis iaceat hic tandem sitis.
Satis hausit ira sanguinis, ferro manet
spoliata vestro Troia. Te generum vocant
Priamusque coniunx Hecuba, tibi regno parant
dotare natam. Quilibet vetus furor
pellatur animo; templa te Phebi manent.
Regalis illic turba coniugium parat
firmare sacrum. Perge; cur dubitas diu?

Ac. Optata quamvis fulserit nobis dies
et vota placidi sumpserint divi, tamen
non coniugale tempus hoc fieri vetat.
Ut flama pelago, marte sic distant faces.

Sa. Erras. Iugalem tempus hoc tedam petit;
cum sevus urbes excitat belli furor
strictique fervor ensis in gentes ruit,
tunc pacis opus est. Bella si semper gerat

same, Cupid has won. O how much love has that boy driven deep in my breast! O daughter of Priam, Helen of the radiant countenance now yields to you as a cause of wars. O hope of Achilles, when Thetis, calling you her daughter-in-law, summons you to be joined to him in a Thessalian marriage bed, all by yourself you will bring peace to both peoples.[25] On their knees in prayer both peoples beg the gods for this marriage. But now the follower of Paris draws near; he seeks out my banners, singing a joyful wedding song with panting voice.[26]

Follower. O glorious offspring of Thetis, O terror of the Trojans, whose highborn fame entered both temples of Phoebus, glory of the Argive fleet, on her knees Troy stretches out her noble hands to you, whose sword grew red with our blood, and with humble prayer sues the captain for peace, so that here at last the cruel thirst for slaughter may end. Your wrath has drunk enough of our blood; Troy has been despoiled through your sword. Priam and his wife Hecuba call you their son-in-law; for your sake they are prepared to dower their daughter with a kingdom. Let your old fury be driven from your mind; the temple of Phoebus awaits you. There a royal throng makes ready to confirm your holy marriage. Go forth: why do you hesitate so long?

Achilles. Although this longed-for day has shone upon us, and the kindly gods have received our prayers, nevertheless the present time is unpropitious for marriage. Like fire and water, Mars and the marriage torches do not mix.

Follower. You're mistaken. These are the very times that demand a wedding. When the cruel frenzy of war stirs up our cities and the fever of the unsheathed sword descends upon our peoples,

mortalis ardor, ulla nec crescat Venus,
peribit orbis. Pastor amittit gregem,
qui semper aris victimas cedit sacris
pecusque nullum reparat. Extingui solet
vetus ira tedis. Unicum Priamus gerit
solamen animo, mille quod tantum rates
tulere generum. Fateor, hoc regem fovet
senio gravatum debili, afflictum malis.
Quod magnus Hector frater atque audax nimis
iacuere, thalamo pensat hoc. Tantum dabis
quantum abstulisti. Priamus Alcide capit
exempla, quamvis unico distent loco:
victo pepercit Hercules, Priamus duci.
Si lesus iram ponit, hunc magis decet
qui lesit, arma. Regna summittet tuo
regenda sceptro, prole nec villi genus
angustus hausit, genere sed claro nitet.
I, Thetide dignam coniugem nurum pete.
Quicunque dona negligit semel deum,
mox vota surdis auribus celo dabit.
Ac. Odiosa cunctis facere sibi soli est nefas.
Sa. Danaisne?
Ac. Danais.
Sa. Longa quos belli mora
patrio carentes detinet fessos lare,
sevus iuvabit bellicus semper labor?
Credas precari celites pacem deos;
sed multa pectore regius celat timor.
Tali salutem fata posuerunt thoro;
utriusque populi sanguis hoc sistet fluens.
Optata perage; numinum prestat favor.
Ac. O quam libens Fortuna seu celi favor
parem superno vexit Eaciden Iovi!

it is then one needs peace. If mortal ardor should always wage war, if no love may grow, the world will perish. The shepherd loses his flock who always sacrifices his victims on the sacred altars and never renews their number. Old anger is commonly allayed by weddings. The only consolation Priam has is that those thousand ships brought him so mighty a son-in-law. I confess, this marriage brings comfort to a king encumbered by old age and afflicted with ills. Now that great Hector and his all-too-audacious brother lie dead, this marriage is his compensation. You will give as much as you have taken away. Priam looks to Hercules as an example, although they differ in only one way: Hector gave pardon to the conquered, Priam to the conqueror. If Priam, the injured party, puts aside his anger, it befits still more the man who has done the injury to put aside his arms. He will surrender his kingdoms to be ruled by your scepter. He did not draw his high descent from a mean or impoverished breed, but is glorious for his noble ancestry. Go, seek a bride worthy to be the daughter-in-law of Thetis. Whoever once neglects the gifts of the gods, soon will be sending up to heaven prayers that fall on deaf ears.

Achilles. It is wrong to do something for oneself alone that is hateful to the rest.

Follower. You mean the Greeks?

Achilles. The Greeks, yes.

Follower. Will the cruel exertions of war always please those whom its long delays keep exhausted and far from their homes? You may believe that they are praying to the gods in heaven for peace; but the king conceals many things in his heart out of fear. The Fates have placed deliverance in a marriage like this; the shedding of blood will stop for both peoples. Accomplish what you have longed for; the gods offer you their favor.

Achilles. O how kindly was Fortune or the favor of heaven to lift the heir of Aeacus[27] to be the peer of celestial Jove! Why should

Quid marte gentes obrutas nostro loquar?
Michi cessit omnis, signa cum cantus mea
animosa cecinit; sola non timuit cohors
peritura ferro. Flebiles vidit deus
celsos canore nobili muros suo,
quis magnus Hector obstitit bello impotens.
Timuere matres inclitum Thetidis genus
solusque Achilis obruit cunctos pavor
Mavorsque tantum bellice sortis potens
nec favit acie. Quicquid optavi, meo
Fortuna fato iunxit. En divi parant
sociare nostros genere regali thoros.
Super astra gradior, celitum sedes premo,
quos nostra semper cura solicitos tenet.
Si michi Tonantum coniugem natus daret
thalamosque fratris negligat Iuno meis
sortisque iudex premium reddat sue
et marte tuto; quelibet Polixene
tibi cedet uxor. Propero, iam more piget.

Ch.G. Armatus gemina fervet arundine
Vulcano genitus, cui Venus est parens.
Immitis puer hic pervolat ocior
excusso manibus fulmine patrui
effusasque sagitas agilis movet,
qua nascens rutila fronte patet dies
et lucem pelagus qua bibit ultimam
et quacunque solum cingitur equore.
Affigit penitus vulnera certior
quam fallax profugi dextera cuspide
Parthi, sive fugas fingere preparet,
seu recte feriat. Viscera pestilens
ignis tota vorat nullaque vulneri
frons est clara; latet sevior Ethneo

I speak of the peoples crushed in our battles? Every man gave way before me when my war chant sang of my proud banners; the troops that did not fear me were destined to die by my sword. The god looked down on the weeping walls that had been raised high by his noble song, the walls before which great Hector stood, powerless to defend them. Mothers feared the famous offspring of Thetis; fear alone of Achilles crushed them all, and not even Mars, so powerful in deciding battle, showed favor to their ranks. Whatever I wished for, Fortune allotted to my fate. And, lo, the gods are ready to link us in marriage to a mighty lineage. I climb above the stars; I thrust my way among the seats of the heavenly gods, whom our ministrations keep ever attentive to our welfare. If the son of the Thunderers, Juno and Jove, gave me his lover for my wife, and Juno left the marriage bed of her brother for mine, and the judge gave up to me the prize awarded him for his choice,[28] and the war was safely over, all wives would still give way before you, Polyxena. I make haste now, I am sick of delay. [*He rushes off to Troy.*]

Greek Chorus. Armed with his double shafts, the boy sprung from Vulcan, whose mother is Venus, bustles with activity. Unrelentingly, he flies more swiftly than the lightning bolt strikes at the hands of his grandfather. Nimbly he scatters arrows where the rising day shows its reddish face, where Ocean drinks in the last light of day and wherever the world is bound by the sea. He drives the wound deep, more surely than the wily hand of the fleeing Parthian's arrow, whether he is preparing to feign retreat or to strike head-on.[29] Cupid's pestilent fire wholly devours the vitals, showing no outward sign of the wound; the heat lies hidden, burning the poor wretches more cruelly than terrifying

inflamans miseros sed calor horrido.
Hoc fervent iuvenes, hic tepidos senes
rursum flore comas cingere concitat
ignotamque iubet querere virgines
matrem. Quid superos? Liber avus nec est.
Heu passum quotiens tela Cupidinis
falsum terra Iovem sensit! In aureo
nimbo fluxit amans. Corpore candidus
cignus plumifero tunc petit thoros
cum nobis genuit bellaque Dardanis
et taurus spolii nomina littori
fratris regna secans pectore tradidit.
Calisto, posuit fulmina te petens
et vultus domine mitior induit.
Prolem, nube latet, dum tenet Inachi;
Alcidem genuit dum iubet Hesperum
hoc nomen solito sumere longius.
Iunonis thalamos linquere Iupiter
est passus, Semelem dum petit inclitam,
cuius vota gemit, fulmine languido
invadens uterum, parte sui gravem.
Ac proles caluit tigribus imperans
Thesei dum spolium curribus attulit,
qui gentes domuit qua prior est dies
delphinesque dedit primus in equora.
Phebus que pueri vulnera dirigant
novit tela. Soror noctivagos regens
currus incaluit. Figere celites
cognatos patitur nullaque gens vacat.
Quem duplex genuit nox, ferus Hercules
implevit calatos stamine coniugis
et clavam posuit, qua domuit feras,
dum fusos tenuit. Quid referam ducem,

Etna. Youths grow hot from it; it arouses old men who have lost their vigor to weave flowers in their hair again and virgins to seek out his mother, Venus, whom they do not know. And what of the gods above? Not even Cupid's grandfather is free from his power. Alas, how many times has the earth seen unfaithful Jove suffer from Cupid's darts![30] As a lover he flowed down in a golden cloudburst. Then, as a white swan with feathery body he sought the bed of Leda when he begot wars for us as well as the Trojans. And as a bull cleaving a path with his breast through the kingdoms of his brother Neptune, he gave to Europa's shores the name of his prey. Callisto, when he pursued you, he put aside his lightning and more gently put on the countenance of Diana. He hides in a cloud as he holds the daughter of Inachus; he sired Hercules while he ordered Hesperus to take that name of his for longer than was his wont.[31] Jupiter let himself leave the bed of Juno while he sought noble Semele, at whose prayers he groaned, and with a drooping thunderbolt pierced her womb, heavy now with his seed. His child Bacchus grew hot with love, guiding his tigers while he bore on his chariot the spoils of Theseus. He dominated the peoples where the day arrives earlier, and he was the first to send dolphins into the seas. Phoebus knows the wounds the boy's arrows are shooting for. His sister,[32] driving his night-wandering chariot, burned with love. He permits himself to strike his heavenly kin; no one is safe. Fierce Hercules, to whom that double night gave birth, filled the baskets of his wife with yarn and put the club down with which he tamed wild beasts, while he tended to her spindle.[33] Why mention the

cuius, thesalicum, Troia dolet manu?
Qui solus populi marte vicem tenet;
cuius fama nitens transit ad ultimas
gentes, Occeanus quas lavat et decus
mille est argolicis puppibus inclitum;
et qui, femineis cultibus abditus,
est fassus tumidos corporis impetus
armorum posuit iura, thoros petens.

: III :

Hecuba, Priam, Cassandra, Chorus Troianorum

He. Superba tandem concidit Troie lues.
Meliore fato celites nostros vident
fessos penates. Quicquid adversum obstitit
clarumque fudit sanguinem, Paridis manu
iacet interemptum. Templa testantur dei.
Ite ite, nati, puppe funesta senex
Acherontis aulam pandet. En vobis iter
quis nunc negabit? Misera quod feci nefas?
Extrema natos fata posuerant loco
tuto, carentes hoste. Felicem putans,
rupi quietem. Forsitan bellum intulit
ad regna Achiles tertie sortis potens;
natum trementi forsitan curru trahit
Cererisque generum terret et sevum Canem
serpente cuius terga villosa obstrepunt.
Quid misera feci? Certa quid Paridis manus?
Magis ipsa videor crimine infausto nocens;
autor cruenti sceleris in culpam incidit.
Adversa sed cur bella natorum putas?

Thessalian leader by whose hand Troy grieves? In battle this one man alone takes the place of his people; his glittering fame extends to the farthest nations that Ocean washes. He is the fame and glory of the thousand Argive ships. The man who, concealed in women's clothing, betrayed the bursting power of his body,[34] has now laid aside the rights of warfare and seeks a marriage bed.

: III :

Hecuba, Priam, Cassandra, Trojan Chorus

[Inside the city of Troy]

Hecuba. [*To herself*] At last, the haughty scourge of Troy has fallen! The heavenly gods see to it that our wearied household gods will have a better fate. Whatever it was that stood against us and shed our noble blood lies slain by the hand of Paris. The temple of the god bears witness. Go, go, my sons;[35] old Charon on his funereal ferry will open up for you the halls of Acheron. Lo, who shall deny you passage now? What evil thing have I done in my heartsickness? The last fates had placed my sons in a safe place, free from the enemy. Though reckoning it happy, I interrupted their repose. Perhaps mighty Achilles brought the war to the realms of the underworld; perhaps he's dragging my son behind his frightful chariot and terrifying Ceres' son-in-law and the cruel hound whose shaggy back bristles with snakes. Wretched woman, what have I done? What has the unerring hand of Paris done? I myself would rather seem to be culpable in this unfortunate deed; it is the author of this bloody crime who bears its guilt. But why do you reckon that your

Quicunque geminam mente perversat vicem
peiora semper cogitat. Natos puta
vicisse dudum thesali manes ducis,
suprema si post fata et extremum diem
servantur odia. Lenta cur Priamum diu
latere patior hostis infandi necem?
Gaudere gentes Ylii tandem decet.

Pr. Magnanima coniunx, fronte quid leta geris?
Hectorea postquam membra consumpsit rogus
emptosque cineres urna compressit brevis,
gaudente vultu nulla te vidit dies.
Hector iacentes erigit quis nunc Friges?

He. Michi restituti latera precingunt mea
nati. Parentem turba consequitur gregis
veneranda nostri. Mitior Ditis manus
leviore precio tradidit matri Hectorem.

Pr. Hec ipsa letam causa te demens facit?
Miseranda coniunx, nullus est Hector tibi.
Horribilius opus Atropos vertens sua
dextra impia sororum opere, sub cuius manet
potentia gens tota, que Iovem trahit,
perfracta nunquam stamina adiungit semel.

He. Nunc si ipse tacitam, qualis Alcides, domum
aperiret Hector, viribus vastis furens
Theseique frater sumeret tractus locum,
vix tanta menti gaudia afflicte daret
Fortuna quantis nostra prelucens viret.

Pr. Effare quicquid pectore hoc leto feras;
absit petitis longa sed, coniunx, mora,
morata quoniam dona villescunt diu.

He. Pirrus nepotis fata comitatur tui
Thetisque nostri socia meroris dolet.

sons' wars are going badly? Whoever turns over twin alternatives in his mind always thinks the worse must be true. Assume that your sons have at long last conquered the ghost of the Thessalian leader—if hate does endure after one's final destiny and last day. Why do I allow myself to delay and keep from Priam the death of our hated enemy? At last, the people of Ilium may fittingly celebrate. [*She approaches Priam*]

Priam. My high-souled wife, why do you show so joyful a face? Not since the funeral pyre consumed Hector's limbs and a small urn enclosed his ransomed ashes has there been a day that has beheld you with a smiling face. What Hector now uplifts the vanquished Trojans?

Hecuba. My sons are restored to me and stand by my side. The venerable throng of our family flock follows its mother. The gentler hand of Dis has given Hector to his mother at a cheaper price.

Priam. Mad woman, is it this that makes you happy? My poor wretched wife, there is no Hector here for you. Atropos,[36] turning her unholy hand to a deed even more horrible than the works of her sisters, and under whose powers every living kind remains and who compels even Jove, never rejoins her threads once they are broken.

Hecuba. Now if Hector himself, just like Hercules, were to unlock the silent house, raging with mighty strength, and if his brother were snatched from hell to take the place of Theseus, scarcely would Fortune have granted such great joys to my afflicted mind as those on whose account our radiant mind now thrives.

Priam. Tell me what it is you are carrying in that happy heart of yours. Let there be no delay in answering me, wife; gifts put off too long become worthless.

Hecuba. Pyrrhus is a companion of the fates of your grandson, and Thetis grieves as a partner in our sorrow.[37]

Pr. Qua peste Achiles? Ense ne an fluctu iacet?
Vindex ne fulmen stravit horrendum caput?
He. Thalamos petebat virginis Polixenes;
gener esse Priami concidit ferro putans.
Pr. Obruere quisnam potuit audaci manu
ferrumque in hostem mittere?
He. Hunc certo Paris
invasit arcu; vulnere haud uno iacet.
Pr. I, gener Achiles, inferum sedes doce
celebrare tedas; nempe cognato Hectori
ostende thalamos. Regios quisnam furens
intrat penates? Lauriger vultus patet.
Cassandra laceras, fronte turbata, comas
insana gestat; dubia quo gressus ferat
recursat amens, qualis amissam petens
prolem gementi cursitat vultu fera.
Cas. Quis me ad penates concitam furor trahit?
Ad quod vocamur carmen? Aut quonam meum
mittam furorem? Phebus ad matrem vocat.
Non fugere poteris thesalas nate faces;
retenta poscet classis; hoc hostis tamen
negabit hosti; coniugem coniunx bibet;
in te redibit ira dum fratrem petes.
He. Iam fessa cecidit, pectus effusum tremit;
huc ferte gressus iuxta, famularis cohors;
relevate mestam. Gelidus hanc foveat latex
per ora fusus. Sensit, en paulo movet
artus, revixit.
Cas. Quis meos sensus furor,
o Phebe, rursus concitat? Cerno nefas
quodnam cruentum? Munus acceptum dei,
et casta, dol[c]eo. Stimulat hunc magis dolor

Priam. [*After a pause*] How did Achilles die? By the sword or does he lie drowned in the sea? Or did an avenging lightning bolt fell his fearful head?

Hecuba. Seeking marriage to the virgin Polyxena and reckoning himself Priam's son-in-law, he fell by the sword.

Priam. Who on earth had the daring to crush him and impale our enemy with a sword?

Hecuba. Paris attacked him with his unerring bow; he lies dead, and by no means from a single wound.

Priam. Go, my son-in-law Achilles, teach the infernal regions how to celebrate a wedding; to be sure, show your kinsman Hector your marriage bed.[38] [*Cassandra enters.*] But who is this, pray, what mad person is entering our royal dwelling? A countenance crowned in laurel appears—it's Cassandra, with stormy brow, her tresses rent, gesticulating insanely; dazed, she runs hither and yon, knowing not where her steps take her, like a wild beast that runs everywhere howling and searching for its lost young.

Cassandra. [*To herself*] What madness is dragging me home in agitation? To what prophetic strain am I being summoned? Where should I utter my mad prophecy? Phoebus summons me to my mother. [*She approaches Hecuba.*] You will not be able to escape, Hecuba, a Thessalian marriage for your daughter. The fleet held back will demand her; nevertheless, one enemy will deny this to the other; a spouse will drink the blood of a spouse. Wrath will return upon you while you are seeking out her brother.[39] [*She falls to the ground.*]

Hecuba. She's now collapsed in exhaustion; her heaving breast trembles. Come over here, servants; help my poor unhappy daughter. Splash some cold water on her face, that will help. Look, she's responding; she's moving her limbs; she's waking up.

Cassandra. What madness, O Phoebus, stirs my senses once again? What bloody sacrilege do I see before me? I accepted the gift of the god, and though chaste, I grieve. A greater sorrow

quicunque fati prescius semper timet.
Occurrere erumnis dulce, prescire est grave.
He. O cara proles, pristinam mentem cape,
depone laurus, gemma prelustret caput
Serumque cultus vellere intextos gere.
Iam cecidit hostis, festus est Troie dies.
Cas. Sacrum Minerve manibus abductum tremo
dextramque iuvenis regius spargit cruor.
Horrenda cerno. Troia bis Priami nurum
veneratur unam; solvit et natus patrem
quodcunque timuit. Sydere haud uno regit
nos nauta. Solus iudicis locus est feri.
Pr. Placate superos. Colla cedantur iugi
ignara tauri; thure sacrato deos
tandem faventes colite et ante aras vigil
persistat ignis: letus est urbi dies.
Ch.T. Iupiter, celi dominator alti,
dardanas tandem meliore fato
despicis gentes. Manibus deorum
quicquid est structum, Genitor, tueris.
Traxit ingentes lira pulsa cautes;
Cadmus, externa comitante vacca,
victor armatas metuens cohortes,
semine ex tanto retinens sodales,
struxit et Thebas simili labore.
Concidit postquam venerandus Hector,
mille quem graie timuere puppes,
affuit semper dolor omnis urbi.
Thesali cedes reprimet dolores
sed ducis; leto vaga turba vultu
regios testis colit et penates.
Quisquis adversis premiturque fatoque
infimas ponti rate vidit undas

afflicts anyone who, knowing the future, is always afraid. To confront troubles is sweet; to know them beforehand is burdensome.

Hecuba. O dear child, return to your former consciousness; take off the laurel, let jewels gleam on your head, and put on your silken garments interwoven with wool. Our foe has fallen now. This is a festal day for Troy.

Cassandra. I tremble at the vision of a sacred image of Minerva, stolen by profane hands, and the royal blood splashed on the youth's hand.[40] I see fearful things. Twice does Troy honor the same daughter-in-law of Priam,[41] and the son destroys whatever thing feared his father. The pilot guides our ship by many stars.[42] There's one place only for the inhuman judge.

Priam. Appease the gods above. Let throats be slit of bulls unused to the yoke; with sacred incense honor the gods who at last are favorable to us. Before the altars an undying flame will stand. It is a happy day for the city!

Trojan Chorus. Jupiter, master of heaven on high, finally you look down on the Trojan people with greater favor. Whatever is built by the hands of the gods, you, Father Jove, protect. By strumming his lyre Amphion hauled gigantic boulders; Cadmus, with an unknown heifer as his guide, victorious, though afraid of his armed troops, kept a few companions from their great seed and built Thebes with similar effort.[43] After the awesome Hector fell—he whom a thousand Greek ships feared—sorrow without end of every kind came upon the city.

But the killing of the Thessalian leader will subdue sorrow; with happy faces a wandering crowd, witness to the slaughter, venerate the royal household gods. Whoever, threatened by adversity and fate, lies prostrate on a ship, staring into the depths

stratus et vultu lacrimat gementi
deserat spem non timidus foventem.
Volvitur semper rota namque fati,
nulla longevi cecinit vetustas
temporis sortem; relevat cadentes
opprimens celsos metuenda colles.
Nulla tam celum tetigit potestas
que diu possit retinere vires.
Quisquis excelsus agitatus alis
nititur summas penetrare nubes,
ocior telo cadit in profundum.
Igneo quicquid magis obstat ingens
fulmini, sevo potius Tonantis
sternitur ictu.
Sive Fortuna regimur rotanti,
sive tu mundum, Genitor, gubernas,
ista lex orbi datur equa nostro.
Quisquis humano saturat cruore
cedis et dire est truculentus autor
parcit et nunquam furibundus ensi,
sed iuvat dextra rutilante terras
sanguine externo maculare semper,
concidet tandem sceleris magister.
Nemo tam fortis valet esse, quo non
fortior assit.
Omnis exemplo sequitur luentes,
quod nefas fecit patitur cruentum.
Hospitum pinguem saturavit aulam
sanguine Alcides rigidi tiranni
et gregem pavit Diomedis ultor
proprio sevi iugulo ministri.
Hectorem stravit Thetidis superbus
natus et gentes domuit feroces;

of the sea, weeping and groaning, should not timorously give up hope of relief, for the wheel of fate is ever turning. All antiquity tells us that one's lot in life cannot long remain the same; the same terrifying wheel[44] that leveled the high hills can raise them up again. Once power touches heaven, it loses force. Whoever wings his way aloft in exaltation and tries to penetrate the highest clouds falls more swiftly than an arrow into the deep. Any greatness that tries to withstand the fiery thunderbolt is instead knocked flat by a savage blow from the Thunderer.

Whether we're ruled by revolving Fortune or whether you, Father Jove, govern the world, this fair law is given to our world: whoever, drenched with human blood, is belligerent and responsible for cruel slaughter and in his fury never spares the sword, but with reddening hand always takes pleasure in staining the earth with foreign blood, will in the end be cut down himself, an example of wickedness.[45] No one can be so strong that someone stronger may not appear.

Every man follows the example of those who are being punished and suffers for what his own bloody wickedness has done. Hercules drenched Diomedes' court, made rich by the plunder of guests, with the blood of that unbending tyrant, and in vengeance Hercules pastured Diomedes' herd of mares on the slaughtered remains of their cruel master.[46] The proud son of Thetis slew Hector and subdued fierce nations, but Paris of the

sed Paris certus violenter arcu
fixit hunc; testis necis est Apollo.
Diva quam spernit sociale regnum,
arbiter pomi rutilantis audax
vindices sprete tribuit sagitas.

: IV :

Nuncius, Chorus Grecorum

Nu. Quis me cruentus nuncium casus gerit?
Quis me in profundo Tartari volvet specu
faciemque visu merget occeano gravem?
Quis fervor Ethne spiritu sevo calens
flamante vultus obruet nostros coma?
Graviora vidi. Caucasus celi premens
furtum rigenti vertice huic levis est malo.
Ch.G. Himenea vultus equidem talis negat;
sed pande quicquid pectore arcano est novi.
Nu. Hec ipsa celeri causa me vexit gradu.
Ch.G. Effare. Sed cur induit pallor genas?
Nu. En trepidus horror languido motu subit
geluque victus torpet in fibris cruor.
Imago tanti sceleris in faciem redit.
Ch.G. Pervince quicquid prohibet atque animum aggravat.

unerring bow pierced him violently. Apollo is the witness of his death. O goddess [Discordia] whom the royal partnership spurns, the rash judge of the bright red apple offers you, O scorned one, the arrows of vengeance.[47]

: IV :

Messenger, Greek Chorus

[In the Greek camp]

Messenger. What bloody disaster makes me its messenger? Who will send me running into the deep cave of Tartarus and sink my face into Ocean, a sight terrible to behold? What blast of Etna, its cruel breath seething hot, will cover my countenance with its flaming mane? I've seen such dreadful things. Even the Caucasus, looming with its icy peak over the thief of heaven,[48] is trifling when compared to this evil.

Greek Chorus. Indeed, such an expression as yours does not bespeak news of a wedding; but reveal whatever is hidden in your heart.

Messenger. This is the very reason that has brought me with so rapid a step.

Greek Chorus. Speak up. But why has the color drained from your cheeks?

Messenger. Lo, a fearful horror slowly steals upon me, and my freezing blood stands still in my veins. The image of an enormous crime appears before me.

Greek Chorus. Overcome whatever it is that stops you speaking and weighs upon your spirit.

Nu. Horrore sceleris lingua prohibetur loqui.
Ch.G. Licet ipse condas, veritas semper patet
facinusque nullum durat occultum diu.
Nu. Te fulminantem, sceptra qui gestas poli,
et qui per altas lumen extendis plagas
et qui tridente cingis humanas tuo,
testor, catervas: concidit regum decus
et mille robur puppis argolice inclitum
orbamque Thetidem sevus hic fecit dies.
Ch.G. Quis mestus aures perculit nostras sonus?
Nu. O clare Titan, cladibus tantis potes
per summa celi spatia lucifero diem
gestare curru? Maius hoc certe est nefas
epulo Thiestis; merge, sed sero, caput.
Scelus hoc tremisco, deserit corpus vigor.
Ch.G. Effare mortis ordinem: erumnas iuvat
audire miseros; nulla celetur lues.
Nu. Procul a pelasgo ereptus est postquam foro
et mille Achiles inclitus liquit rates,
non arma sumpsit qualis his fictus tumens
invasit acies: pectoris sevos clepens
ictus vacavit; nulla vibrata est manu
armata verticem asta nec texit caput
fidele tegmen, membra complexus negant
induere tutos; solus est lateri comes
receptus ensis; turba non sequitur ducem
animosa ferro. Qualis himeneum decet
hic templa querit; Thetidis et Pelei nurum
thalamosque claros regie stirpis putat
celebrare Troiam. Callidi fictor doli
simulante vultu thesalo perstat duci.
Decipere amantes facile. Si semper vagas
pulsare Scirtes, puppe si fracta horridum

Messenger. My tongue is kept from speaking in horror at the deed.

Greek Chorus. Although you may keep it hidden, the truth will always out, and no crime stays hidden for long.

Messenger. I call you to witness, you who thunder and bear the scepter of heaven, and you who spread the light through the lofty regions, and you who girdle the lands of us humans with your trident.[49] The glory of kings and the noble strength of a thousand Argive ships has fallen. This cruel day has made Thetis childless.

Greek Chorus. What sad sound is this that strikes our ears?

Messenger. O radiant Titan, amidst such great disasters can you even carry the daylight through the high reaches of heaven on your glistening chariot? This sacrilege is surely greater than the meal served to Thyestes. Sink your head in Ocean, although it is too late! I tremble at this deed; strength leaves my body.

Greek Chorus. Tell us how he died. It gives relief to the wretched to hear of afflictions. Let no detail of the disaster remain concealed.

Messenger. After renowned Achilles tore himself from the Greek camp and left the thousand ships far behind, he did not carry arms of the sort he would put on when aflame to attack a battle line. He had no shield against savage blows to the chest; he shook no well-tipped spear in his hand, nor did he cover his head with a trusty helmet. His limbs refused to don armor. The only companion he took was the sword at his side. No throng of men, spirited in arms, followed their captain. He made straight for the temple, as befits a bridegroom. He believes that Troy is celebrating the illustrious wedding of a royal daughter and the daughter-in-law of Thetis and Peleus. The inventor of the sly deception stands looking with his lying face at the Thessalian leader. It's easy to trick those who are in love.

sulcare pontum, sydera et celum aggredi
amor imperaret, nullus obstaret pavor.
Superare novit celites viros feras.
Ut seva fulsit dardani Phebi domus,
Peleus cacumen vidit huc velox gradum
tum concitabat. Astra vergebant ducis,
horrenda fata miserant summum diem.
Namque in potentes astra ius magnum tenent;
in fata properat quilibet libens sua.
Ecce ecce tetigit liminis sacri fores.
Non thure flama pinguis ante aras micat;
non est sacerdos more dardanio colens
secreta divum; nullus aspicitur, gregis
rector ferocis, taurus immunis iugi
sparsurus aras. Dux stupet, tandem subit.
Tunc patuit omnis fraudis yliace dolus.
Armigera utrinque cinxit en latus cohors,
quos inter omnes summus emicuit Paris.
Quicunque Achilis Hectorem laudi canit
urbesque fusas impetu tantum suo,
parum arma novit atque virtutem ducis.
Hic nempe vires summus explicuit dies.
Non ille pavidus supplici vitam genu
tot inter arma querit et victus iacet;
sed fortis iras pectore ex toto capit;
qualis feroces libicus extendit leo
animosque rigidas concutit fervens iubas
cum cernit hostes, obvius ferri minas
poscit; timere puduit et virtus malis
erigitur ingens. Prospero fortes loco
celantur animi: adversa virtutem probant.
Delubra sonitu bellico tota obstrepunt
fremuntque galee; solus hic centum ferit

If love commanded them to pound the shifting Syrtes, to cut through the perilous sea on a crippled ship, and to climb up to the stars and heaven, no fear would hold them back. Love knows how to conquer gods, men, and beasts. As the cruel temple of the Trojan Apollo gleamed, the son of Peleus saw its dome and quickened his pace. The stars of Achilles were setting; the fearful Fates had sent him his last day on earth. The stars hold binding authority over potentates, to be sure, but everyone hastens willingly to his own fate. Behold, behold, he has reached the doors of the sacred threshold. No flame fed with incense sparkles before the altars; there is no priest tending to rites of the gods in the Trojan manner. No bull is to be seen, master of his wild herd, not subject to the yoke, who will wash the altars with his blood. Achilles is bewildered, but at last he enters. Then all the treachery of Troy revealed itself. Lo, on either side, a cohort of armed men surrounded him, among whom Paris stood out as their chief. Whoever sings of Hector in praise of Achilles and of the whole cities he routed by his assault alone, knows little of the military skill and courage of this captain. This day, Achilles' last, revealed his might without question. He was not afraid and did not beg on bended knee for his life in the midst of overwhelming arms, nor cringe in defeat, but called up the passionate force of a brave man from his whole breast. Just as the Libyan lion enlarges its ferocious spirit when he sees enemies and angrily shakes his shaggy mane, so facing them, Achilles welcomes the threat of their swords. It shamed him to be afraid, and his huge courage was aroused by these evil acts. Brave souls lie hidden in prosperity; adversity tests courage. The entire shrine reverberates with the sound of battle, and helmets clash. A single man, Achilles wounds a hundred men, and their thousand weapons cause not

et mille solum tela non vulnus gerunt,
non fixa pendent. Quicquid emittunt, retro
inane fertur, qualis inpulsu cadit
maris unda saxi. Dubia dum martis labat
sors, inquit: 'Hec est prolis Assaraci fides?
Hec iura thalami? Pacis hec false quies?
Sed ante nostros cimba quam manes ferat,
multi nepotis nuncient vires avo
paremque servet manibus nostris locum.'
Hec fatus, ensem pariter in cunctos gerit
humilem ac ferocem; largus exundat cruor;
iaculatur omnis tela nec tantis sat est
vulneribus unum pectus. O miserum diem!
Vix patitur animus horridum scelus eloqui.
Tandem subactus pronus Eacides ruit,
qualis regentem premium rota afferens,
superata falsis axibus. Cecidit tamen
nec totus, astat genibus erectus potens.
Barbarica resonant vocibus templa horridis;
non querit ultro bella nec cedem invenit;
satis est tueri et ensis in clipei loco
defendit ora. Nullus est ferro aggredi
vicinus audax; tela sed Paris manu
sublimis aptans, inquit: 'I, nunc, thesalos,
superbe, currus pondere Hectoreo preme.
Hac hac sagita nulla te eripiet Thetis.'
Haud dixit ultra. Cornibus iunctis volat
sagita, vulnus, morte permixta, ferens.
Ut ille sensit, languido vultu cadit
terramque fusus ore prostrato ferit;
decus omne clari corporis telo perit;
mutata facies pallet et totum iacet
humo cadaver. Nullus est vulgo pudor:

a single wound; they bounce off him. Whatever they throw at him comes back at them, futile blows, like the waves of the sea crashing on a rock. While the outcome of the battle was still in doubt, Achilles said, "Is this the good faith of the race of Assaracus?[50] Are these the rites of marriage? Is this the repose of your pretended peace? But before the ferry of Charon bears my shade below, many men will bring report to my grandfather of his grandson, and Peleus will reserve a place for me worthy of my shade." Speaking thus, he turned his sword, short and fierce, against them all alike. Oceans of blood pour forth. All hurl their weapons at him, and one breast is not proof against so many wounds. O heartbreaking day! My soul can scarce suffer to relate the revolting crime. Overcome at last, Achilles crashes to the ground, like a chariot bearing the winner of the race, collapsing from a broken axle. Achilles falls, but not entirely; he is able to stand upright on his knees. The barbarous temple echoes with dreadful shouts. He stops attacking but does not find death; his look is enough, and in place of a shield his sword defends his face. No Trojan dares to attack him up close with a sword, but haughty Paris, fitting an arrow to his bow, says, "Go, now, proud Achilles, load up that Thessalian chariot of yours with Hector's weight. Thetis will not rescue you from *this* arrow!" He said nothing more. From his taut bow the arrow flew, carrying a wound mixed with death. As soon as he felt it, his countenance relaxed and he fell, striking the ground face downward. All the beauty of his noble frame died with that arrow. His face changes, going white; and his whole corpse lies on the earth. The vulgar mob has no shame. Still

saturata nundum membra divellit manus.
Ubi regnat odium, spernitur pietas, fides.
Ch.G. Ut Phebum sequitur soror,
sic letos animos dolor.
Dum clari renitent poli
et nimbis gravibus vacant
nec lucis tegitur nitor,
at solis radios capit
mundi purpureus decor,
auster nubifer advolat
pulsus carcere saxeo,
lucem protinus excutit,
obscurans nitidum iubar
celum nubibus induit;
sic cum leta virent, levis
casus precipitat rote
et luctus revehit. Diu
non stant numina prospera,
nulla est in superis fides.
Cum Phebus gerit aureos
currus loraque dextera
fulgenti resecans plagas
celi luciferas regit
preceps fertur et occidens
invadit subitus, caput
ac mergit pelago nitens,
aufertur nitidus dies,
noctis nuncius Hesperus
obscure exoritur prior;
sic risus lacrime vorant
et lucem tenebre obtegunt.
Sit quisquis cupiat potens
aula magnus et inclita

not satiated, they tear him limb from limb. Where hatred reigns, piety and good faith are scorned.

Greek Chorus. As his sister follows Phoebus,[51] so sorrow follows happy souls. While clear skies shine and are free from gravid clouds, and the brightness of the day is not overshadowed, but the rosy beauty of the world seizes the rays of the sun, the cloud-bearing south wind blows in, expelled from its rocky prison. At once, it blots out the light, hiding the bright sunshine, and dresses the sky with clouds. So, too, when happy times are green, a slight mischance sets fate's wheel in motion downward, and sorrow turns back upon us. Not for long do the gods remain favorable; there's no relying on them. When Phoebus drives his golden chariot and with his shining hand takes the reins as he cuts through the light-filled realms of heaven, he is borne headlong and suddenly lands in the West, sinking his shining head in the sea; the bright day is done. Hesperus, the messenger of gloomy night, rises earlier. Thus, tears devour laughter, and darkness covers light. Whoever so desires, let him

et fortes acies ducum
sublimisque tumens regat.
Plebeus satis est michi
cultus, me teneat casa.
Est felix locus infimus;
in glisca tenui cibus
secure capitur. Quies
me parvi foveat laris.
Nam quicquid volat altius
momento rapitur brevi.
Excelsus penetrans nimis
alis Icharus ethera,
mandati patris immemor,
languens in pelagus ruit.
Pheton curribus arduis
indocta retinens manu
phebei iuga ponderis,
ustus fulmine concidit
fraterneque soror necis
luctu cortice inhorruit.
Pelides genitus dea
olim qui timor Ylios
sublimis stetit incliti,
cesus templa rigat suo
ferro sanguine Apollinis.
Paucos sicca duces trahit
mors ad vincula Tartari.
Vivit sancta fides procul
semper limine regio.

be powerful and great at a famous court, and let him rule from on high, swelling with pride, the captains' mighty battle lines. For me, the life of a commoner is enough; let a cottage shelter me. The lowest place is happy; at a poor table dinner is eaten without fear. May the quiet of a small home content me. Whatever soars too high in a brief moment is pulled down. Icarus, flying too high through the air on his wings, unmindful of his father's command, fell helplessly into the sea. Phaëthon in his lofty chariot tried to control the weighty team of Phoebus with an unskilled hand, but fell, scorched by a thunderbolt. His sister, in grief over her brother's death, became wrinkled with bark.[52] Achilles, born of a goddess, who once was the awful terror of renowned Ilium, has been slain by the sword and drenches the temple of Apollo with his blood. A bloodless death drags few captains to the chains of Tartarus. Sacred trust always dwells far from the thresholds of kings.

: V :

Agamemnon, Menelaus, Calchas, Chorus Grecorum

Ag. Fortuna gentes que regis cunctas potens,
Titan calenti quas ferit primus rota
mergensque nitidum fessus Occeano diem,
tu blanda nunquam ducibus argolicis faves,
simul atque Frigibus prospero vultu diu.
Inclitus Achiles bella dum ple<c>tro vacans
torpente dira sperneret dulci manu
superabat Hector, gentis yliace decus.
Obstare quisnam potuit? Hec dextra impotens
armata facibus pene consumpsit rates,
quarum alta noster vela perflavit cruor.
Pavidus iacebat quisquis; hic tutus pari
furebat Hector; sanguine argivo tumens
yliaca pinguis Xantus intravit freta.
Traxere postquam thesale Hectoreos rote
Achilis artus ense prostratos fer<r>o
preciumque nati Priamus amittens dedit,
vicere achivi marte felici duces.
Sors equa sed nunc, cede geminata, capit
utrumque populum. Natus hinc pelagi dea,
est Hector illinc. Concidit Paridis manu
decus omne grai nominis, spes et fides
periere templo. Pateris hoc divum sator?
Cur cessat alto fulmen emissum polo?
Tonare decuit. Horridum impune est nefas?
En sacra Phebi templa maculavit cruor.
Sed cur Tonantem fulmina ut mittat rogo?
Violata non sunt cede funesta Iovis,
sed templa Phebi. Lucis o clare arbiter,

: V :

Agamemnon, Menelaus, Calchas, Greek Chorus

Agamemnon. Fortune, who rules in power over all peoples that Titan first strikes with his flaming wheel before sinking, exhausted, with a flash into Ocean, you never give your kindly favor to the Greek leaders and at the same time turn your propitious countenance on the Trojans for long. For as long as noble Achilles scorned cruel war and with languid hand plucked at his sweet lyre, Hector was in the ascendant, the glory of the Trojan race. Who could stand up to him? Armed with firebrands, his indomitable hand nearly destroyed the fleet, whose high sails our own blood had filled.[53] Every man cowered in fear; Hector raged on, having no equal to challenge him. The Xanthus was swollen richly with Argive blood as it entered the straits of Ilium. After the Thessalian wheels dragged Hector's limbs, cut down by Achilles' cruel sword, and Priam, bereft of his son, paid a ransom for his corpse, the Argive captains were triumphant in battle.

But now an equal lot, with twin slaughter, befalls both peoples: on our side, the son of a goddess of the sea, on theirs, Hector. The entire glory of the Greek name perished by the hand of Paris; our hope and our faith died in that temple. Father of the gods, will you allow this? Why does the heaven-sent lightning not strike? It is fitting that it thunder. Is this awful crime to go unpunished? Lo, blood has stained the sacred temple of Phoebus. But why do I ask the Thunderer to send his lightning bolts? It is not the temples of Jove that have been desecrated by deadly slaughter, but those of Phoebus. O judge of radiant light, who ever controls the cycles of the fading year,

qui semper anni iura precipitis tenes
pateris cruento scelere fedari tuas
inultus aras? Certius sancta manu
tendatur arcus, Paridem et Ylios pete,
Phitonis atras qualis infesti iubas
olim petisti, tabe cum dira fluens
sanguis veneni spargeret nigri solum;
vel cum parente dextra contempta furens
equate Niobes sterneret prolem deis.

Me. Germane, Danaum cuius imperio favent
tot arma, prolis Tantali clare decus,
haud invocati punient scelus dei.
Impune superi non diu linquunt nefas.

Ag. Iam lesit ipsos celites Priami sator
fidemque rupit. Traxit ingentes cheli
ad saxa cautes Phebus et locum sibi
fecere cantu. Regna qui sorte ultima
primaque cessans divus equorea obtinet,
firmavit arces dextera intactas sua.
Caruit negato numinum precio labor
fraudemque gemino Laumedon struxit deo
etiam sagitis fluctibus pena vacans.

Me. Cur mille superos vindices poscunt rates?
Extrema cogunt querere auxilium deos.
Hec una superest nulla cum superest salus.
Viget alta Danaum prospero bello cohors;
hac dextra Paridis vindice in penas cadat.

Ag. Accendit animos causa Pelide tuos,
an causa thalami?

Me. Me utraque in bellum trahit.

Ag. Magis iste fervet pectore insano furor;
repetis iugales marte violento faces;

will you permit your altars to be defiled by a bloody crime without taking vengeance? Unerringly you should stretch your bow with your sacred hand, take aim at Paris and Ilium, just as you once took aim at the dark crest of the terrible Python[54] — its blood drenched the ground flowing with the dire contagion of its black poison — or just as when your furious right hand, out of contempt for their mother, slew the offspring of Niobe who had claimed equality with the gods.[55]

Menelaus. Brother, whose command so many Greek arms obey, glory of the noble race of Tantalus, the gods will punish this crime, even unasked; not for long do the gods above leave wickedness unpunished.

Agamemnon. Already the father of Priam[56] injured those heavenly gods and broke his word. With his lyre Phoebus dragged huge boulders to the stone walls and made a place for them with his song. The god who passed on the first and last offer and accepted the watery realms[57] strengthened the inviolate citadel with his own hand. The gods' labors went without their promised reward, and Laomedon committed fraud against the pair of divinities, even managing to escape punishment from arrows and waves.

Menelaus. Why do the thousand ships petition the gods above for vengeance? Such extreme evils as these force us to ask help from the gods. When there is no other means of salvation, this one only remains: the noble army of the Greeks flourishes in a successful war. Let Paris in punishment fall by this avenging hand of mine!

Agamemnon. Is it because of Achilles that your courage grows hot or because of your marriage?

Menelaus. Both draw me into conflict.

Agamemnon. This frenzy of yours burns the more because of the insanity in your heart. You are laying claim again to the torches of marriage by means of martial violence. The grief you feel for

te solus urit coniugis rapte dolor.
Me. Iuste dolet quicunque pro thalamo dolet.
Ag. Proh seva fata, dura, truculenta, aspera!
Quod mille puppes sydus horrendum freta
per tumida vexit? Graia mercedem petit
quam marte tellus? Sanguine huc veni meo,
Thetidis recedam. Causa que belli datur?
Me. Iuste arma lesus, coniuge abrapta, movet.
Ag. Clitemestra veteres Tantali lares tenet.
Me. Regem tueri regis ignoti interest.
Ag. Infesta quicquid classis ancipiti petit
vel marte, detur pacis et crescat quies.
Tot sparsa regum membra, tot Danaum rogos
supplebit Helena? Sanguine effuso leves
hec una satis est premere titubantes rates?
Vigebit alto Tindaris solio potens.
Orbata lacrimas fundet eterno Thetis
Itacique fraudem callidam semper gemet.
Me. O, vera fateor, candidi proles Iovis,
tu prima danaas causa movisti rates;
nunc tota Achili bella debentur. Tibi
detraxit odia thesali cedes ducis;
pugnabit ultrix graia non pro te manus.
Ag. Nos fata miseros undique infausta opprimunt.
Iacet ille cuius cecinit argolicas deus
inserere arene, dextra si deesset, manus.

the ravishing of your wife is the only thing that is torturing you.

Menelaus. His grief is just who grieves for his marriage.

Agamemnon. O cruel fates, unyielding, ferocious, harsh! What fearful star brought our thousand ships through stormy seas? What gain does the land of Greece seek in this war? I came hither by spilling the blood of my own child; by shedding the blood of Thetis' son shall I return. What reason is there for this war?

Menelaus. Recourse to arms is just when a man has been injured by the theft of his wife.

Agamemnon. Clytemnestra, *my* wife, dwells still in the ancient home of Tantalus.

Menelaus. It is in the interest of a king, even a humble one, to protect a fellow king.

Agamemnon. Whatever the hostile fleet demands, even though the outcome of the battle is in doubt, let it be granted, and may the tranquillity of peace increase. Can Helen take the place of the many royal limbs strewn everywhere and the innumerable funeral pyres of the Greeks? Is this one woman enough to ballast our bobbing fleet, made light by the shedding of so much blood? She will thrive in power on the high throne of Tindareus.[58] Childless Thetis will weep forever and always lament the wily deceits of Ulysses.[59]

Menelaus. O child of bright Jove,[60] I speak the truth, you were the original cause that dispatched the Greek ships; now, the whole war is in debt to Achilles. The death of the Thessalian captain has lessened hatred for you; the Greek forces will no longer fight to avenge your ravishing.

Agamemnon. On every side unpropitious fates oppress us in our wretchedness. That man is dead of whom the god prophesied that the Greek army would be sown like seeds in the sand if his

Quisve igitur ultor? Ylios nunquam ruet?
Me. Calcas salutis limen ostendet; sequar.
Ag. Sospes ut Horestes vivat, et Calcas canat.
Cal. Vox nostra regis sanguinem nullum petit.
Ag. Effare
Cal. et aras nullus asperget cruor.
Ag. Exprome quicquid Phebus Argivos docet.
Cal. Generosa Achilis suppleat proles locum:
hanc fata poscunt. Iuvenis hic Troiam obruet.
Ag. Paterna Pirrus nobilis castra oppetet;
sed mesta Danaum luctibus resonet cohors
et mille feriat interim clamor rates.
Ch.G. Ad quos fletus Fortuna vocat!
Heu quo nostras lacrimasque vehit!
Lugere decet, fortis Achile.
Feriant planctus mille carinas;
sonet ydeis vox nostra iugis.
Reddere fletus non satis Echo est:
findant gemitus ethera nostri.
Capiant gemini mesta Tonantes
verbera, planctu feriente chaos.
Perdant seva fila sorores,
metuat custos vallata gerens
terga colubris imique Iovis
stupeat coniunx, Alecto gravi
pinumque metu furibunda sinat.
Linquat puppem trepidante manu
pressus nostro clamore senex;
fugiant proprios manesque locos,
non traitia resonante cheli.
Tempus lacrimis manet eternum.
Non laurigero vertice currus
in thesalicas te feret urbes,

hand was not with us. Then who is the avenger? Will Troy never fall?

Menelaus. Calchas will light the threshold of salvation. I shall follow.

Agamemnon. Provided Orestes is safe, let Calchas sing. [*They approach Calchas*]

Calchas. Our voice asks for no royal blood . . .[61]

Agamemnon. Speak . . .

Calchas. . . . and no blood will stain the altars.

Agamemnon. Reveal whatever it is Phoebus has to teach the Greeks.

Calchas. The noble offspring of Achilles should take the place of his father; the Fates demand him. This youth will conquer Troy.

Agamemnon. Noble Pyrrhus will come untimely to his father's camp; but meanwhile let the mourning army of the Greeks resound with lamentation and let wailing resound from the thousand ships.

Greek Chorus. To what weeping does Fortune call us? Alas, whither does she draw our tears? Brave Achilles, it is fitting to grieve for you. Lamentation should resound from our thousand ships; let our voice reecho from the peaks of Mt. Ida. To return our mourning, Echo is not enough; our grief should pierce the ether. May the twin Thunderers[62] take up their sad lashes as our plaint strikes down into Chaos. May the cruel sisters lose their thread, and may the guardian of hell, his back bristling with snakes, grow fearful, and the spouse of infernal Jove[63] be dumbfounded. Let Alecto, maddened, drop her pine bough out of heavy fear. May the old ferryman, besieged by our clamor, leave his boat, his hand trembling; let the shades flee from their proper places, and let the lyre of Orpheus resound no more. The time for tears is eternal. No chariot, once cumbered with

olim Hectoreo pondere pressus;
et non frigii tua signa duces
clara sequentur; non thura deis
post tanta dabis premia belli.
Nec thesalice tibi dona ferent
urbes, festos turba penates
colet egregio plausura duci.
Non aurata clarus in aula
leges populis et iura dabis;
obvia nato non magna Thetis
oscula fundet. Quid plura feram?
Te Troia cadet.
Sed te rigidi tenet ora dei,
virtus Stigios si petit amnes,
aut Elisio tutus in arvo
felixque vires si letheas
non bibis undas: semper populi
tua fata canent. Nunquam stabilis
Fortuna iaces: rota precipiti
humana vehit cursu fata.
Nichil in miseros, Fortuna, potes,
que seva tenes frena potentum.
Tu que Stigias incolis umbras
seva sororum, graviore manu
stamina versans, impia cuius
dextera frangit quicquid Cloto
Lachesisque gerit, vertis nimium
fata virorum properante colo.
Cunctos recipit cimba Carontis
vertere cursum nullique licet.
Cum letheos haustus tetigit,
iura relicti negligit orbis,
omnia carpit superumque fides;

Hector's weight and bound with laurel, will carry you into the Thessalian cities, and no Trojan captains will follow behind your noble banners. No incense will you offer to the gods after so many spoils of war. Nor will the cities of Thessaly bring you gifts, nor will the throng honor your household gods in festival, applauding their renowned leader. You will not nobly issue laws and privileges to the people in a golden court, nor will great Thetis pour kisses on her son when you meet. Why should I say more? Troy will fall because of you.

But the shores of the stern god hold you back. Whether your courage brings you to the river Styx or whether, safe in the Elysian fields and rejoicing in your might, you drink not of the waters of Lethe, men will sing forever the story of your fate. Fortune, you never rest in one place; your wheel bears the human fates on their precipitous course. You can do nothing, Fortune, against the wretched, but you control the mighty with your cruel reins. You who dwell among the shadows of the Styx, the cruel one of the sisters,[64] turning the threads with your deadlier hand, whose unholy right hand breaks whatever threads Clotho and Lachesis spin, you play too much with men's fates on your speedy spinning wheel. The ferry of Charon receives all, and no one can change its course. When his ship touches the waters of Lethe, it abandons the laws of the world

impia nulli dextera parcit.
Qui sublimi nitet imperio
fronte superba populosque regit,
rumpi metuit fila sororum.
Nullus tantis viribus audax
nullus tantis opibusque viret,
quem non rapiat furibunda manus.
O mors cuius sorbet hyatus
quicquid Phebi gignit et auget
calor auxilio, Neptune, tuo
quicquidque Jovem naribus efflat,
heu quot properas metuenda modis!
Quid, cum vacuas liber in auras
spiritus intrat miserumque sinit
funere truncum corpus, remanet,
nisi terra levis?
Nullique suum vitare licet
quem fata diem summa dederunt.
Ponite vanas spes soliciti,
ponite timidi simul atque metus:
fata gubernant mortale genus
et prima dies ultima novit.
Quicquid gerimus sydera volvunt
cursusque poli mundana regunt.
Non ipse deus mutare potest
quicquid Fatis nectitur altis.

Anthonii de Luschis de Vicentia tragedia
explicit Achiles.
Laus sit Deo.
Amen

it left behind, and faith in the gods above consumes all things. Alecto's unholy hand spares no one. The man who shines with exalted power and rules peoples with haughty demeanor, fears that the thread of the sisters has snapped. There is no one so bold and strong nor so flourishing with great wealth that the angry hand of Fate may not seize him. O Death, whose gaping mouth swallows whatever the warmth of Phoebus begets and is nurtured with your help, Neptune, and whatever breathes Jove from its nostrils,[65] alas, in how many ways do you hasten what must be feared! When the freed spirit enters the empty air and leaves its wretched body, cut off by death, what remains of it except dust? It is not allowed for anyone to avoid the day which the highest Fates have appointed as his last. Put aside vain hopes, anxious men, and at the same time put away your fears, ye timid: the Fates do govern mortal kind, and the first day knows already the last. All our acts depend on the turning stars, and the course of the heavens rules all things on earth. Not even a god himself can alter whatever is woven by the Fates on high.

Here ends the tragedy *Achilles*
of Antonio Loschi of Vicenza.
Praise be to God.
Amen

GREGORII CORRARII

PROGNE

Argumentum

1 Huic tragoediae titulus est Progne. Argumentum huiusmodi: Tereus, rex Thraciae, boellum Pandioni, regi Athenarum, intulerat. Demumque inter reges, firmata pace, convenerat ut Tereus uxorem duceret Prognem, maiorem natu filiam Pandionis: hoc scilicet haud leve pacis stabilimentum rati, si mutua necessitudine devin-
2 cerentur. Duxerat, igitur, Tereus Prognem. Natus erat Ythis, iam quinquennis puer. Progne (interim crescit desiderium Philomenae sororis, quae domi innupta erat) exorat coniugem ut sibi eius visendae copiam faciat. It Tereus, impetrat a patre virginem. Navigant e Graecia, Thraciam deveniunt, urbi appropinquant. Amat Tereus, infert vim virgini, lacessitur convitiis, puellam elinguem facit, clausam servari iubet, comites eius necat, detur ut fallaciae locus. Solus Pistus, puelle alumnus, fuga eripitur.

3 Ita, re gesta, Tereus ad Prognem venit, mentitur lacrimas, refert sororem, vi maris gravatam, defecisse. Credidit Progne. Sed diu

GREGORIO CORRER

PROCNE

CHARACTERS

Diomedes, *a Thracian king, now a shade*
Tereus, *king of Thrace*
Procne, *his wife*
Philomena,[1] *Procne's sister*
Chorus
Pistus, *a faithful companion of Philomena*
Nurse
Itys, *male child of Tereus and Procne*
Messenger

Argument[2]

The title of this tragedy is *Procne.* Its argument is as follows: 1
Tereus, king of Thrace, had waged war with Pandion, king of the
Athenians. Finally it was agreed that in order to ensure peace between them, Tereus would take Procne, the older daughter of
Pandion, as his wife; they believed it would strengthen the peace
considerably if the two of them should be bound together by mutual obligation. So Tereus married Procne. A boy named Itys was 2
born to them, now five years old. Procne in the meantime has a
growing desire to see her sister Philomena, who lived at home,
unmarried, and begs her husband for some means of seeing her.
Tereus goes and requests the maiden of her father. They sail from
Greece, arrive in Thrace, approach the city. Tereus, enamored of
Philomena, rapes her. Provoked by her reproaches, he cuts out her
tongue, and orders that she be locked up. He kills her attendants
so that the treachery could take place. Only Pistus,[3] the girl's dear
companion, escapes by fleeing.

This done, Tereus comes to Procne, lies to her, telling her in 3
tears that her sister died in a shipwreck. Procne believed him. But

tantum scelus latere non potuit: venit sororis alumnus, omne scelus detegit.

4 Forte tunc orgia Bacchi repetita triennia suadebant. More igitur sacri exit in silvas Progne, Bacchantes sequuntur. Deveniunt ad locum ubi servabatur Philomoena, occiduntur custodes. Ducitur puella more sacrorum ornata. Furit Progne, per abominandum scelus ulciscitur: natum unicum interimit patrique epulandum ponit.

5 Dictum autem poetice Tereum ex Marte genitum, ob saeviciam boellorum et ex nimpha Bistonide, ab eo per vim oppressa. Fictum etiam Prognem conversam in hyrundinem, Philomoenam in avem sui nominis, Tereum vero in uppupam, cuius facies cristata est, ut indicet regium caput. Vivit autem e stercore propter memoriam comesi nati.

6 Imitatur in hac tragoedia Senecam in Thieste, ut ibi Tantalus ab inferis veniens introducitur, ita hic Diomedes, thrax tyrannus.

Genera metrorum totius tragoediae

7 *Lucos et amnis desero inferni Iovis:* carmen archilogicum, trimetrum iambicum achatalecticum, assumit in disparibus quidem locis: iambum, choreum, spondeum, dactilum et anapaestum; in paribus autem iambum, choreum et anapestum. Hic vero videlicet anapestus apud tragicos rarius, apud comicos frequentius invenitur, ita tamen ut multarum brevium iunctura vitetur.

8 *Orte Saturno pelagique rector:* in hoc choro continentur duae metri diversitates. Prima enim carmina, usque *Rex victus* [. . .], dicuntur saphica trochaica: constant enim trocheo, spondaeo, dactilo et

so great a crime could not be hidden for long; her sister's dear companion [Pistus] comes, and the whole crime is exposed.

At that time, it chanced that the secret rites of Bacchus, which recurred every third year, were calling. Thus in accordance with the ritual Procne goes out into the woods, followed by the Bacchantes. They arrive at the place where Philomena is being kept. The guards are killed, and the girl is taken away, decked out in the manner of the rituals. Procne is enraged and is avenged by means of an abominable crime: she kills her only son and serves him to his father at dinner. 4

It is said by the poets that Tereus was the son of Mars, because of his cruelty in war, and of the nymph Bistonis, whom Mars raped. They also invented the story that Procne was turned into a swallow, Philomena into a nightingale,[4] and Tereus into a hoopoe,[5] which is crested to indicate that his head is a royal one. However, he lives on excrement as a reminder of the son he ate. 5

This tragedy imitates Seneca's *Thyestes*. Just as in that play Tantalus, coming from Hades, is brought on stage, so here Diomedes, the tyrant of Thrace. 6

Types of Meters used throughout the tragedy[6]

Lucos et amnis desero inferni Iovis (1): Archilochean verse, iambic trimeter acatalectic, that in odd feet has: iamb, tribrach, spondee, dactyl and anapest. In even feet, however, it has: iamb, tribrach and anapest. It is easy to see, however, that the anapest is rather rare in tragedies, but is found more frequently in comedies; still, a succession of many short syllables should be avoided. 7

Orte Saturno pelagique rector (68): In this chorus two varieties of meter are included. The first verses, up to *Rex victus . . .* (82), are said to be in the lesser sapphic: it consists of a trochee, spondee, 8

duobus trocheis. Reliqua vero dicuntur gliconica: constant autem spondaeo, choriambo et pyrrichio.

9 *Nulla mortalis tenuit voluptas:* hic chorus continet duas metri diversitates. Prima quidem est ut in primo choro *Orte Saturno* [. . .]. Intermixtum est vero carmen adonicum, quod constat primo dactilo, secundo spondaeo sive trocheo, quoniam ultima ponitur indifferenter in omni metrorum genere.

10 *Sacra Thyoneo repetita triennia suadent:* hic chorus continet novem metri diversitates. Primum genus metri heroicum exametrum dactilicum, ut *Sacra Thyoneo* [. . .]. Secundum saphicum est: constat autem primo trocheo, secundo spondaeo, tertio dactilo, quarto choriambo, quinto spondaeo sive trocheo, ut *Huc ades proles Iovis*. Tertium constat primo dactilo, secundo amphymacro, tertio epitrito quarto, quarto pyrrichio sive iambo ut *Ex utero praeustae* i[. . .]. Quartum *Te te Thraca vocat* [. . .], ut in primo choro *Rex victus* [. . .]. Quintum, asclepiadeum choriambicum: constat primo spondaeo, secundo et tertio choriambo, quarto pyrrichio sive iambo, ut *Huc formose puer* [. . .]. Sextum constat primo paeonetertio, secundo spondaeo, ut *variosque lincas*. Septimum, *Tercia sacris* [. . .], ut in primo choro. Octavum constat primo anapesto, secundo iambo, tertio spondaeo, quarto anapesto, quinto pyrrichio, sexto trocheo, septimo spondaeo sive trocheo, ut *Hedera virenti* [. . .]. Nonum, adonicum, ut intermixtum est in secundo choro, ut *Lactea colla*.

11 *Huc e latebris procede soror:* in hoc carmine continetur unicum genus metri, quod dicitur archilogicum. Constat autem spondaeo, dactilo et anapesto indifferenter in omnibus quattuor locis.

dactyl, and two trochees. But the remaining verses are called glyconic; they consist of a spondee, a choriamb, and a pyrrhic.

Nulla mortalis tenuit voluptas (300): This chorus contains two varieties of meter. The first is the same as in *Orte Saturno* . . . (68) in the first chorus. But intermixed is adonean verse, which consists of an initial dactyl, followed by a spondee or a trochee, since the final foot is an anceps, a variable foot in every kind of meter. 9

Sacra Thyoneo repetita triennia suadent (487): This chorus contains nine varieties of meter. The first type of meter is the heroic dactylic hexameter, as in *Sacra Thyoneo*. . . . The second is the sapphic; it is composed of a trochee in the first foot, a spondee in the second, a dactyl in the third, a choriamb in the fourth, a spondee or a trochee in the fifth foot, as in *Huc ades proles Iovis* . . . (489). The third meter consists of a dactyl in the first foot, an amphimacer in the second, a fourth epitrite in the third, a pyrrhic or iamb in the fourth foot, as in *Ex utero praeustae* . . . (490). The fourth meter, *Te te Thraca vocat* . . . (491), is like that of the first chorus *Rex victus* (82). The fifth is the lesser asclepiad which consists of a spondee in the first foot, in the second and third feet a choriamb, in the fourth a pyrrhic or iamb as in *Huc formose puer* . . . (492). The sixth meter is made up of a third paeon in the first foot, a spondee in the second, as in *variosque lincas* (495). The seventh meter, *Tercia sacris* . . . (497), is the same as in the first chorus. The eighth consists of an anapest in the first foot, an iamb in the second, a spondee in the third, an anapest in the fourth, a pyrrhic in the fifth, a trochee in the sixth, a spondee or a trochee in the seventh foot, as in *Hedera virenti* . . . (498). The ninth meter is the adonean, as it is intermixed in the second chorus, as in *Lactea colla* (511). 10

Huc e latebris procede soror (560): in this verse is contained a single type of meter, which is called the anapestic dimeter. It consists of a spondee, dactyl and anapest used indiscriminately in all four feet. 11

12 Edidi Mantuae, anno aetatis meae decimo octavo.

Pedes quibus constant supradicta metra

Pyrrichius ∪ ∪	Iambus ∪ –	Dactilus – ∪ ∪
Spondaeus – –	Trocheus – ∪	Anapestus ∪ ∪ –
Epitritusquartus – – – ∪		Choreus ∪ ∪ ∪
Paeontertius ∪ ∪ – ∪		Amphymacrus – ∪ –
Choriambus – ∪ ∪ –		

Diomedes

Lucos et amnis desero inferni Iovis,
ad astra mittor supera convexi poli:
neque enim inter umbras noxius visus furor
est ullus aeque. Thracia, heu, solus potest
explere Furiis corda Diomedes. Nefas
odisse liceat, crimini datum est satis
satisque sceleri. Deprecor sontis plagas,
amare liceat. Addite ad poenas meas,
siquid potestis, dira Furiarum agmina.
Titana pubes exuat vinclis manus
caelo rebelles, aeneis nodis premar.
Nil iam recuso: Sisyphi premat lapis,
me ludat amnis Tantali, vel Isionis
iaculetur orbis, crescat in poenas iecur.
Parum videtur? Torqueat per me suas
Phlegeton harenas, igneo torrens vado.
Cur me innocentem facitis alterna vice
sceleris nefandi Thraces? Agnosco scelus!

Published at Mantua, in my eighteenth year. 12

Feet which form the meters cited above

pyrrhic ∪ ∪
spondee – –
fourth epitrite – – – ∪
third paeon ∪ ∪ – ∪
choriamb – ∪ ∪ –
iamb ∪ –
trochee – ∪
dactyl – ∪ ∪
anapest ∪ ∪ –
tribrach ∪ ∪ ∪
amphimacer – ∪ –

: I :

Diomedes[7]

[*Thrace*]

I leave behind the groves and streams of infernal Jove; I am sent to the stars in heaven's dome above, nor among the shades below is there any destructive rage to be seen like it. Alas, only Diomedes can fill Thracian hearts with the madness of the Furies. Let it be possible to hate a wicked act. Enough has been paid for the crime, enough for the offense! I beg the regions of the guilty: may it be allowed me to love. Add on to my own punishments, if there is anything else you can add, you cruel ranks of Furies. Let the Titans' company strike off the chains from the hands that rebelled against heaven; let me be weighed down by the bronze bonds.[8] Now I refuse nothing; let the rock of Sisyphus burden me, let the waters of Tantalus mock me, or let the wheel of Ixion toss me about, let my liver keep growing as my punishment.[9] Does this seem too little? Let Phlegethon, burning in its fiery channel, torment me with its sands. Why, Thracians, do you make me seem innocent by the recurrence of unspeakable wickedness? I see the crime! A

Pars iam peracta est, noster explebit nefas
adventus. Unde hoc? Omnis arescit seges,
(sensere terrae), deficit pratis color
quacumque gradior fontibusque humor solitus
deest, cavernis intimis quaerens fugam.
En alta cerno decora natalis soli
thracosque muros: regiae est illinc locus
atque hinc superbus alta pro templo pater
Gradivus ipse limina horrendus tenet.
Pudet referre: facinus agnosco meum
stabulumque, quo me victor Alcides feris
obiecit ipse, pabulum armentis ducem.
Sed ecce subeo regiae limen domus
aulamque Terei. Quid hoc est? Fugiunt retro
versi penates, decidunt flores novi
numinibus ipsis. Misera ne trepida domus:
venio coactus. Quis novus cogit furor
dirum profari facinus? Agnosco nefas.
Nunquam vacabit scelere Diomedis domus,
nunquam nocentes leviter Thraces erunt.
Peccatur omne scelere quod vincat scelus,
semperque veteris preterit formae modum
crimen quod oritur: obruit recens vetera
parvumque quod fuit scelus, dum fit novum.
Matris furorem cerno et eversam domum
miserumque patrem. Video crudelis focos
et sparsa pueri viscera et diras dapes.
Mensae parentur, sacra splendescat dies:
abominandum, pessimum, horrendum, novum,
otrisia facinus prima concipiat domus,
suumque vincat scelere crudeli genus.
Vix cum peractis saeculis olim polus
ardebit, ignis cum mare et terram ambiet,

part of it has already played out, and my arrival will complete the evil. What is the cause of it? All the crops dry up (the lands feel it). Wherever I walk, the meadows lose their color, and the liquid that is wont to flow from the springs dries up, seeking refuge inside its caverns. Lo, I see the beautiful heights of my native land and the Thracian walls; on one side is the site of the palace, and on the other proud father Mars himself stands terrible on the high threshold before the temple. I am ashamed to recall it, but I recognize my misdeed and the stable in which the victorious Hercules himself threw me to the wild animals and made me, their master, food for my own herd. But, behold, I am passing over the threshold of the royal house and into the court of Tereus. What is this? The household gods turn round and flee, and the fresh flowers honoring their divinities are wilting. Fear not, O house of wretchedness! I come under compulsion. What new madness compels me to give warning of an awful deed? I see an act of great wickedness. Never will the house of Diomedes be free of crime, never will Thracians commit petty harms. Every crime committed is surpassed by another crime, and each new crime that springs up exceeds the measure of the old; the recent evil defeats the old ones when what was a small crime is committed anew. I see the rage of a mother, a household ruined and a wretched father. I see cruel hearthfires and the scattered vitals of a boy and a repellent meal. Let the tables be set; let the sacred day become bright; let the royal house of Thrace be the first to produce this abominable, utterly evil, repellent, unheard-of deed, and let it surpass its own ancestry in cruel wickedness! Though the heavens shall one day be set on fire at the end of time and fire shall cover the sea and the earth, another such

numeretur aliud, vixque posteritas fidem
datura famae. O semper infamis domus!
Sileatur omne veteris errati scelus:
stupra in nefanda vile sint crimen domo!
Satis ne dixi? Iam satis: facto est opus.
Obsedit animos impius mentis furor,
flagrat cupido turpis. Inventa est via:
scelus patebit. Carbasa extendat Zephirus,
vellis citatis prospero cursu natet.
Tandem favebo Thracio regi: redeat.
Redisse nollet! Ecce solemni prece
Tereus vocatur. Appara festum diem,
germana venit. Ora quis quatit mea?
Vocat flagello me me ad infernos lacus
Erynnis. Onere tellus infaesto diu
nostro levetur, caetera explebit Furor.

Chorus

Orte Saturno pelagique rector,
qui levi curru gradiens per aequor
temperas pontum quatiens tridentem,
sterne secura pelagus quiete;
tuque ventorum domitor procellas
qui regis duro reserasque saxo,
(te timent nautae trepidique adorant),
tu potes actum pelagus tumultu
sternere atque idem super astra ferre.
Tu pater nimbos nebulasque torques,
thraciae plebi faveas, precamur.
Adsit actutum Tereus citata
puppe, nec vellis cadat aura, donec
thracios portus teneat tyrannus.

crime may scarcely be counted,[10] and posterity will scarcely credit the story. O house forever disgraced! Let every crime of ancient error be silent, let these acts of shame be a contemptible crime in this unspeakable house! Have I said enough? Now, yes, enough! Deeds are what is needed now. An unholy madness of the mind besieges the spirit, shameful desire is ablaze. A way is discovered: the crime will out! Let Zephyr stretch sails, let him float with swift sails on his prosperous voyage. In the end, I shall be favorable to the Thracian king: he may return. If only he had not wished to return! Behold, Tereus is summoned with solemn entreaty. Prepare the festive day, a sister comes! Who strikes my face? With their whip the Erinyes summon me—me!—to the infernal lakes. May my hostile presence no longer cumber the earth; madness will fulfill the rest.

Chorus

Sprung from Saturn and ruler of the sea, O Neptune—you who control the waves with a shake of your trident as you pass on your light chariot across the sea—cause the waters to subside into untroubled tranquillity; and you, lord of the winds, Aeolus, you who rule storms and release them out of the hard rock (sailors fear you and, trembling, worship you), you can make the sea subside when it is driven by tumult and carry the waters beyond the stars,[11] you, father, who whirl the clouds and the mists, show your favor to the people of Thrace, we pray. Let Tereus appear without delay on his hastening ship, nor let the wind slacken in his sails until the tyrant reaches the Thracian harbor.

Rex, victus prece coniugis
reginae, pelago caput
commisit fragili rate;
venti perfidia nihil
cunctatus, soceri domos
portu mosopio petit.
O qualis pietas thori!
Nutritur face mutua
sacrati thalami calor.
Orpheus, Euridicem suam
Quaesitum, petiit lacus
Averni et miserae Stigis
vectus flumina trans novem
interfusa vadis. Lyra
motus portitor aurea,
orantum immemor heserat;
illum ut Tartareus canis
ripa prospicit ultima,
cauda deliniens, stetit.
Mirantur fidibus novis
Manes, nec sitiens senex
curat flumina Tantalus,
non ales Ticii iecur
hesitque Isionis rota.
Saxo Sisyphus insolens
Insedit, stupet Eacon,
et cum coniuge lurridus
Pluton, qui quociens velit
irasci, tociens prece
placatus, Lachesim iubet
vitae stamina nectere.
Adsit mitior Orpheo
Tereus, caelicolum genus.

Our king, persuaded by the entreaty of his wife the queen, entrusted his life to the sea on a fragile boat, unhesitating despite the fickleness of the wind, and seeks the dwellings of his father-in-law at the Athenian port. O what devotion to his marriage! The warmth of their sacred marriage bed is nourished by a mutual torch. Orpheus, seeking his wife Eurydice, searched for her amid the pools of Avernus and the wretched Styx,[12] conveyed across the nine rivers interspersed with fords. Charmed by Orpheus' golden lyre, the ferryman froze, unmindful of those begging for passage; just as the hound of Tartarus, when he saw Orpheus on the furthest bank, stopped wagging his tail and stood still. The shades are amazed by the new strains; thirsty old Tantalus takes no thought for the river water nor the bird for Tityus' liver, and the wheel of Ixion stops rolling. Sisyphus, strangely, sits down on his rock; Aeacus is dumbfounded; and with his wife Proserpine, ghastly Pluto—placated by prayer every time he tries to be angry—orders Lachesis to join together the threads of life. Let Tereus, of the race of the

Omnes, principe reddito,
solvent vota calentibus
aris et tremuli senes
spargent pocula Lesbii
et cum virginibus simul
insontes pueri canent.
Ecco, montibus abdita,
respondet Rhodope iugis,
quacumque et Tanais rigat,
qui cum frigore duruit,
plaustri conteritur rotis.
Nuper remige percitus,
duro fert equitem vado.
Omnis Thraca decentibus
saltabit cytharae modis,
templa et Bistonii tegent
sertis et viridantibus
ramis, in medio sidet
faestus laeticiae deus.
Sed quis profecto strepitus e portu sonat?
Accurrit unde haec turba? Puppi regia
en arma praefixa, en Tereus adest, procul.

: II :

Tereus

Gradive, gelidis sive sub Rhodope iugis
fessos iugalis pabulo recreas novo,
aut nubifer ubi verticem Hemus exerit
aut Otris ingens, aut ubi ilicibus nigris
Pangaea resonant, sive per populos agis

gods,[13] be present, still more kindly than Orpheus. Once our prince returns, let all discharge their vows on smoking altars, and let tremulous old men sprinkle cups of wine from Lesbos, and let innocent boys together with maidens sing. Echo, hidden in the mountains, returns their song from the peaks of Rhodope and reechoes wherever the Tanais flows—the river that crunches beneath wagon wheels when it freezes in winter. While earlier in the year it resounds to the oar, it now affords the horseman a hardened path.[14] All Thrace will dance to graceful measures of the zither, and the Thracians will festoon their temples with wreaths of flowers and fresh boughs; in their midst the festive god of joy will squat down.[15]

But what is that clamor coming from the harbor? Where is this mob of people running? Look, a ship in the distance, displaying the royal arms! Look, Tereus is at hand!

: II :

Tereus

[On board ship approaching Thrace]

Mars, whether you revive your wearied steeds in fresh pastures under the frigid slopes of Rhodope, or where the summits of cloud-capped Haemus or great Otris emerge, or where Pan-

currus cruentos, inclitum cernis, pater,
gnatum. Tremiscunt ultimi vires meas
Thraces et omnis regio glacialis poli
me me tremiscit; arma Cecropidae mea
timuere, nata vixque Pandion socer
pacem impetravit. Nunc quoque e soceri solo
conspicuus hospes remeo: tot spoliis ducum
praeclara puppi tecta prospicio libens.
En alta decora patriae cerno domus
gratosque muros; iura quo reges solent,
agnosco templum, sceptra gestantes, dare.
Verum minime in patriam reducis animum gero:
deiectus animo, traherer in Syrtis velut,
aut exul undis classe barbarica premerer.
Conscia, licet nullus premat, mens se premit.
Quid anime segnes? Quod fuit summum, tibi
dedere superi; siquid erravit furor,
fac ipse liceat, facile quod reges solent.
Non cernis alta decora natalis soli?
Gratare tandem: non decet regem timor.
Sed ecce littora remige assiduo sonant:
laetantur omnes, obviam cuncti ruunt
aderitque Progne. Quas misera voces dabit,
postquam sororem cernet absentem, sibi
diu expetitam? Consilia tegent nefas.
Simulabo victam turbine immensi maris,
demum peremptam: lacrimae facient fidem.

Tereus, Progne

Te. O fida consors, multa post maris virum
pericla cernis!

gaea reechoes among the black ilexes,[16] or whether you drive your bloody chariots in the midst of the peoples, father, you watch your illustrious son. The most distant Thracians tremble at my power and every region under the icy pole fears me—me! The Athenians were afraid of my arms: my father-in-law Pandion lately sued for peace by means of his daughter. Now too, as his renowned guest, I return from the soil of my father-in-law, and I look out with satisfaction from my ship at our homes, distinguished with numerous spoils of warlords. Look, I see the noble insignia of my father's house and its welcome walls; I see the temple where kings, bearing scepters, are accustomed to make laws.

But I do not carry with me at all the emotions of a man returning to his country: I am depressed, as though I were being pulled into the Syrtes,[17] or as though I were an exile on the high seas, beset by a barbarian fleet. No one besets me; it is my guilty conscience that besets me. Why are you so torpid, mind? The gods above gave you what was best; if madness went astray in something, cause it to be permissible yourself—something kings are wont to do easily. Do you not see the noble insignia of your native land? Rejoice at last; fear does not become a king. But, look, the shores resound with busy oars; everyone is rejoicing; they are all rushing out to meet me, and Procne will be there. What cries will the poor heartsick woman utter when she sees that her sister is not here, the sister she has awaited so long! My schemes will hide the crime. I shall pretend that her sister was swept away by a storm on the high seas, then lost; tears will make me credible.

Tereus, Procne

Tereus. O faithful wife, you behold your husband after many dangers at sea.

Pr. Laetor incolumem, sed hae
lacrimae loquentis (talis in patriam redis?)
cur ora complent? Ubi vel est soror mihi,
optate coniunx? Vivit an morte occubat?
Effare aperte, maeror augescit mora.

Te. Pelago perempta est (hi mei reditus!) soror.
Vellis citatis, prospero cursu ratem
Strimonius Aquilo vexit ad soceri domos;
egressus adii. Forte tunc rex Palladis
ad templa summae praesidem orabat deam,
opima feriens colla stat comptus caput
vitta sacerdos; ipse sacratis focis
spargebat arae thura solemni prece.
Tunc me lacertis senior affusis ait
complexus: 'Ut, ut te, gener, dum spiro adhuc,
iuvat videre! Nunc reiuvenesco senex.
Valet ne Progne? Superat et carus nepos?'
Sed quid moramur plura? Vix multa prece
gnatam impetravi; spondeo celerem reditum
aegro parenti, ast olli in amplexu ultimo
singultus ora patria oppressit gravis.
Aptant carinam socii et antemnas ligant.
Decrescit omnis terra paulatim, undique
caelum et mare: secat spumeum pontum ratis
ac pone placidus exultat delphin salo.
Et iam diei finis: in nubem cadens
sol, passus oculos, mergit occeano rotas,
rubicunda Phoebe surgit ac stellae cadunt.
Et ecce nubes densa ceruleum aethera
involvit, altis montibus fragor sonat
et tunsa late saxa latratu gemunt.
Caligo caelum texit et crebri micant
Ignes; at Eurus surgit orientem movens.

Procne. I rejoice that you are safe and sound, but why are your cheeks covered with tears as you speak? Is that how you come back to your country? Where is my sister, my long-desired husband? Is she alive? Or can it be that she lies dead? Speak freely; sorrow increases through delay.

Tereus. Your sister was lost at sea—such is my homecoming! With our sails quickening, a Strymonian[18] north wind carried our ship on a favorable course to the dwellings of my father-in-law; I left the ship and went to the house. By chance the king was praying at that moment to his tutelary goddess at the temple of highest Minerva; the priest stood, his head adorned with the sacral fillet, slaughtering sacrificial victims, while the king scattered incense on the sacred hearths of the altar, uttering a solemn prayer. Then the older man, embracing me with his outstretched arms, said, "O how it pleases me to see you, my son-in-law, while I am still alive; an old man, I have now become young again. Is Procne well? And is my dear grandson still alive?" But there's no need for many words. Without numerous entreaties I succeeded in obtaining his daughter, promising her quick return to the ailing father, but in the final embrace, a deep sob overwhelmed the father's face.

My crew prepared the ship and tied the yardarms in place. Little by little, the land grew smaller, giving way on all sides to sky and sea; the ship cut through the foaming seas as a carefree dolphin played in the saltwater behind us. And now it was day's end; the sun, enduring our eyes, was falling into a cloud, and submerged its wheels in the ocean; blushing Phoebe rose, and the stars began their descent. And, behold, a thick cloud cloaked the blue sky, thunder resounds from the mountaintops, and the rocks groan far and wide with the roaring and crashing of the sea. Darkness covered the heavens, and lightning glittered continuously, but Eurus arose, stirring the East. Sud-

Repente pluviae, nubibus ruptis, cadunt;
tumescit aequor, latera navigii tremunt
collisa. Pulsat sidera et harenas ciet
vis vasta pelagi: saepe, deducto freto,
immergit et nunc erigit caelo trabem.
Conclamo: 'Socii, ponite antemnas, labat
carina.' Et ecce desuper turbo rapax
ferit rudentis, pontus in puppim niger
fertur, procella malus immani tremit.
Non grata nautis occidens nunquam micat
glacialis Arcthos, sidus Arthophilax tuum
texere nubes: omnis eripitur polus.
Erramus, adeo cursus incerti, neque
noctem diem ve digeri sinit polus.
Haec inter, acri percita stomacho, soror
devicta demum est, evomit: membra labant,
nec alitur ullo corpus infirmum cibo.
Non is genarum fulgor, ut olim decens:
tumor per artus abiit afflictos gravis.
Tandem revoluta posuit in sinu caput
loeto gravatum: solvitur corpus gelu,
anima per ora flentis ad Manes fugit.
Necdum omnis abiit fulgor, in vultu pio
mors quoque placebat. Talis in viola nitor,
cui forma nondum fugit et prato caret.
Non hos dolores fluctus invisi minae,
sed dii dedere: testor imperii decus.
Vix clausit oculos destra, cum ventus minas
posuit, resedit omnis extemplo furor,
cessere nubes, vasta tempestas perit.
Lentantur ecce remi et antemnae cadunt.
Optata miseris quarta cum luce astitit
infausta tellus: quassa dilluvio ratis

denly, rain began to fall from the broken clouds; the sea began to swell, and the ship's ribs shake beneath the blows. The vast strength of the sea strikes the stars and stirs up the sand; the ship often sinks down as the waves split apart and now it rises up to heaven. I shout, "Crewmen, strike the sails, the hull is going to break up!" And, behold, from above, a destructive whirlwind tears all the ropes, the black sea comes over the stern, and the ship's mast shakes from the brutal blast. The frozen constellation of Ursa, an unwelcome sight to sailors, never shone in the west; clouds covered the star of Boötes;[19] all heaven is snatched from view. We wander about, unsure what course to set; the sky won't let us tell night from day.

In the midst of the storm your sister is overcome with seasickness and vomits; her body begins to faint from lack of food, her cheeks lose their former attractive color; a sickly swelling spreads through her afflicted limbs. In the end, falling back, she rested her head, heavy with death, on her bosom; her body is undone by the cold, and before my weeping eyes her soul flees to the shades. Her beauty was not entirely gone; on her holy countenance even death seemed fair.[20] Such is the violet's brightness, which still keeps its beauty when plucked from the meadow. I swear on my royal honor that the hateful threats of the sea did not cause these sorrows; the gods did.

Scarcely did my hand close her eyes in death when the wind put aside its threats, and immediately all its fury was calmed. The clouds dispersed, and the vast tempest died out. Behold, our oars are bent while our sails hang idle. On the fourth day, an ill-omened shore appears before us which we have longed for in our misery. Our ship, damaged by the storm, drops anchor;

subsedit anchoris, latere pontes cadunt.
Est collis altus, ultimi Thraces serunt,
praerupta rupes eminet ponto media,
curvata vallis humida et sterilis iacet,
utrimque silva claudit ac montis tegit
cupressus alta funebri ramo virens.
Hoc ubi potiti, quisque tabentis salo
siccavit artus. Horret et littus quoque,
nec credit ullum gravibus erumnis locum.
Tunc funus egomet manibus instruxi meis:
ferro bipenni pinus impulsa eruit,
cadit cupressus, nemora cum silvis trahunt
late ruinam. Structa sublimis pyra
caelo minatur: flamma per ramos sonat
ac fumus ater nube funerea coit.
Stridunt favillae. Maestus umbratur dies.
Circum omnis adstat veste funerea caput
amicta turba, lacrimae et planctus sonant.
Manes vocantur, turba ter rogos obit.
Postquam solutus debitus flammis honos,
tegitur sepultus aggere excelso cinis.
Pr. Quid turba comitum superat? Ubi Pistus senex?
Te. Ut carpsit ignis avidus appositam struem,
cadaver uri coepit ubi stratum super,
ultra dolores ferre non potuit senex:
irrumpit igni seque in eodem iacit.
Qualis securem taurus attonitus fugit,
aut qualis acri concitis Maenas iugis
agente Baccho fertur insano gradu,
talis rogos petivit afflictus senex,
fidusque alumnae cineris ut foret comes
passus cremari. Sed reor summum sibi
fuisse, ut unus ignis arriperet duos.

the gangplanks are let down from the sides. There is a high hill (the furthest distant of the Thracians cultivate it); a sheer cliff rises from the midst of the sea; a curving valley, wet and barren, lies there; a forest encloses it at both ends, and a grove of tall cypresses covers the mountains, verdant with their funereal boughs. Gaining the shore, each of us, wasted by the salt water, dried out his limbs. The shore frightened us, and each of us believed it offered no place for men with grave troubles.

Then I myself arranged the funeral with my own hands; a pine was cut down with a two-headed ax; a cypress was felled; a wide grove was cleared in the forest. A lofty funeral pyre was constructed that menaced the sky; its flame crackled through the boughs, and black smoke thickened in a deathly cloud. Sparks from it hissed. The sorrowful day was overcast. Our whole company stood around in funeral garments, covering the head; tears and laments resounded, and the shades of the dead were summoned. Thrice the men approached the pyre. After due honor had been paid by the flames, her ashes were buried beneath a high mound.

Procne. What became of your companions? Where is the old man Pistus?

Tereus. As the raging fire consumed the structure that had been built, when it began to consume the corpse laid upon it, the old man could not bear his grief any longer: he rushed impetuously into the fire and threw himself upon it. Just as a bull dazed by a blow flees the sacrificer's ax[21] or just as a Maenad on the raving mountaintops, driven[22] by keen Bacchus, is borne along with maddened step, just so the afflicted old man besought her pyre and suffered immolation, so as to be the faithful companion of her dear ashes. But I think it was his greatest

Alii reversi nuntii dirae necis.
Pr. O mors acerba! O multa frustratae preces!
O saeva maria! O mortis horrendum genus
et morte peius! Quam dolor capiet viam
crudelis? Ubinam gravibus erumnis modum
statuam? Sorore quid enim restat mihi
morte occupata? Quid queror demens? Ego,
ego te peremi. Causa nostra est haec, soror,
crimenque nostrum: namque dum propero nimis
unam videre, pene dispersi duos.
Me, me, procellae, ferte in abruptum mare
scopulosque Syrtis, ferte disiectam undique,
ubi nives alta canet aeterno gelu,
aut ubi propinquus pabulum feris negat
sol, ubi venena, ubi herba pestifera viret.
Me pontus, aether, me premat dirum chaos.
Utinam sororis pariter arsissem rogo!
Ubicumque iaceat Pistus, invideo tibi.
Nec te sororis morte culparim, Tereu:
sors ista fati debita, ut funus tuum,
soror viderem. Quamvis hoc vetuit deus,
potuere mortis fata largiri moram
brevem sorori. Moestus, heu, forsan pater
dat thura templis: ipsa iam Lethen bibit,
secura mortis. Tollite ornatus mihi
regalis auri, veste funerea dolor
utatur. Istas ventus involvat comas,
feriat lacertos invicem exertos manus.
Sed cur monilli colla scithonio nitent?
Auferte famulae.
Te. Tollite ad thalamos heram
pocius iacentem. Reddat huic animum thorus.

desire that one fire would absorb two people. The rest returned to become messengers of her dreadful death.

Procne. O bitter death! O my many frustrated prayers! O cruel seas! O the repulsive manner of her death, even worse than death! What path will this cruel grief take? Where in the world will I find some limit to these heavy sufferings? What is left for me with my sister dead? Why do I complain? I am out of my mind. I, I have destroyed you! Sister, this is my fault and my crime: for while I was in too great a hurry to see one person, I have come close to drowning[23] two. Storms, carry me into the deeps of the sea, to rocks and quicksands, scatter me in all directions, where snow whitens the high places with perpetual ice, or where the neighboring sun denies food to wild beasts, where there are poisons, where plague-bearing plants grow. Let the sea, the sky, and dreadful Chaos crush me! If only I too might be cremated on my sister's pyre! Wherever you may lie,[24] Pistus, I envy you. Nor should I blame you, Tereus, for the death of my sister: this evil lot must be charged to fate, that I, sister, should behold your death. Although God has not allowed it, the Fates could have bestowed a brief stay of death for my sister. Alas, perhaps her sorrowing father is scattering incense in the temple; now she is drinking Lethe's water, secure in death. Remove my garb of royal gold; let grief avail itself of mourning weeds. Let the wind entangle the locks of my hair, let my hand strike in turn my bared arms. But why does my neck gleam with Thracian necklaces? Maids, take them away! [*She faints*]

Tereus. Rather, carry your prostrate mistress to her bedchamber. May sleep restore her spirit! [*The servants carry off Procne*]

Chorus

Nulla mortalis tenuit voluptas
longa, nec unquam miseros tenebit:
laeta dant nobis adimuntque Parcae,
praepeti semper rapiente fato.
Nemo tam foelix spacium senectae
finit intactus. Modo natus infans
inter hos vitae miseros tumultus
lege pensatur: sedet atra cunis
Cloto, venturi comes usque fati.
Nil fit aeternum solidumque nil est
rebus humanis: variae voluptas
quota pars vitae est? Subeunt labores
et graves curae miserique luctus.
Nuper, insigni comitata turba,
thracias inter veneranda matres
ibat, e collo radiante gemma
maesta nunc deflet miseranda Progne
fata sororis,
victa quae saevis pelagi procellis
virgo defecit. Feriat licebit
ipse vocali cythara querellas
Orpheus, nunquam superos videbunt
cum semel leves animae natarunt,
una quas vexit feriente remo
cimba, deductis tociens lacertis.
Typhis, invicti domitor profundi,
mortis invenit nova fata primus:
ante nec pontum secuere puppes,
nec gravis fluctus timuere nautae.
Quisque securus placidis in agris
vixerat, necdum senior marinos,

Chorus

No mortal pleasure lasts for long, nor will it ever last for wretched men; the Parcae grant us happy moments and take them away: fate, flying swiftly, is always snatching them away. No one is so fortunate as to complete the span of old age unscathed. An infant new born among these miserable turmoils of life is weighed by this law. Black Clotho roosts on cradles, companion of the fates that are to come. Nothing is eternal, nothing secure in human affairs. How small a part of inconstant life is pleasure! Toils and heavy cares and wretched grief afflict us.[25] A moment ago, Procne was going among the Thracian mothers, a venerable presence, accompanied by a noble throng, a gleaming jewel about her neck; now, grief stricken and wretched, she mourns the fate of her sister who was overcome by the savage winds of the sea, dying a virgin. Although Orpheus himself may strum plaintive notes on his tuneful lyre, insubstantial souls shall never see the gods above once they have begun to float in the single bark that bears them with plashing of oars, their arms extended piteously.

Tiphys,[26] tamer of the unconquerable sea, was the first to discover new fates of death; before him, ships had not cut through the seas, nor had sailors feared the relentless waters. Each man had lived securely on his peaceful lands; nor yet had the man of old, leaving his own shore and his homeland's har-

300

305

310

315

320

325

littus egressus patriaeque portus,
noverat casus scopulosque saevos
arte latentis.
Ille tranquillae placidaeque vitae
ocia movit,
primus e terra resecare funem
ausus et ligno fragili natare;
iussit antemnas religare malo
primus et tortos statuit rudentis,
ac sinus laxos, feriente Choro,
tradidit audax.
Credulae pontum secuere puppes,
nauta tum ventos varios notavit
et minas caeli posuitque pictis
nomina stellis.
Naufragus picta vehitur carina,
suppara e summo religavit audax,
anchoram ignota statuitque terra.
Hoc genus leti miseros manebat!
Currat hinc illinc alius per aequor,
solis occasum videatque et ortus,
monstraque et saevos pelagi labores
garrulus tuta referat sub umbra.
Me domus dulci saturet quiete
parva, nec terras numeret remotas
nostra senectus.

bors, come to know the mischances of the sea and its cruel rocks, so artfully hidden. Tiphys disturbed the leisure of a tranquil and placid life; he was the first who dared cut his mooring cables to the land and to float on a fragile bark; the first to order the yardarms to be bound to the mast, the first to set up the twisted ropes, and, rash man, to betray slack sails to the beating of the north wind. Trusting ships cut through the sea; then the sailor took note of the variable winds and dangerous storms, and gave names to the painted stars. The shipwreck borne on a painted bark—rash man!—has tied his kerchief to the top and dropped anchor in an unknown land. This was the kind of death awaiting wretched men!

Let another man run hither and yon throughout the seas; let him see the rising and the setting of the sun; let him bring back tales of monsters and cruel struggles on the deep, chattering about them while safe beneath the shade. A little house and sweet tranquillity will satisfy me; let not our old age count up the distant lands it has seen.

: III :

Pistus senex, Nutrix, Progne

Pi. Quam gravia passus defero e silvis gradum
infaustus hospes, nuntius diri mali.
O sors acerba! Vix mihi sufficiunt pedes
rectoque ducunt tramite errantem gradum.
Nut. Quid portat iste trepidus e silvis senex?
Ni fallor ipse est Pistus.
Pi. O nutrix, ubi
regina?
Nut. Fare, Piste, quod portes malum?
Pi. Ad hoc malorum nuntio misero est opus
ipsaque Progne ex me sciat tantum nefas.
Sed ecce venit.
Pr. Fidus extinctae comes
olim sororis, numquid a maesto venis
Phlegetonte? Namque te quoque extinctum Tereus
edixit: iste prorsus inferni situs.
Pi. Me longus error, luctus et silvae pavor
deformat: illic teter increvit rigor,
sparsus per humeros crinis, attractae genae
et crura dumis lacera.
Pr. Quid causae fuit
tentare latebras? Ede fortunam, senex,
et quae sorori cura morituræ fuerit.
Pi. Utinam perempta!
Pr. Numquid impositum aggerem
erexit humeris umbra, remeata Stige?
Effare aperte, quicquid est. Timeo omnia
et te (fatebor), ipsa vix credo mihi.
Quae clades ista? Numquid et peius nece?

: III :

Pistus, Nurse, Procne

[Near the Thracian woods]

Pistus. Having suffered the worst of all experiences, I make my way out of the woods, an inauspicious guest, a messenger of horrific evil. O bitter fate! My feet can scarce sustain me, scarce lead my wandering step on a straight path.

Nurse. What brings that shaking old man out of the woods? Unless I am mistaken, it is Pistus himself.

Pistus. O nurse, where is our queen?

Nurse. Speak, Pistus; what evil tidings do you bring?

Pistus. There needs a wretch to tell these evil tidings, and only Procne herself must learn the monstrous crime of me. But look, she comes.

Procne. Faithful companion of my late sister, are you come from sorrowful Phlegethon? For Tereus reported that you, too, were dead, and Phegethon, surely, is the place of the dead.

Pistus. It is long wandering, grief and fear of the forest that disfigure me. It is from the forest that I gradually acquired my repellent stiffness; my long, straggling hair; my sunken cheeks and my legs, scratched from prickly bushes.

Procne. Why did you investigate these dens? Tell me your story, old man, and what care was taken of my sister, destined to die.

Pistus. Would that she had died!

Procne. Is it really possible that her ghost shouldered aside the mound laid upon her and recrossed the Styx? Speak openly, whatever it is. I am afraid of everything and (I shall confess) of you; I scarcely trust myself. What was that disaster? Surely it was not worse than death?

Pi. Mors ipsa votum. Vivit, hoc ipsum dolens.
Pr. Cui lucis odium?
Pi. Cui decus, melior sui
pars, periit. Utinam corpus extinctum nece,
salvo pudore: corporis periit quoque
pars magna.
Pr. Mitte verba perplexe loqui.
Quis hic stuprator virginis clarae fuit?
Pi. Quem, si rescieris, scire poeniteat quidem.
Pr. Effare aperte, moeror augescit mora.
Pi. Heret palato lingua, pulmonem gravat
attractus aer: totus horresco memor.
Aliquo procellae deferant mersum caput,
dum es innocens adhuc.
Pr. Fieri nocens
cupio, nefandi sceleris ulciscar modo.
Pi. Vicina tellus nobilem portum efficit,
unde omnis urbis pateat aspectus, nisi
opposta Rhodope brachium extendat mari,
fluctu protervo rupes exesum latus
ostendit. Hic nos ponere antemnas Tereus,
cursu peracto, littus ad notum iubet.
Paremus omnes, sceleris ignari, ocius.
Vix prima tellus coepit, (heu dirum nefas!),
abominanda scelera molitur Tereus.
Instat puellae, qualis armenius leo
cervae paventi, viribus vastis fremens.
Tentata precibus restitit virgo diu,
coacta donec, saepe clamato patre,
saepe et sorore, stupra violente pati.
Tunc scissa crinis, ora pudibunda obtegens,
acclamat: 'O crudelis, o verum genus

Pistus. Death is the very thing she prays for. She is alive, and this very fact causes her pain.

Procne. Who is there who hates life?

Pistus. The one for whom honor, the finer part of oneself, has perished. Would that her body had been destroyed by death and that her chastity had been saved! An important part of her body has perished as well.

Procne. Enough of such obscure talk. Who was it that defiled the noble maiden?

Pistus. If you should find out who, it would make you very sorry indeed.

Procne. Speak openly; grief increases with delay.

Pistus. My tongue cleaves to my palate, the air I breathe burdens my lungs. The memory of it fills me all with horror. Would that storms would take me off somewhere and drown me, while you were still innocent of the deed.

Procne. I want my innocence taken away, so long as I may take vengeance for the unspeakable crime.

Pistus. A nearby stretch of land makes a fine port from which all sides of the city would be visible if the mountains of Rhodope opposite did not stretch an arm into the sea. A rocky crag showed one of its sides eaten away by the wild surge. Here along the familiar strand, having finished our voyage, Tereus bade us lower our sails. We obeyed with alacrity, not knowing the act of wickedness he was planning. Barely had he set foot on land (alas for the horrible deed!), when Tereus contrived abominable crimes: he forced himself on the girl like an Armenian lion, roaring with its vast strength, attacking a frightened doe. For a long time the maiden, assailed by his entreaties, resisted, calling often for her father, often for her sister, but in the end she was forced to endure a violent rape. Then tearing her hair and covering a face suffused with shame, she cried out, "O

Thracum nefando scelere, quid primum querar?
Non te parentis tenuit afflicti fides,
non destra, non cognata proximitas neque
sacrum pudoris movit intacti decus!
Pellex sororis igitur amisi decus.
At tu superbus sceptra gestabis manu
post stupra? Nullus scelere pro tanto deus
persolvet ultor debitas grates tibi?
Non sic abibis! Ipsa per populos loquar,
aut, si tenebor clausa custodum manu,
movebo saxa et conscios facti deos.
Testor pudoris numen adversum mihi,
hac labe careo: corpus hoc tantum tulit.
Germana, te, te si parum soror movet,
contaminatis aude pro thalamis aliquid
quod ipsa laudem. Stabo et implebo nemus'.
Vix haec. Tyranno maior increvit furor,
ut saevus anguis, forte compressus pede,
tumet veneno, lubrico lapsu ferox.
Stabulum propinquae rupis apparet cavo.
'Servabit hic te fida famulorum manus,
istas cathenas auferat soror tibi!'
Nec plura fatus. Forcipe apprensam secat
linguam puellae, faucibus radix micat
et murmur (heu me!) voce pro solita dedit.
Cruenta lingua palpitat moriens, velut
longae colubrae cauda, quae, celeri rota
traiecta, partem quaerit ereptam sibi.
Post haec paventum caedis effrenae impetu
obtruncat ipse cassa praesidia comitum,
ne quo resciscas nuntio tantum scelus.
Hoc vile solus, fateor, e cunctis caput
a tam parata morte subduxi pedibus,

cruel man, true offspring of the Thracians in the wickedness of your crime, where to begin my plaint? You were not restrained by the trust my sickly father placed in you, by the right hand of friendship, by our family connection! You were not touched by the sacred honor of virginity! Thus have I lost my honor and have become my sister's rival! But will you proudly wield the scepter after the rape? Will no avenging god pay you the thanks you deserve for this enormous outrage? You won't get away with this! I shall tell the people myself, or if I am kept under guard, I shall move the rocks and the gods who witnessed your deed! I swear to the divinity who has charge of chastity—my enemy—that I am free of stain; only my body has borne this shame. Sister of my blood—if the mere word 'sister' moves you too little![27]—dare to carry out some deed that I myself might praise in return for the contamination of your bed! I shall stand firm and fill the woods with my lament!"

Scarcely had she spoken when a greater fury filled the tyrant, like a wild serpent who is stepped on and swells with venom, fierce in its slimy slithering. A stable is visible in a cave under the nearby cliff. "A trusty band of attendants will keep you here—let your sister strike *these* chains off you!" He spoke no more, but he seized the girl's tongue and cut it off with a pair of tongs. The base of her tongue quivered in her throat, and she gave out a gurgle (O alas!) in place of her usual voice. Her bloody tongue wriggled as it died, just like the tail of a long snake which looks for its severed part after a swift wheel has run over it. After this, Tereus himself cut down the ineffectual guard of her frightened attendants in a burst of reckless slaughter, lest there be anyone from whom you could learn of his monstrous deed. I confess that I alone, out of all of them, escaped with this worthless life of mine by running away from

tentare latebras ausus ignotas mihi.
Montis per altos ducor ex illo vagus,
silvas et amnis lustro permixtus feris,
herbae et rubeti poma solantur famem.
Rami caduci pariter et flatus movent
strepente folio, somnus in nuda fuit
tellure. Demum huc appuli fessus malis.
Pr. O machinator fraudis! O crudelior
Diomede thraco (sanguinis verus parens
ille est nefandi)! Siccine obtendis dolo
commenta mortis funera? Et tantum nefas
speras inultum? Magna delicta diu
latere nequeunt: sequitur a tergo comes
vindicta. Scelere nemo laetatur diu.
Tereu, nefanda strage turbasti domum,
post stupra fletus ausus ordiri novos.
At nunc superbus regio luxu incubas;
lingua recisa, carceris duri solo
germana nudo recubat, ubi sueti greges.
Non sic iacebit clara Pandionis domus
illusa, misera: tollet aliquando caput.
Prodesse miseri facile si nequeunt, nocent:
invenit odium saepe quem arma nequeunt.
Indulge, quaeso, facinus hoc nuper, soror,
ad nos redundat; aderit actutum tibi
vindicta, poenas impius coniunx luet.
O ter quaterque morte foelicem invoco
te, te parentem! Genitor evixit super,
restaret ut hoc tempore infoelix pater:
in hunc dolorem fata servabant senem.
Speranda iam tum scelera, cum hosti barbaro
sociata cessi. Superat hic animus sibi.
Utinam dehiscens tellus hoc olim caput

the death intended for me. I dared to seek out hiding places unknown to me. I made my way from that place wandering through the high mountains, moving in different directions; I moved confusedly through forests and rivers, sharing woods and streams with wild beasts; grass and brambleberries slaked my hunger. Falling branches and the wind howling through the leaves agitated my mind; I slept on the naked ground. At last, wearied by my ills, I arrived here.

Procne. [*She addresses Tereus*] O scheming deceiver! O man more cruel than Thracian Diomedes (the true father of your unspeakable bloodline)! Is this the way you veil in deceit those fictitious funeral rites? Do you hope that such a crime will go unavenged? Great offenses cannot hide for long: retribution is a companion who follows you from behind. No one revels in crime for long. Tereus, you have roiled our house with an unspeakable act of violence; after your act of rape you have dared to cause fresh tears to flow. But now you nest arrogantly in royal luxury, while, with her tongue cut out, my sister lies on the bare ground of a hard prison where flocks of animals are wont to be kept. Not so shall the noble house of Pandion lie prostrate, deluded, wretched: some day it shall raise its head. If the wretched are not able easily to be helpful, they will be harmful: hate often finds the man whom arms cannot. Please, sister, allow that this recent outrage shall come back upon us; vengeance will swiftly be at hand for you, and my evil husband will suffer punishment. O thrice and four times happy in death, I call upon you, my mother.[28] My father has survived you so that he might stay behind to be unhappy now. The Fates preserved the old man for this sorrow. Crimes were already to be expected when I left home to be joined to a barbarian stranger. This courage prevails over itself. Would that this earth had gaped open then and swallowed my life in Orcus when first this impudent youth made war on us! Alas, I was the

mersisset orco, boella cum primum intulit
iuvenis protervus! Pacis heu pignus fui,
ut hoc viderem facinus! In thalamis meis
cruenta Erynnis crine vipereo stetit.
Hac, hac ministra, facta sum dudum parens
uteroque semen impiae prolis tuli.
Iterum sorori spargere has comas iuvat.
Quo cedis, anime? Num soror lacrimas petit?
Agedum, sororem quaere per montis ocius,
everte silvas, carcerem horrendum erue!
Simulabo Bacchi: maior hic lateat furor.

Chorus, Progne

Ch. Sacra Thyoneo repetita triennia suadent,
mollia Nisea cingamus tempora vite.
Huc ades, proles Iovis aetherei, matris
ex utero praeustae direpte puer,
te, te Thraca vocat tua.
Huc, formose puer, rite propicius,
vultu virgineo dirige, nebride
praecinctus, viridis rotas
variosque lincas.
Lucidum caeli iubar astriferi veni.
Tercia sacris remeavit aestas:
hedera virenti ornare iuvat madidos capillos,
seu iubes spargi sine lege ventis.
Te decet flavos religare crinis
floribus vernis madidosque mirra
tergere ferro et cohibere mithra;
te decet molli religare zona
luteas vestes tirio colore;
tu, puer, ludo placidaeque rixae

pledge of peace, so that I might witness this crime! A bloodstained Fury stood on my marriage bed with her serpent hair. It was through her ministrations that I at length became a mother, and bore the seed of an unholy race in my womb! I would like a second time to loose my hair for my sister. Whither do you depart, mind? Is there not a sister asking for your tears? Come, seek out your sister through the mountains, and swiftly, fell the forests, unearth her frightful prison! I shall pretend to rave like a Bacchante: let this greater madness lie hidden.[29]

Chorus, Procne

Chorus.[30] The rites of Bacchus, recurring every three years, call to us; let us bind our soft temples with Nysaean vines: be present here, offspring of ethereal Jove, you boy, ripped from the womb of your scorched mother.[31] Your land of Thrace summons you, you! Send hither, handsome boy, duly propitious, with your girlish face, girt with faun skins, send hither your verdant chariot and spotted lynxes. Come, bright radiance of the star-bearing sphere! The third summer has returned for your sacred rites: it is pleasant to adorn dewy locks with growing ivy or, if you command it, to scatter our disordered hair to the winds. It suits you to fasten your yellow hair with spring flowers and wipe it wet with myrrh, holding it back with your turban; it suits you to fasten your golden garments with a soft girdle dyed with crimson from Tyre. You, boy, always smile at

semper arrides, tibi mota pulsant
timpana et ferro spoliata buxus.
Naiades blandae Satyrique molles
usque mirantur niveos lacertos
et genas puras placida iuventa et
lactea colla.
Huc adsis, formose: vocant nemora omnia circum,
vitisator, quamvis te decolor India iactet
orgiaque in toto resonent triaterica Gange.
Tyrsos spargere nunc levis
intextos hederis iuvat,
Bacchis lampade nos vocat
Euboe, Oggigie, adveni!
Mater Pentheos impii
non hic commaculat manus,
avellens humeris caput.
Hic cum Calliope satum
fudissent miserae matres,
moestum cum gemeret nemus,
digna pernicie scelus
pendunt, vindice te, improbae.
Te Rubrum timuit mare
et quae decolor India
cingit tempora pampino;
Termodunciaci chori
victoris genua incliti
addunt sceptriferas manus.
Quacumque et niveus rigat
Ganges flumine lucido,
quicquid sol nitidus videt,
quodcumque occeanus lavat,
laudes, Bacche, tuas canit.

gentle, playful tussles; the tambourines are shaken for you, and for you the boxwood is carven with the knife.[32] The charming Naiads and lascivious satyrs marvel utterly at your snowy shoulders and your unspoiled cheeks, your untroubled youth, and your milk-white neck. Come hither, lovely boy; all the woods around beckon you, planter of vines, even though sunburned India may boast of you, and the triennial orgies may resound over all the Ganges. Now it is pleasant to sprinkle the light thyrsus interwoven with ivy. Bacchis[33] calls us with her torch. O Euboean, O Ogygian,[34] come! It is not here that the mother of unholy Pentheus[35] defiles her hands, tearing his head from his shoulders; here is where the wretched Thracian matrons squandered the seed of Calliope, as the mourning woods groaned, immoral women expiating a crime worthy of perdition, with you its avenger.[36] The Red Sea feared you, and the temples which sunburned India girt with vines; the Amazonian choruses put their sceptered hands on the knees of their famous victor.[37] And wherever the snowy Ganges flows with its clear stream, whatever the shining sun looks down upon, whatever land Ocean washes, it sings your praises, Bacchus. When

Naxon cum peteres tuam,
Chiae nobilis insulae
solam littore virginem
fovisti placido sinu.
Mundus serta decentia
munus, Bacche, tuum tulit.
Idem perfida pectora
fudisti pelago, puer,
frustra brachia dum student
lentare; in tenebras quoque
te Mineides improbae,
dum spernunt, fugiunt citae.
Dirige pampineas circum nutante corimbo,
Bacche, rotas; turpi veniat Silenus asello.
Ad mare thraicio dum flumine defluet Haebrus,
dum Rhodope nivibus stillabit vere solutis,
sacra Thyoneo repetita triennia mittent.
Pr. Eruite propere carceris duri minas
atque hos ministros regii iussus neci
mandate! Maior victima his cadet manibus!
Eruite propere: iam satis Baccho datum.
Insaniendum est nunc mihi, instigat furor.
Pr. Huc e latebris procede, soror,
hic dies, hic est (germana venit)
quo violenti stupra tyranni
datur ulcisci. Eia, comites,
hederis frontem cingite Bacchi,
de more caput vitta coherceat
nebride sacra latus instructa,
tyrsum vibret. Soror ornatus
hos cape mecum. Quid moesta tegis

you were headed for your dear Naxos,[38] you comforted the lonely girl on your contented bosom by the shore of the noble island of Chios.[39] The cosmos accepted your gift as a becoming garland, Bacchus.[40] Again, you threw the faithless sailors into the sea, boy, while they vainly tried to swim;[41] into the darkness also the wicked daughters of Minyas[42] quickly fled after spurning your rites. Arrange the vine leaves in circlets with nodding ivy berries, Bacchus; may Silenus[43] come on his disgusting donkey. As long as the Hebrus[44] will flow down in a Thracian flood to the sea, as long as Rhodope will drip with melting snows in the spring, let the triennial rites sacred to Bacchus be set free.

Procne. [*At the cave where Philomena is being held*] Quick! Tear down the menaces of this cruel prison and send these ministers of the royal command to be put to death! A greater victim shall fall by *these* hands! Tear it down quickly! Enough has already been done for Bacchus; now I must go mad on my own account. Rage provokes me.

Come here, sister, out of your dark hiding place: here is the day, here is the day (your sister comes!)[45] on which you are given vengeance on the violent tyrant for rape! Heigh-ho, companions, encircle her brow with Bacchus' ivy; in accordance with custom bind her head with the fillet, and wearing the holy fawn skin, let her shake the thyrsus. Sister, take these adornments with me. Why do you cover your sorrowing face?

ora? Quid lacrimas fundis inanes?
Attolle, soror, pudibunda solo
lumina, casto libet amplexu
fudisse pias per colla manus.
Hic ne genarum roseus fulgor?
Oculi ne hi geminum sidus? Cur
hirtae squalent per colla comae?
Unde haec macies foedoque pedes
pedore graves? Vix agnosco
membra sororis. Silet infoelix,
pallida vultus etiamque timet,
vocis damnum muta fatetur,
conscia tantum numina monstrat
caeloque gemens spargit aperto
livida duris brachia nodis.
Flete, heu, miseram Cyconum matres,
siqua est pietas, feriatque humeros
manus exertos. Sentiat aether,
siqua aethereis numina regnis
humana regunt curisque piis
auris praebent inque superbos
acris mittunt fulguris ignes.
Strimonis undae fletu nostro
crescant: gelidas visere ripas
iuvat et ventis iactare comas:
decet hic habitus casus nostros.
Sed quid trepidas, miseranda soror,
Laribus nostris inferre gradum?
Etiamque times Terea dirum?
Testor tenebras noctis opacae
Ditisque domos et Tartarei
trina ora canis Stigiosque lacus.
Omnis quaeram scelerum formas,

Why do you pour out empty tears? Sister, raise your shame-filled eyes from the ground, I want to put sisterly hands around your neck in a chaste embrace. Where is the rosy glow of your cheeks? Where the twin stars that were your eyes? Why is your hair so rough, lying squalid on your neck? Why so thin, why are your feet caked with foul grime? I scarcely recognize my sister's limbs. She makes not a sound in her unhappiness, and even her pale face shows her fear; mute, she proclaims the loss of her voice. She only points to the witnessing gods and groaning, spreads to the open sky her arms bruised by the cruel ropes.

Weep, Thracian mothers, alas, for this wretched woman; if you have any sense of decency, let your hand flagellate shoulders laid bare. Let the upper air hear it, if any divinities in the ethereal regions rule human affairs, and if they listen to our pious concerns and loose thunderbolts against the proud. Let the waters of the river Strymo[46] swell with our tears; it gives pleasure to see his chill banks and to launch our hair into the winds: this is the appearance that suits our miserable state.

But why are you afraid, my pitiable sister, to take the road homeward? Are you still fearful of dread Tereus? I call to witness the shadows of blackest night and the abodes of Dis and the triple maws of the Tartarean dog and the Stygian lakes. I

scelus ulcisci cupiens, omnis
fugiet pietas; per scelus omne
eat in poenas ferus hic animus.
Huc viperea valle sorores,
adeste. Voco. Dabit ista dies
aliquid longo semper in aevo
immite, ferum. Vincite dirae
coniugis artes maiusque aliquid
excute Progne. Femina vincat!

Nutrix, Progne

Nut. Vultum furoris pelle, ne prodat furor.
Pr. Heu, quis dolori sit satis tanto furor?
Quae poena Tereo digna? Quis regi queat
nocere diro? Tota splendescat licet
acthea ferro tellus et summae parent
arces Cyclopum boella, desertis licet
campis colonus arma Bistoniis ferat,
frustra hunc lacessant. Parthicas olim timuit
Cecrops pharetras, gentis effrenae impetus
audaxque boelli notus est dudum Tereus
viresque regni. Scilicet nullus premat,
natura finis ipsa custodit loci:
hinc alta Rhodope nutat excelsis iugis,
hinc vasta Syrtis geticum inversat mare,
Maeotis inde stringit Arcthoos sinus.
Quas spes inanes volvis? Ha nescis, misera,
vindicta quo constet loco: me, me est opus,
ego vel Athenis sola sum potentior,
ego sum timenda. Desinant reges licet,
ex hoc timere coniuges discant patres.
Ego, dum nefando coniugi reddam vices,

shall seek out every kind of crime in my desire to avenge crime; all sense of right will flee. By means of every crime may this furious heart of mine seek vengeance. Come here, sisters, from your snaky pit! I summon you. This very day shall yield a deed merciless and wild, lasting for a long age, forever! You Furies, surpass the wiles of a dreadful spouse! Throw out something even greater, Procne! May the woman conquer!

Nurse, Procne

Nurse. Take that look of rage off your face or it will betray you.

Procne. Alas, what rage is enough to match the great pain I feel? What punishment would be good enough for Tereus? Who could harm this dreadful king? Even should the whole land of Attica glitter with swords and the high citadels of the Cyclopes prepare for war, even if the farmer should leave his Bistonian fields to bear arms, they would assail him in vain.[47] Long ago, Cecrops[48] feared the Parthian quivers, the attacks of wild people, while Tereus has long been notorious for his audacity in war and the power of his kingdom. One may be sure that no one would threaten him. Nature itself guards the boundaries of his realm: on this side towering Rhodope nods from its lofty peaks; on the other side the Thracian Sea turns into dangerous shoals, and from there on, the Bay of Maeotis hugs the northern coastlines.[49] What empty hopes are you pondering? Ah, wretched woman, you don't even know in what place you may base your vengeance! It's up to me, me! I alone am more powerful even than Athens. I am someone to be feared, though kings may fail. Let fathers learn from this to fear their wives! While paying back my unspeakable husband, I shall go further and fill

pergam et nefando scelere complebo domum.
Bene instituto fiat exemplo nocens
uxor mariti: coniugem agnoscet suam!
Nut. Quo, misera, pergis, quove furibundam rapis,
alumna, mentem? Rebus afflictis decet
praebere fortis: unica est mali salus
nescire vinci, quoque demissa est magis,
vires doloris opprimunt mentem magis.
Pr. Fluctu doloris obruor: non sum mea.
Talis carina fertur, amisso duce,
cum saeva pelagi forte tempestas rotat.
Vos o recentes, caede miseranda obruti,
adeste Manes: facinus explebo ocius
quocumque tantus iusserit dolor modo.
Vindex sororis dicar, ulcisci libet.
Nut. Et vindicanti saepe vindicta obfuit.
Pr. Quem nam timebo, fata si nihil movent?
Nut. An non timebis Bistonum vires, mulier?
Non hic Athenae! Patrio tutam sinu
fortasse credis? Tellus hostilis premet.
Pr. Nihil morabor, perfidus luat modo.
Nut. Moriere.
Pr. Moriar ulta.
Nut. Fama te moveat.
Pr. Non it ad umbras fama, nec curant leves
post fata Manes fama quid vulgi ferat.
Nut. Perimes, cruenta, morte crudeli virum?
Pr. Perimam, et nefando sanguine hic poenas dabit.

our home with unspeakable wickedness. May the wife be made a criminal, well instructed by the example of her husband: the husband will recognize her as his wife!

Nurse. Poor woman, where are you heading? Where, dear one, are you taking that infuriated mind of yours? In such travails it is fitting to be brave; the one salvation from evil is to be unconquerable; the more despondent you are, the greater the power of suffering to crush the heart.

Procne. I am overwhelmed by a flood of sorrow. I am not myself; I am like a ship that, having lost its pilot, is carried along when a savage storm at sea chances to spin it round in circles. Come, O you shades who have but lately been undone by pitiable slaughter. I shall quickly carry out an outrage in whatever way my great sorrow demands. I shall be called the avenger of my sister; I want to avenge her.

Nurse. Vengeance is often harmful to the avenger too.

Procne. Whom, pray, shall I fear, if death leaves me unmoved?

Nurse. Aren't you afraid of Thracian power, woman? This isn't Athens! Do you believe, perchance, you're safe in the bosom of your own country? A hostile land may crush you.

Procne. I shall not hesitate, so long as this treacherous man suffers punishment.

Nurse. You will die.

Procne. I shall die avenged.

Nurse. Concern for your good name should stop you.

Procne. One's good name does not go down to the shadowy realms, nor do insubstantial ghosts care what the vulgar say about them after death.

Nurse. You will destroy your own husband with a cruel death, you bloodthirsty woman?

Procne. I shall destroy him, and he shall pay the penalty with his own unspeakable blood.

Nut. Lassat sacrilegas urna Bellides neque
pensatur ullo fine tam tetrum facinus.
Si nil movet te, respice at gnatum, parens!
Pr. At qui sororem? Iam ipsa cum gnato patrem
cremabo flammis, ipsa iaculabor faces
in regna Terei: tota splendescat domus
regalis. Omnis eruam stirpis notas,
super ipsa iaciar. Eia membratim occidat
discerptus ipse: iam iuvat linguam trahere
trucis tyranni. Meruit hic quicquid potest
irata mulier.
Nut. Siste vesanos, precor,
regina motus: maius hoc ira malum
tuisque maius viribus. Rex est Tereus,
multum paterni roboris saevus gerit.
Pr. Non si ipse clipeum genitor opponat sibi,
poena vacabit. Quisque contemnit necem
rex est tyranni: moriar, ut mortem oppetat.
Nut. Horrore quatior, crinis erectus, pavet
animus, reliquit ossa consuetus calor.
Quodnam hoc malum est? Quis tantus instigat furor?
En, ora torquens, mater aspectu truci
furibunda natum spectat, invicem quoque
vultus sororis. Superat et crescit dolor.
Pr. Quid hoc furore maius accrescit malum?
Libet experiri, quicquid est, quod me monet
ultrix Erynnis. Ora Furiarum intuor,
et ipsa Alecto, crine vibrato, sinu
iniecit anguem. Lubricus venis meat.
Hortamur. Eia, quod mare et terra horreat,
invade facinus: auctor audendi furor.
Quaenam haec sororum funebre inversat manu

Nurse. The vases weary the sacrilegious daughters of Danaus;[50] the expiation of so foul a crime never ends. If nothing else stops you, at least[51] consider your son, mother!

Procne. But who is there to consider my sister? Now I myself shall immolate by fire the father along with his son; I myself will hurl fiery torches at the kingdoms of Tereus; may the entire royal palace be glowing with fires. I shall destroy all traces of his lineage, and I myself shall leap upon flames. Ah, let him be struck down and torn limb from limb! Now I would like to pull out the cruel tyrant's tongue. The man deserves whatever an angry wife can do to him.

Nurse. Stop this insanity, queen, I beg you: this evil deed is something greater than your anger and greater than your strength. Tereus is a king, a brutal man who wields much of his father's power.

Procne. Even if his father, Mars himself, were to protect him with his shield, Tereus will not escape punishment. Whoever despises death is king over a tyrant. I shall die so that he will meet his death.

Nurse. I shake in horror, my hair stands on end, my soul stands aghast, the accustomed warmth leaves my bones. Pray, what evil thing is this? What great fury is driving her? Look, her face twisted, a maddened mother glares cruelly at her son, then in turn at the face of her sister. Sorrow increases and overflows.

Procne. Why is a greater evil growing out of this fury? I would like to find out what it is that the avenging Erinys is telling me to do. I gaze upon the faces of the Furies, and Alecto herself, with her hair waving, has implanted a serpent in my breast. Slithering, it courses through my veins. I encourage it. Ah, plunge ahead with a deed that makes both land and sea cringe in horror! Let rage be the author of daring! Which one of the three sisters turns over the sword of death into this hand?[52] I

ferrum? Tremisco. Quis matrem impellit manus
maculare duras impia nati nece?
Crudelis ille est: meruit ut facerem scelus.
Fecisse pudeat! Quo fugit coeptus furor?
Hoc, hoc libet quod timeo, vel siquid mali
est peius usquam: non placet primus furor.
Tereus supersit, vivat, ut vivat miser
optetque mortem: peius est votum nece.
Discede pietas. Prima concipiam nefas,
quod omnis aetas horreat; post me pia
sit nulla mater. Hoc sed est etiam parum.
Maedea Cholchis caede puerili manus
maculavit. Addam maius huic sceleri scelus!
Magnum est quod animus fluctuat, quid sit tamen
ignoro. Perge, furor, prope est, par est scelus.
Nil quaero supra: coniugem hoc decet meum
nostrisque thalamis dignus est tantus furor.
Animum parentis pelle, siquid est tamen:
eversa dudum coniugis nostri fides.
Evicit ille, siqua fit sceleris mora
pietate matris; vinco, si propero scelus.
Quemcumque sceleris miseret auctorem, miser
est ipse pariter. Quicquid hic fuerit pium,
quicquid morabor. Crimini tantum hoc detur.
Eia, anime, meditata aggredi cessas! Satis
tempus querellis, iam satis tempus datum:
parentur epulae, sacra splendescat domus.
Manibus parentis innocens cadat puer,
ut ipse genitor viscera exedat sua!

Nut. Per has seniles deprecor mammas, hera,
per spes anilis perque maiores deos
desiste coeptis. Quae barbara ulla immanitas
commisit unquam facere quod properas scelus?

am trembling. Who is forcing a mother to stain her hard hands with the impious killing of a son? The man is cruel; he deserves that I should commit this crime. It should shame me to have done this! Where has my earlier rage fled? I want to do this very deed that I fear, or an even worse one, if there is one.

I don't like my first mad plan. Let Tereus survive. Let him live so that he may live in wretchedness and hope for death: the wish for death is worse than the reality. Let all sense of reverence for the gods and for family leave me. Let me be the first woman to contrive an act of unspeakable wickedness at which every age may shudder. After me, let no mother be dutiful. But even that is too little. Medea of Colchis stained her hands with the murder of her children;[53] I shall add a greater crime to hers! It is a great crime indeed which is bubbling up in my mind, but I don't yet know what it is. Come on, rage—it's almost there—a crime equal to his! I seek nothing beyond that: that is what befits my husband, and a great act of fury is what our marriage bed deserves. Drive out the love of a parent, if there be any still; the trust due my husband was ruined long ago. He has won if maternal piety causes any delay in the crime; I win if I hasten it. Whoever feels pity for a crime he has committed is himself pitiable. Let my scruples and my hesitation here be set down only to the greatness of the crime. Ah, my soul, stop brooding; enough time has been spent airing grievances, you've had enough time. Let the banquet be prepared; let the holy house be resplendant. By the hands of a parent let an innocent boy die, so that his father may devour his vitals!

Nurse. I beseech you, mistress, by these old breasts of mine and by the hopes of an old woman and by the more exalted gods, desist from these plans! What agent of barbarous brutality has ever committed the crime you are rushing to do? What you are

Factura deinceps omne femineum genus
nocens? Recedat impius mentis furor,
nec tale facinus clara Pandionis domus
inusitatum, pessimum, horrendum paret.
Vindicta quovis abeat, hanc partem sine.
Pr. Altrix (fatebor), pectora attonitae labant
vario tumultu. Talis incerto ratis
trahitur fragore, boella cum venti movent
diversa rapidi. Si intuor poenam levis,
si crimen ingens. Gemina me pietas movet
cogitque pietas. Matris hinc nomen vetat.
Indulge, soror, ha, potius impune hoc ferat.
Spes una miserae matris hic solus puer,
uterique nostri cara progenies Ythis,
pignus parentis, unicum afflictae domus
levamen, etsi genitor invisus mihi
in omne facinus excitet mentem feram.
Quid enim tyranni liquit intactum furor?
Oblitus ille decoris et nostri quoque
miserique patris, virginem oppressit comitem,
fideique pignus. Nec placet tantum scelus,
nisi scelus addat: virginis socios necat
ipsique linguam forcipe apprensam rapit.
Post haec paventem clausit immani specu
simulatque mortem, lacrimas struxit quoque
periurus: haec est coniugis nostri fides.
Post ista dubitas sceleris ulcisci, misera,
per omne facinus? Pereat hic, non est meus
diro parenti similis (ha nimium) puer!
Disce ex marito denique insigne facinus
audere, Progne! Fluctuat pectus neque
meminit parentis: tota sum, fateor, soror.
Furor relinquat corda, si facerem scelus

about to do will hereafter harm the reputation of the entire female sex. Let this impious madness subside; let not the noble house of Pandion bring forth a crime so unprecedented, so utterly evil, so repulsive. Let retribution go where it will; let this part of earth alone.

Procne. Nurse, I confess it, my heart is wavering, stunned as I am by the confusing uproar, like a ship being rowed amid haphazard crashing when howling winds make war on it from different directions. If I consider the punishment, it seems light; if the crime, enormous. Twin loyalties move me, anger drives me. On one side, the name of mother forbids me. Indulge me, sister—ah, rather, let this thing go unpunished. The one hope of a wretched mother is this one boy, the dear progeny of my womb, Itys, the pledge of a parent, the one solace of an afflicted household, although his father, whom I hate, arouses my wild mind to every sort of enormity. What indeed has the tyrant's rage left unscathed? Heedless of honor and of me and my wretched father too, he attacked a virgin who was a companion entrusted to his care. And this act of wickedness did not please him unless he added another to it: he murdered the girl's attendants and ripped her tongue out with a pair of tongs. After that he shut the frightened girl up in a cave fit only for beasts and with manufactured tears pretended she was dead, perjuring himself: such is the good faith of my husband. After acts such as these do you hesitate, wretched woman, to avenge his wickedness with an outrage of any kind? Let him die! He is not my boy, he is like—ah, too like!—his dreadful father. Learn from your husband at last the daring needed for an infamous deed, Procne! My heart is seething and forgets that it is a parent; I confess that I am nothing but a sister. Let madness

male sana. Pereat fructus, irarum est satis.
Ego sum furore peior. Emittat licet
pestes Averni dirus umbrarum arbiter,
ipsas fugabo. Non capit sedem dolor.
Utinam tulissem foeta natorum gregem
utero capaci, posset ut numerus matris
saciare mentem! Quod tamen venter tulit
redeat in patrem: nil sit ex illo meum.
Nut. Mater, necabis unicum gnatum tuum?
Pr. Est nempe Terei.
Nut. Cur necem meruit puer?
Pr. Scelere paterno gnatus emeruit mori.
Nut. Iniqua racio est crimine alieno pati.
Pr. Cum iusta quaerit ira paulatim cadit:
non est furoris capere mensuram sceleri.
Gravis ira sontem respicit, poenam levis.
Nut. Alumna, quaeso, nulla te pietas movet?
Poteris, nefanda, caede puerili manus
maculare? Poteris, ipsa, per pueri caput
vibrare ferrum? Deprecor, mentem exue
diri furoris: mater es.
Pr. Soror quoque.
Nut. Alias nocendi moeror inveniat vias:
enses, venena, flamma vel sontem premat
animamque saevus egerat.
Pr. Tellus prius
gestabit astra lucida et caelum feras
priusque luci preerit noctis dea
tenebrisque Phoebus, quam meus mutet dolor
decreta mentis.
Nut. Facere quo properas modo?

leave my heart if I should carry out this mad crime. Let the fruit of my womb perish, and rage will be satisfied. I am worse than rage. Let the dreadful judge of shades send out the plagues of Avernus and I shall put them to flight. My grief finds no resting place. Would that when I was pregnant I had given birth to a whole flock of boys in my capacious womb, so that their number could gratify a mother's thoughts! Let what my womb has borne, nevertheless, return to its father: let nothing I have from him be mine.

Nurse. Mother, you will kill your only son?

Procne. He is Tereus' son, surely.

Nurse. Why does the boy deserve to die?

Procne. The son has earned death through his father's crime.

Nurse. It is unjust to suffer for another's crime.

Procne. When one is seeking justice, little by little anger subsides; it is not the way of madness to take the measure of the crime. Deep anger has regard to the guilty party; light anger to the punishment.

Nurse. My dear, please, do the claims of piety not move you at all? Will you be able, unspeakable woman, to stain your hands with your boy's slaughter? Will you be able, yourself, to swing the sword through your boy's neck? I beg of you, strip your mind of this terrible rage: you are a mother!

Procne. I am a sister too.

Nurse. Let your grief find other ways of avenging her: swords, poisons or flames might assail the guilty man and fiercely carry off his soul.

Procne. Sooner will the land be spangled with bright stars and the heavens be filled with wild beasts, sooner will the goddess of the night escort the day and Phoebus the night, than will my grief alter the decrees of my mind.

Nurse. How quickly will you do this?

Pr. Faestus propinquat thracio regi dies,
quo mos adire coniugi tantum dapes
mensasque regis. Aggredi licet patrem
dapibus nefandis: sanguinem bibet suum.
Huius diei faxo sit semper memor!
Commissa, nutrix, occule!

Nut. Hoc annis mea
solet senectus tarda: praestabo fidem.

Chorus

Quaecumque extat fortuna nimis
altoque ferit vertice nubes,
placido regnet licet in ocio,
finisque suos ambiat unda
Tagus aurata et gemmifer Hyster,
nullo rerum pondere pressa,
corruit in se, nec capit unquam
placidae regnum limina vitae.
Animos regum turbine versat
fortuna suo, rapit ambicio
vulgique favor, pluris mergunt
nimii luxus luxusque comes
dira libido. Castus vixit
Iuppiter olim, cum dicteo
pauper in agro patrem fugeret,
ast ubi fregit sceptra parentis
vacuoque sedens solus Olimpo
sub se terras vidit apertas
tractusque maris et vaga sidera,
tunc Iunonem, fallere coepit.
Nunc Alcmenem capit Amphitrio
cessasque tuos, Lucifer, ortus

Procne. A feast day is nearing in honor of the king of Thrace, on which it is the custom for the wife alone to approach the banquet table of the king. I shall be allowed to approach the father with a monstrous meal: he will drink of his own blood. I'll see to it that this day is memorable! Nurse, keep secret what I've told you!

Nurse. My slow old age is long used to this: I shall prove my loyalty.

Chorus

Wherever she is found, Fortune strikes the clouds with her over-lofty head and though she reigns in peaceful ease and the Tagus circles her borders with its golden waters and the gem-bearing Hister,[54] still she collapses upon herself, crushed by no weight of affairs, nor does her realm ever cross the threshold to a life of tranquillity. Fortune with her whirlwind turns round the thoughts of kings; ambition and the favor of the mob capture them; excessive luxury and lust, luxury's dread companion, drown the greater part of them. Once upon a time Jupiter lived chastely, when as a pauper he fled his father on the Dictaean plain,[55] but when he broke the scepter of his father and was seated alone on empty Olympus, seeing the open lands beneath him, the expanses of the sea and the wandering stars, it was then that he began to cheat on Juno. Now, as Amphitryon, he seduced Alcmena, and, you, Lucifer, morning star, were bidden

iussus longam ducere noctem;
nunc pharetratae virginis arma
humeris sumpsit, crura coturno
stringens, tenui subligat auro
per colla comas; modo littoribus
nivei simulans membra iuvenci
equitem dorso per freta tulit;
candida plumis brachia movit,
placido fundens gutture carmen
improbus ales. Pauci reges
sacrata colunt iura pudoris.
Non ullius foedera lecti
animos tardant, odere thoros,
nec cognato sanguine virgo
tuta est; pronus furor in vetita
vetitumque nihil. Maxima pars est
quae nullius numinis aras
colat atque animae restare nihil
post fata putet, nec tartareis
horrida flagris verbera curet.
Magno miseri iudice causae
librantur nostrae: Eacon umbras
ipse fateri crimina vitae
subigit. Quicquid gessimus olim
patimur: nulli crimina parvo.
Nec prosunt tituli ordine certo:
purpura damnat. Mediae turbae
pauci nigro livida fondo
aequora verrunt. Foelix pauper,
qui contentus modico vivit
nullique gravis tempora ducit.
Pauperis intrat limina nunquam
immunda Venus: vincere somnos

to extend the long night and delay your rising; now, he took on his shoulders the arms of the virgin goddess' quiver, fitting her buskin boots to his own leg and binding his hair behind his neck with her golden band. Now on the shore, pretending to be a milk-white bull, he carried a rider on his back across the straits; he put plumage on his white arms and — the shameless bird — poured out a song from his ingratiating throat.[56] Few are the kings who honor the sacred laws of chastity. No treaties of marriage hinder their passions — they despise marriage — no virgin is safe, even if a blood relative; their madness is prone to whatever is forbidden — and nothing is forbidden. The greatest part of them spurns the altars of every divinity and thinks that after death nothing of the soul remains, nor do they care about horrible beatings from the whips of Tartarus. As for us wretched men, our cases are weighed by the great judge. Aeacus himself forces shades to confess their crimes. We suffer for whatever we have done in life; no one gets a discount on his crimes. Nor are titles in their fixed hierarchy an advantage: purple robes are a source of condemnation.[57] Few of the middling throng skim over the grey waters in black hulls. Happy is the poor man who lives content with little and lives his time, a burden to no one. Unclean Venus never crosses the threshold of the pauper; his

studio coniunx rustica temptat,
servat castos horrida mores
casa, nec nimiae solvunt epulae.
Mox, cum placidae fata senectae
ultima cursus egere suos,
foelix moritur, nec marmorea
corpus in archa balsama servant.
Pauci reges ultima vivunt
tempora vitae, pauci sicca
morte recedunt. Alius diri
signa comaetae trepidet; nullis
territa monstris nostra senectus
spacium vitae finiat actae.
Sed quid trepido nuntius ore
portat? Dubios ede tumultus!

: IV :

Nuntius, Chorus

Nun. Terrore quatior: sceleris ante oculos trucis
imago pendet. Totus horresco memor!
Heret palato lingua.
Ch. Quid portas novi?
Nun. O thraca tellus, scelere perpetuo nocens
quamque omnis aetas damnet! O dirum nefas!
Quae Cholchis unquam, qui ve dispersi Scithae,
quae regio tantum fecit aut credet nefas?
Abominandus ipse Diomedes minus.
O sors acerba, scelere punitum scelus!
Eversa cuncta.

country wife tries to conquer his sleepiness with her ardor; a rough hovel keeps mores chaste, and luxurious banquets do not corrupt them. Presently, when inevitable death has completed the course of his tranquil old age, he dies happy, and spices do not embalm his body in a marble vault. Few kings reach the last ages of life, and few escape a bloodless death. Let another man fear the portents of the dreadful comet; let our old age bring an end to life's full span without terror of monsters. [*A messenger approaches*] But what news does this messenger bring with trembling lips? Tell us of tumults uncertain!

: IV :

Messenger, Chorus

Messenger. I shake in horror; the image of a brutal crime is suspended before my eyes. The memory makes me tremble all over! My tongue cleaves to my mouth.

Chorus. What news do you bear?

Messenger. O land of Thrace, ever guilty of crime, a land which every age shall curse! O dreadful offense! What did Colchis ever do, what did the scattered Scythians, what land ever committed so monstrous a crime or will ever believe it? Abominable Diomedes himself did less. O bitter fate, wickedness punished by wickedness! Everything is turned upside down.

Ch. Mitte perplexe loqui.
Post prima scelera nemo mirari solet
siquod secundum maius exoritur scelus.
Nun. Me, me procellae, ferte disiectum undique,
ubi Caribdis Scicula disturbat freta,
ubi Scilla canibus latrat accincta rabidis.
Ch. Effare aperte, nos pariter et te leva.
Nun. In parte regiae ultima stabulum latet,
ubi Diomedes, pecoris impii dominus,
humana saevus pabulum diris feris
secabat ipse viscera et capita sanie
madida superbus alta figebat manu
foribus tremendis; semper infaustus cruor
undabat, ipse donec armenti dominus
suo scelere peremptus ac poena nocens.
Hic nocte tota voce ferali gemunt
umbrae vagantes, strepitus horrendum intonat
tractae cathenae. Fremere crudeles ibi
fama est leones: saepe latratu specus
reboat, tremiscit terra, discordes deae
quatiunt rogalis igne funesto faces.
Inhumata regis saepe despecti premit
Manes flagellis turba. Quo, postquam furens
regina subiit, parvulum trahens Ythim,
Philomena subiit. Spectat hanc primum soror,
deinde natum mater aspectu truci.
Paulum morata: 'Quid,' inquit, 'tempus iuvat
conterere lacrimis? Tempus ulcisci venit
thalamos pudici coniugis, stupra et scelus.
Germana, temet excita: hunc similem patri
iuvat esse, dum perficio quod struxi nefas.'
Sic fata, Furiis concita, infantem trahit
de more vituli, quem aspra lactentem rapit

Chorus. Stop speaking in riddles. No one is usually surprised if, after initial crimes, some second, greater crime arises.

Messenger. Winds, carry me, scatter me everywhere, where Charybdis churns the Sicilian straits, where Scylla barks, ringed with rabid dogs.[58]

Chorus. Speak openly. Unburden yourself and us alike.

Messenger. At the farthest point of the palace a stable lies hidden where Diomedes, lord of the unholy herd, himself used brutally to cut up human remains as food for his awful beasts, and by his own hand used proudly to affix human heads, dripping with gore, high upon its fearful gates; the accursed blood gushed always until the master of the herd himself was destroyed by his own crime and suffered punishment. Here all night long wandering shades groan with wild voices; the sound of chains being dragged makes a dreadful noise. It is said that cruel lions roar there; the cave often echoes with barking, the earth trembles, the discordant goddesses shake funereal torches lit with deadly fire. Often the unburied throng assail the shade of the loathsome king with whips. Here the mad queen came, dragging little Itys, followed by Philomena. The sister looks first at her, then the mother looks at her son without pity. After hesitating a moment, she said, "What good is it wasting time with tears? The time has come to avenge the defiled marriage bed of a chaste wife and my husband's rapes and crimes. Rouse yourself, sister. It helps that the boy looks like his father, while I'm finishing off the monstrous deed I've planned." Thus she spoke and, spurred by the Furies, dragged the child like a nursing calf

hyrcana tigris. Ille blanditur matri
parvis lacertis genua complexus puer.
Dimitte matrem, fata te expectant tua,
dimitte. Non est mater irata mulier,
ferior leena foeta quae catulos trahit.
Spes vana patriae, deperis parvus Ythis,
generosa proles gentis actheae, nepos
Mavortis, unum thraciis rebus decus,
pietatis in quo plus tamen fuerat avi,
animos feroces quamvis a stirpe traheres.
Non tu tenebis sceptra Thraicia, puer,
non iura populis patrio solio dabis,
quod si pararunt fata tam miseram necem,
dum mater amens quaerit ulcisci scelus
maiore scelere, fata non facient tamen
te te nocentem. Nescius culpae cadis.
Utcumque moritur innocens, foelix moritur.
Ch. Quis, ede, durus raptor infantis fuit?
Nun. Mater citato transilit ferro latus.
Quod tam cruentum dirus admisit nefas
Diomedes? Ultro cecidit in matrem puer:
ferale stabulum gemuit.
Ch. O novum scelus!
Nun. Utinam scelere contenta desistat truci!
Immota mater properat hinc aliud novum,
ut hoc prematur scelere maiori scelus.
Ch. Quid ultra atrocius potuit? An pabulum
inhumata pueri viscera exponit feris?
Nun. Utinam, feroces quod solent irae, rogo et
humo arcuisset, tradat epulandum feris!
Pietas vocetur illa. Si quaeris nefas,
—o dira fata!—nobili trunco caput
Tereo secatur, caetera in partis rapit,

which the fierce Hyrcanian tiger seizes.[59] The boy smiled at his mother and embraced her knees with his little arms. Let go of mother. Death awaits you. Let go. The angry woman is no mother, but is more ferocious than a whelping lioness dragging her cubs. Die, little Itys, vain hope of your country, noble offspring of the Attic people, grandson of Mars, unique glory of the Thracian state! Though you had more piety in you, you derived the fierce spirit of your grandfather from their stock. You will not hold the scepter of Thrace, boy; you will not give laws to your people from your father's throne. But if the fates have prepared for you a wretched death, while your insane mother seeks to avenge a crime with a greater crime, nonetheless the fates will not find you guilty. You die without experience of guilt. In whatever way an innocent person dies, he dies happy.

Chorus. Tell us, who was the merciless abductor of the boy?

Messenger. His mother. She stabbed him swiftly through the side with a sword. What act of wickedness so bloody did even dreadful Diomedes commit? Of his own accord the boy fell upon his mother. The spectral stable groaned.

Chorus. O unheard-of crime!

Messenger. If only she had been content with this brutal crime and had stopped. Pitiless, the mother hastened from this to another unheard-of outrage, so that this crime would be rivaled by an even greater one.

Chorus. How could atrocity go any further? Did she expose the boy's unburied viscera as food for wild beasts?

Messenger. If only she had merely forbidden him the funeral pyre and burial, something fierce anger is wont to do, and given him to wild animals to feast on! That might be called piety.[60] If you are looking for monstrous wickedness—O dreadful fates!—she severed the head from his noble trunk for Tereus, tore the rest

artus calentis tractat et fibras manu,
nec flexit oculos. Adiuvat Prognem soror:
costas trucidat, pectoris crates rapit,
humeris lacertos amputat ferro levis.
Pars haec aheno volvitur, aestu laticem
miscente, at illa, verubus affixa, ingemit.
Fumus Penates obsidet totos niger.
Disponit ipsa lancibus diras dapes,
gnatum parenti. Viscera edisti tua
ignarus: etiam hoc deerit et scies miser!

Idem chorus

Ch. Omnis vincunt dira Promethei
semina Furias. Iam nihil est quod
postera credant saecula vetitum.
Credimus iras
quascumque ferunt Cholchidos: omnis
scelerum formas tellus nostra
vicit. Sed tu, miserande puer,
vadis ad Manes, culpae nescius,
diros. Maneant digna parentis
praemia facti, quamquam digna es
tu poena, puer: impiae matris
victima caesus dirique premis
viscera patris.

in parts, handles the still-warm limbs and sinews without averting her eyes. Her sister helps her. She hacks at his sides and tears the ribcage out of the breast, cuts his slender arms off his shoulders with a sword. This part is thrown into a cauldron of boiling water; the other part is spitted and hisses as it roasts. Black smoke laid siege to all the household gods. She herself lays out the dreadful meal on platters, a child is feast for a father. You are eating your own flesh and blood, ignorant of your fate! But soon you will lose your ignorance too, you wretch![61]

Chorus

The dreadful seeds of Prometheus[62] overcome all Furies; now there is nothing which future ages will consider forbidden. We believe in the wrathful acts which they say are of Colchis;[63] our land wins at every form of wickedness. But you, pitiable boy, go to the deadly shades unconscious of guilt. May worthy rewards for parental deeds be in store, though you yourself are a worthy punishment, boy: slaughtered as victim by an impious mother, you burden the vitals of a dreadful father.

: V :

Tereus, Progne

Te. Faestum diem celebrare quid vetat mihi
animumque turbat mobilem incerto metu?
Quid heret animus? Prospero regnum in statu est.
Ego quid tremiscam nescio, timeo tamen.
Modo inter aras, sacra cum ferrem deis,
repente cecidit regii capitis decus.
Vidi cruorem verti in obscenum pariter
Bacchi liquorem, flevit in templis ebur,
emicuit ara, flamma per totam domum
erepsit. Etsi timeo nil, piget tamen
sacri nefandi. Sed quid horresco? Procul
secede, terror. Quisque praesagit sibi
vanos timores, meruit in veros cadere.
Pocius retexe fronde viridanti comam,
indulge Baccho, voce faestiva cane.
Pr. Vide ut superbus regio solio incubet,
nec credit ullo posse devinci malo.
Conviva laetus, exple sacratis famem
dapibus, cruore pelle natorum sitim!
Sic te superbe!
Te. Solus afferre solitam
gnati quietem posset aspectus mihi.
Pr. Philomoena posset sola solamen mihi
afferre.
Te. Segnis inter exanguis iacet.
Pr. Idem inter umbras natus exangues cubat.
Te. Omitte, coniunx, ista.
Pr. Coniugem vocas,
nefande Tereu?

: V :

Tereus, Procne

[In the royal palace]

Tereus. What is preventing me from celebrating the feast day and troubles my inconstant mind with nameless fear? Why am I in difficulties? The kingdom is in a prosperous state. I don't know why I am trembling; nevertheless, I am afraid. Just now, amid the altars, as I was offering sacrifices to the gods, suddenly my royal crown fell to the ground. Likewise I saw the wine changed into loathsome gore, the ivory in the temple weeping tears, an altar flash, and a flame snaking through the whole palace. Though I fear nothing, the desecration of rites is disturbing. But why am I so afraid? Be gone, terror! Every man who has forebodings of baseless fears deserves that real ones befall him. Rather should we bind up our hair with a green garland, drink deep, and sing with festive voice.

Procne. See how proudly he nests on his royal throne and trusts that he cannot be conquered by any evil. Happy dinner guest, satisfy your hunger with sacred foods and slake your thirst with the blood of children![64] Let it be so for you, arrogant man!

Tereus. Only the sight of my son could restore my usual calm.

Procne. Only Philomena could bring me solace.

Tereus. She lies unmoving among the bloodless dead.

Procne. So, too, your boy reclines bloodless among the shades.

Tereus. Wife, stop saying such things!

Procne. You call me wife, wicked Tereus?

Te. Quod malum audio?
Pr. Nequeo
crudele gaudium ferre; per totos rigor
artus cucurrit. Iam iuvat vultus patris
spectare primos.
Te. Quicquid est, parcat meo
gnato.
Pr. Bene est. Scelus peractum est: hunc amat.
Te. Vocetur. Ubi natus latet diu mihi?
Pr. In te latitat.
Te. Ubi est Ythis?
Pr. Scies.
Te. Ubi est?
Pr. Stupro sororem qui violat, effer quoque,
linguam trucidat virginis, socios necat,
epulatus ille est impia natum dape.
Philomoena, pueri profer extincti caput
in ora patris. Hunc ne cognoscis, pater,
magis an sororem?
Te. Sustines, rerum sator,
tam gravia scelera? An vanus in gentis timor
fulmen coruscas? Misce dilluvio omnia:
fluvii rapaces, fontibus ruptis, meent.
Dimitte habenas, merge ad infernos lacus
animas nocentis, pondus invisum rape,
dehisce tellus, Tartari fondo occule.
Me, me trisulco fulmine invisum pete,
sator deorum, quo trium moles cecidit,
erecta caelo montium atque hostes feri.
Sum fulminandus ignibus sacris ego,
ego sum cremandus. Si, pater, natum paro
mandare flammis, quas, miser, voces dabo?

Tereus. What is this evil I hear?

Procne. I can't bear the cruel joy of it; all his limbs have stiffened. How I enjoy watching the father's first facial reactions!

Tereus. Whatever is going on, spare my son!

Procne. Good; the crime is finished; he loves this boy.

Tereus. Let him be summoned. Where is my son hiding from me for so long?

Procne. He is hiding inside you.

Tereus. Where is Itys?

Procne. You will find out.

Tereus. Where is he?

Procne. The man who raped my sister — bring it out![65] — who also cut out a maiden's tongue, killed her companions, that man has feasted on his own son in an unholy meal. Philomena, put the head of the dead boy before his father's eyes. [*Philomena places Itys' head in front of Tereus*] Don't you know him, father, or is it my sister whom you know better?

Tereus. Creator God, why do you allow such monstrous crimes? Do you flash your lightning bolt, an empty terror among the nations? Send a flood over all the earth! Let destructive rivers from broken springs pass over! Release the reins, send guilty souls to the infernal lakes! Earth, seize their hateful weight, yawn, and hide them in the pit of Hell. Creator of the gods, aim your triple thunderbolt at my hateful self. It was by that thunderbolt that the pile of three great mountains, raised against heaven, was knocked down and your savage enemies as well.[66] I myself should be stricken with the sacred thunderbolts, consumed by fire. If, father, I prepare to send my son to the flames, what words should I speak, wretch that I am?

En ora cerno quodque de toto est super
caput cruentum! Scelere materno occidis,
culpa parentis. Hanc ego merui necem.
Hunc te, Ythi, genitor video? Quis fleat satis
meas miserias? Tumulus est nati pater.
Quis inhospitalis Caucasus tantum nefas,
aut quis Procustes, qui ve contemptor deum
Busiris unquam, quae barbara ulla immanitas
commisit? In me natus innocens iacet,
destra parentis caesus. Hoc uno pater
superos timebam. Genitor explevi sitim
gnati cruore. Da, pater nostri nimium
oblite Mavors, tela, vel coniunx dabit:
eviscerabo corpus, ut gravis redeat
cibus. Negatur? Hoc negat Progne mihi?
Philomoena praebe! Si miser non sum, nega.

Pr. Iam summa voti contigi: Tereus dolet.
Nunc restitutum credo germanae penitus
raptum pudorem, nunc meis thalamis fidem.
Erepta ferro lingua nil curo, miserum
dum muta videat. Virgines stupro opprime,
commenta mortis funera et fletus para,
dum te nequiciae pigeat aliquando tuae.
Advenit ecce tempus et dies mihi
quo te, superbe, dum nihil times, premerem.
Manibus parentis cecidit his natus tuus,
partita pueri corpus in partis soror:
pars haec aheno volvitur aestu laticem
miscente, at illa, verubus affixa, ingemit.
Post haec cruorem miscui sacro mero.
Poterat sine ulla caede puerili peragi
Vindicta, poteram temet in flammas dare
oculosque pressis unguibus ruere aut aliquam

Behold, I look upon his face and bloody head, all that is left of him. You died because of a mother's crime, a father's guilt. I myself deserved this death. Is this really you I see, Itys, I, your father? Who could shed tears enough for my misery! The father is the tomb of the son. What inhospitable Caucasus ever committed so monstrous a crime, what Procrustes,[67] what Busiris,[68] scorner of the gods, what agent of barbarous brutality ever did such a thing? My innocent son lies within me, slaughtered by the hand of a parent. For him alone, as a father, I used to show fear of the gods. A father, I have slaked my thirst on the blood of my son. Give me a spear, father Mars, you who have forgotten me too long, or my wife will give me one: I shall disembowel my body so that the burdensome food may come back. Is this denied me? Does Procne deny me this? Give it to me, Philomena! If I be not wretched, deny me!

Procne. [*To herself, triumphantly*] Now I have reached the summit of my desire: Tereus in pain! Now, I believe, the chastity stolen from my sister has been entirely restored; now there is integrity in my marriage bed![69] I care nothing for the tongue the knife cut out, so long as the mute may see him wretched. [*She addresses Tereus*] Rape virgins, make ready fictitious funerals and false tears, so long as some day you may be sick of your own wickedness! Lo, the time has come, the day is here for me, when you suspect nothing, when I may crush you, arrogant man! Your son was killed by the hands of his mother; a sister divided the boy's body into parts. One part was put into a kettle with boiling water; the other hissed on a spit. Then I mixed his blood into the holy wine. Vengeance could have been carried out without the boy's death, I could have burned you alive, killed you by scratching out your eyes, or contrived some other kind of death, but whatever punishment put an end to your

instruere mortem, poena sed visa est levis
quaecumque finem ponit aerumnis nece.
Hunc cerne, genitor.

Te. O novercales manus,
quae Cholchis unquam tanta commisit scelera?
Immitis, atrox, illa se tantum nece
contaminavit: scelere vicisti scelus
et morte maius ausa post mortem nefas.
Tuum est quod hausi crimen, horrendas dapes,
ignarus.

Pr. Insons criminis nomen fugit.

Te. Quo, quo profanus civium aspectus fugiam?
Quae latebra misero tuta? Quo praeceps ferar?
Me, me procellae trans quoque occeanum rapite,
quo nullus hominum, nec ferae, nec sol meet,
aut inligato Rhodope sub Thressae iugis
ales Promethei tundat aeternum iecur.

Pr. Rhodopen poposcis? Cara post stuprum est tibi,
periure Tereu. Virgines stupro opprimis?

Te. Tu, saeva, natum?

Pr. Fateor, et iuvat tuum.

Te. Quid meruit infans?

Pr. Gnatus emeruit mori
tuapte culpa.

Te. Vindices testor deos.

Pr. Pocius pudoris numen intacti voca.

Te. Te te sequentur Furiae.

Pr. Ythis solus patrem.

sufferings through death seemed too light. Look at him, father!

Tereus. O stepmotherly hands! What Medea ever committed such an outrage? Merciless, terrible though she was, she tainted herself only by death; you have beaten her crime with one of your own, and after death dared a crime greater than death. It is by your criminal act that I, unawares, have consumed this horrible meal.

Procne. The guiltless person escapes all charge of crime.

Tereus. Where, where shall I flee from the sight of my citizens, unholy man that I am? What dark den will be safe for a wretch like me? Where shall I betake my headlong steps? Winds, seize me, carry me even across Ocean where no men nor wild beasts nor sun travels; or tie me up beneath the ridges of Thracian Rhodope, and let the bird of Prometheus eternally attack my liver!

Procne. You are asking for Rhodope? The place is dear to you, is it, after the rape, lying Tereus? You rape virgins, do you?

Tereus. You killed our son, didn't you, cruel woman?

Procne. I confess it, and I'm glad he was yours.

Tereus. Why did the child deserve to die?

Procne. Your son deserved to die because of your own guilt.

Tereus. I call upon the gods to avenge me!

Procne. You'd do better to call upon the god of chastity.

Tereus. The Furies will pursue you!

Procne. Itys alone will pursue his father.

LEONARDI DATHI FLORENTINI

HYEMPSAL

[*Argumentum*]

Leonardus Dathus cuique lecturo salutem. Quo facilius meam hanc Hyempsalis tragoediam habeas, haec tibi fuerint argumenti loco.

1 Masinissa, rex Numidarum, post bellum Punicum secundum in amicitiam populi romani receptus, treis procreavit filios: Gulussam, Manastabilem et Micissam. Manastabiles suscepit Iugurtham filium ex concubina. Micissa duos reliquit liberos, Adherbalem et Hyempsalem, quos moriens una cum Iugurtha, viro strenuo, instituit heredes regni. Post exequias, cum reguli atque Iugurtha de rebus regni consulturi convenissent, Hyempsal, tumido et elato ingenio preditus, Iugurtham despiciens, dextra Adherbalem adsedit ne medius honore dignaretur, qui apud Numidas habetur maxi-
2 mus. Deinde, cum de rescindendis decretis, quae Micissa per egritudinem edidisset, inter se statuerent, ex sua id agi sententia Hyempsal dixit, quod per id temporis Iugurtha esset in regnum

LEONARDO DATI OF FLORENCE

HIEMPSAL

CHARACTERS

Asper, *Numidian nobleman*
Polymites, *Numidian nobleman*
Hiempsal, *son of Micipsa and brother to Adherbal*
Adherbal, *son of Micipsa*
Jugurtha, *son of Manastabilis, adopted by Micipsa*
Chorus
Messengers
Ambition
Modesty
Phoenician Woman
Phitonissa, *Libyan priestess of Bacchus*
Ammon, *Numidian nobleman*
Discord
Perfidy
Matrons

[Argument]

Leonardo Dati to the reader, good health. That you may have better understanding of this tragedy of mine, Hiempsal, the following will take the place of an argument.

1 Masinissa, king of the Numidians, was accepted as a friend of the Roman people after the Second Punic War. He begot three sons: Gulussa, Manastabilis, and Micipsa. Manastabilis begot Jugurtha by a concubine. Micipsa left two sons: Adherbal and Hiempsal. On his deathbed he appointed them, together with Jugurtha, a man of valor, as heirs of the kingdom. After the funeral, when the new kings and Jugurtha met together to discuss the affairs of the kingdom, Hiempsal, who was endowed with a proud and arrogant spirit, despising Jugurtha, made Adherbal sit on his right to prevent Jugurtha from being honored by the middle seat, regarded as the highest place among the Numidians.
2 Then, as they were deciding among themselves about rescinding the decrees which Micipsa had issued during his illness, Hiempsal said that, in his

adoptatus. Qua ex re Iugurtha vehementer commotus curavit ut noctu per satellites Hyempsal necaretur. Inde regnum Libyae calamitatibus obrutum conruit. Per hanc historiam, quae late ac fuse apud Sallustium enarratur, ipsa de qua secundo in coronario dis-
3 ceptaturi sumus, invidia describitur. Sunt actus quinque. Primo dicimus quid qualisque sit invidia. Secundo quid ea possit in animis eorum quibus insit. Tertio quales sint invidi, erga eos quibus invident. Quarto quales reddat invidia eos quos invidi lacessierint. Ultimo quantis malis invidia ipsa universum genus hominum afficiat. Prima scaena succincte quodammodo explicat huius ipsius tragoediae argumentum. Lege foelix. Romae MCCCCXL.

Moralis

Ambitio genuit Invidiam. Invidia genuit Discordiam. Discordia genuit Perfidiam, qui cum Inopia, Furtum, Rapina consequuntur.

Poesis

Ambitio caelum petens et ex tonitruo Invidiam gignens terrisque deiecta filiam ipsam, quod informis esset, in scopulum relegavit. Quae tandem adnavit terras Ambitionemque matrem prosequta est et per sylvam Ericthoniam et per omnes terras, etiam per aedes Micissae regis. Inde, inter Hyempsalem et Iugurtham simultas suborta peperit caedem Hyempsalis et regni stragem.

view, this was to be done because Jugurtha had been adopted as an heir during that period of time. Jugurtha was infuriated by this statement, and as a result Hiempsal was murdered at night by Jugurtha's assassins. Thereafter the kingdom of Libya suffered calamities and collapsed in ruin. Through this story, which is narrated extensively and in detail by Sallust, envy is depicted, the very quality about which we are to contend in this second competition.[1] There are five acts. In the first we state what sort of a thing 3
envy is. In the second are described its possible effects on minds where envy is present. In the third we show how the envious behave toward those whom they envy, in the fourth the reactions of those who have been injured by the envious. In the final act we see how many ills envy itself causes for the entire human race. The first scene briefly explains the argument, as it were, of this tragedy. Enjoy reading it. Rome 1440.

Moral

Ambition begot Envy. Envy begot Discord. Discord begot Treachery, from which follow Poverty, Thievery, and Plunder.

Poetry

Ambition, seeking heaven and begetting Envy from thunder, hurled her own daughter to the earth because she was deformed and abandoned her on a rock. At long last, Envy swam ashore and pursued her mother Ambition through the Ericthonian[2] forest and through every land, even through the palace of King Micipsa. As a consequence, a rivalry arose between Hiempsal and Jugurtha which caused the death of Hiempsal and the destruction of the kingdom.

[*Praefatio*]

Ad colendissimum dominum suum, dominum Prosperum cardinalem Columnam. in Hyempsalem tragoediam Leonardi Dathi florentini, episcopi massani, praefatio.

Ad dulce praesidium meum, ad certum domus
altae Columnae et unicum Romae decus,
ad Prosperum tendes, *Hyempsal,* et pede
grandi. At licet nec compta nec forsan ferax
sententiis, ut decet, ei tamen, ut reor,
quoniam mea es, futura grata principi:
nam et mitis est et me Dathum valde probat.
Tum pande quanti est invidia tenax mali,
quae regna scindit funditus, fratres necat;
quando et ita pestilens venenum livor est,
ut vitia tantum caetera excedat lue,
virtute quantum Prosper excellit viros.

: I :

Ambitio et Modestia

Amb. Per et profundum et fulgidum et castum polum
molleque solum aetheris et per alitum vias
delapsa terris, huc, ad hos veteris meos
lauti hospites regni, dea et terra et mari
iactata confugio: ita me infensa et procax
partu sata meo, Invidia, prosequitur dolis,
monstrum vel inferis et invisum et grave.
O me parentem miseram, iterum et iterum miseram! Tot latebris totque in orbis arcibus,

[*Preface*]

To his most worshipful lord, Lord Prospero, the Cardinal Colonna,[3] *a preface to the tragedy Hiempsal by the Florentine Leonardo Dati, Bishop of Massa.*[4]

Go, *Hiempsal,* with stately tread to my sweet protector, to the indisputable glory of the exalted family of Colonna and the singular ornament of Rome, go to Prospero. You may not be elegant nor, perhaps, rich in maxims, as is fitting, but nevertheless I think that, because you are mine, you will be well received by that prelate, for he is kind and values me, Dati, a great deal. Then reveal how implacably evil Envy is, who splits kingdoms apart from their foundations and kills brothers. So deadly a poison is Envy that she exceeds all the other vices as much as Prospero in his virtue excels all other men.

: I :

Ambition and Modesty

[*A palace in Numidia*]

Ambition. Through the deep, bright, pure sky and the gentle region of the ether and through the pathways of birds I have fallen to earth, and buffeted on land and sea, goddess though I am, I take refuge with these my hosts, to whom belongs this ancient, wealthy kingdom. Thus my own hostile and wayward seed, Envy, persecutes me with her trickery, the monster, hateful and cruel even to those below. O what a wretched mother I am, twice and thrice wretched! No safe place is granted me in

ad me tuendam nullus est datus locus:
quocumque tendo, nata perturbat viam.
Mo. Tibi quidem, fastu hoc tuo posito, tuis,
o Ambitio, si temporibus obtemperes,
quoad poteris, ipsa consules. Stat enim mihi
vetus sacellum, quo deum pater atque rex
monstra atque curas progredi vetuit graves.
Amb. Erumna ab ipsis infimis mortalibus
malo vel ex parte minima levarier,
quam omni a deorum grege gravi malo eripi.
Nam ab his quidem levi relato munere
pro maximo beneficii merito eximar.
At quis deorum est qui uspiam sibi esse par
putet relatum, ubi me suis meritis deam
devinxerit? Nempe insolens divum est genus,
quod in dies parvo moveri munere
dediscimus superi. At quid altas aedium
sedes inurentem intus Invidiam audio?
Inde adeo iam, quoad fors feret, mihi consulam.
Cedam furenti: namque cedendo furor
frangitur. Abibo hinc ad Lares intro abditos.
Mo. Ast ego? Meam quo me urbis artifices pii
locaverant sudore sordidam petam
aram, ut protervam hanc et domum et gentem suum
ruentem in excidium subinde rideam,
quando hic quidem nostri apud eosdem numinis
ita nunc colendi ratio curave excidit.

Asper et Polymites

As. Etenim, sator deorum et hominum, Iuppiter,
qui aethera potes mari atque terras aetheri
miscere nutu, numquid haud satis est tibi,
iras trisulca si exeris tuas face,

the many refuges and citadels of the world. Wherever I go, my child frustrates my course.

Modesty. O Ambition, if you would put aside this arrogance of yours and adapt yourself to circumstances as much as possible, you would be doing yourself a favor. I have an ancient chapel where the father and king of the gods has forbidden monsters and grave anxieties to enter.

Ambition. I prefer to be relieved of my griefs, even in the smallest way, by the very humblest of mortals than to be rescued from every evil by the solemn assembly of the gods. For men will relieve me and consider even a small gift given in return a great benefit. But which of the gods will ever think himself adequately requited when he has obligated me, goddess though I am, by means of his services? Indeed, the race of the gods is an arrogant one, because we gods unlearn each day how to be influenced by small offerings. But why do I hear Envy raging like fire within the lofty chambers of the palace? From now on I shall consult my own interests, as far as fate allows. I shall yield to her frenzy, for madness is broken by yielding. I shall retreat from here to the hidden Lares[5] within.

Modesty. And what of me? I shall seek out my altar, filthy with sweat, where the pious builders of the city with their toil had placed me, so that now and again I may laugh at this perverse house and its clan rushing to ruin, since here they have now lost the custom and practice of worshipping my divinity.

Asper and Polymites

Asper. Truly, Jupiter, father of gods and men, is it not enough for you—you who can intermingle sky with sea and earth with sky by a nod of your head—that you discharge your anger with your three-pronged lightning bolt, your right hand hurling

flammas et hinc et inde iaculans dextera
ni vel feram hanc hominumque perniciem ultimam
terris feras? O et tu, olympicum decus,
qui pulcher alta templa gemmis fulgidis
expicta lustras, fervidis praeceps rotis,
vincisque dum libet atque prosternis feras,
crinite Phoebe, usque adeo ne hos miseros potes
odisse mortalis, ut et quos Lucifer
praemissus abs te quemque nuncians diem
dulci a sopore matutinus excitet,
et quos tu agas exerceasque laboribus
sine fine duris atque morti concites,
eos item a feralibus foede undique
monstris sub oculo gaudeas tuo premi?
Profecto sub te, Phoebe, respirat nihil
durius homine; vel quos homo tandem sibi
faciles habebit, usque tam exosus diis?

Po. Immo et quidem sub sole delitiae deum
est homo, modo se hominem velit, non belluam.

As. Quodcunque vescitur aura et incolit globum,
quem premimus ipsi, plus diis cordi est quam homo.
Siquidem fames, langor, dolor, quae caeteris
extrema sunt mala, nos apud capita ultimis
angustiis obmersa non mala prima sunt,
adeo angimur solliciti et innumeris malis.
En stant comae mihi atque ab imis spiritus
praecordiis gelat. Heu cado, heu desum mihi
perculsus horrore, omnibus nervis fluens!
O dulce, letum refugium, a diis datum
nostris malis! Per te quidem erumnas graves,
maerorem, inopiam ponimus; per te fera
monstra et refertam maximis vitam malis
fugimus beasque quo minus sero obvenis.

flames hither and yon, unless you inflict on the earth this ferocious and final ruination of mankind? And you, O glory of Olympus, who traverse the lofty temples, spangled with brilliant jewels, riding headlong on blazing wheels, and who subdue and knock down wild beasts whenever it suits you, Apollo, so handsome with your long hair, can it be that you have hated these wretched mortals so much that even those whom the morning star,[6] sent out before you and announcing each day's arrival, awakens from their sweet sleep, and those whom you send to their endless hard labors, driving them to their death—do you rejoice to oppress foully even these poor mortals with feral monsters on all sides under your very eye? Indeed, beneath you, Phoebus, nothing breathes that is more long-suffering than man. Who will man have, in the end, to be kind to him, if he is so completely hateful to the gods?

Polymites. On the contrary, beneath the sun man is the delight of the gods, so long as he chooses to be a man and not a beast.

Asper. Whatever feeds on air and inhabits the world on which we ourselves walk is much dearer to the gods than man. If indeed hunger, weakness, and grief are extremely distressing evils for others, for us who are completely overwhelmed with the most desperate anguish, these are not our primary afflictions, so much anguish and care do we have from innumerable ills.[7] Look, my hair stands up straight and my spirit turns to ice in my vitals! Alas, I fall, alas, I faint, struck by the horror that flows through all my nerves! O sweet, joyful refuge, given for our ills by the gods! Thanks to you we put aside our heavy sorrows, our sadness and our need; through you we escape savage monsters and a life filled with the greatest of evils, and bless more quickly the one you succor.

Po. Sapiens statuet hoc munus in vita sibi
se se ut ferat, cum nullus adversus magis
homini aut molestus est magis, quam homo met sibi.
Tum qui suas apte volet res ducere,
is muniet mentem artibus bonis suam:
qua fretus haud ullas cohorrebit feras.
Virtuti opem superi ferunt: nocet nihil.
As. Immo dii summi, infimi ac medioxumi,
virtutem odio habent, quando livorem impium
monstrumque virtuti insidens non amovent.
Vos ne, dii, hanc tam pestilentem bestiam
publicaque privataque volutantem loca
sinitis nec arcetis, dii, ne lurido
sacra et prophana omnia pedore polluat?
Exanimor hoc equidem! Sed, o superi, probe
vestrae hinc saluti est additum: Invidiam simul
iecistis orbis monstruosi ad incolas
eique thalares fero monstro leves
vetuistis alarumque ventivolas iubas.
Quod si supernum volitet attingens polum,
non dubito quin audax comam Baccho secet,
discerpat ex humeris Dianae arcum aureum
pharetramque distrudatque clangifragam tubam
ensemque cornipedemque Mavorti fero,
Phoebo lyram altiboanteque a maris deo
tridentem et ex tua, o Tonans, fulmen manu
vertat, novum, horrendum atque inauditum nefas,
caelumque caelicolasque non secus ac domum,
Lares, Penates Masinisse dissipet.
Ita, quam timent luem et relegant dii procul,
virtute fretus quispiam, qui homo sit, feret?
Po. Nunquam, dum erunt homines, erit non foeta humus

Polymites. The wise man will establish this as his goal in life, that he may endure his own self, since no one is more hostile or harmful to a man than he is to himself. Then he who wishes to conduct his affairs properly will furnish his mind with noble arts.[8] Trusting in his mind, no beasts will paralyze him with fear. The gods lend aid to virtue; it is harmful to nothing.

Asper. On the contrary, the gods above us, below us, and in these middle regions hate virtue, since they have chosen not to cast out that hateful monster, Envy, that weighs so heavily on virtue. Don't you, gods, allow so pestilent a beast as this to roam about in public places and private? Do you prevent it, gods, from staining all things sacred and profane with its ghastly filth? This really takes my breath away. But, O gods, it was clever of you to protect yourselves by this precaution: at the same time you hurled Envy down to live among the inhabitants of this monstrous world, you forbade this savage monster from wearing speedy, winged sandals or wind-borne pinions of wings. But if she should fly up and reach the heavens, there is no doubt that, daring as she is, she would cut off the hair of Bacchus and rip the golden bow and quiver from Diana's shoulders, steal the clanging trumpet, sword and horse from savage Mars, the lyre from Phoebus, and from the deep-resounding god of the sea his trident, and from your hand, O Thunderer, she would take the lightning bolt — a new, horrifying and unheard-of crime. She would completely destroy heaven and the gods there no differently than she does the home, Lares, and Penates of Masinissa. Thus, can any human being, however armed with virtue, endure the pestilence that the gods fear and banish far from themselves?

Polymites. Never, as long as men exist, will the earth not be rank with horrifying monsters. For men call forth monsters of their

monstris nefandis: nam ultro monstra hi provocant
passimque blandiuntur et coalunt sinu.

As. Ergo libet hinc effugere ab omni hominum grege.

Chorus

Quicquid sub pelago natat
tetrum, quicquid in ultimis
speluncis libycis siti
squalens ac nocuum latet,
horrendum est minus ac minus
quam Livor, scelerum deus.
Cuius cum faciem canis
infernus videat, tremet
omnesque Eumenides simul.
Olli frons riget hispida
cervixque hirtis aspera setis,
subcrispat rabiem rugis,
protense et grave pendule
dependent ciliis cavis
alae geminae, atrae, pannosae,
noctua quales nocte fatigat,
retrusosque oculos brevi
succludunt luteos sinu.
Cum nox vellere tingitur
et Phoebe iacet abdita,
tum monstrum hoc acie valens
distorto ad lucem capite fremit
aeternumque leves circum deductitat aures,
ac tabo et sanie madens;
rumore alitur fraudis iniquae,
et studia hominum cordaque passim
scrutans vincit nare canum vim.

own free will and everywhere delight in them and nurture them in their breasts.

Asper. For this reason it's better to get away from here, from every assemblage of men.

Chorus

Whatever monstrosity swims beneath the sea, whatever thirsty thing, squalid and deadly, hides in the most distant caves of Libya is much, much less horrible than Envy, the god of crime. Let the hound of hell[9] see the face of Envy and he will tremble, and all the Eumenides[10] along with him. Envy's shaggy brow is coarse and her neck rough with hairy bristles; her face is distorted with rage. From her hollow eyelids hang large and heavily drooping twin wings, dark and ragged, such as those bats beat in the night, and they cover their murky, sunken eyes in their small openings. When the night is tinged with its fleecy mantle and the moon lies hidden, then this monster of keen vision, with her head twisted toward the light, shrieks. She forever turns her tiny ears around and, steeped in rot and gore, she feeds upon rumors of wicked deceit. Better than a dog following a scent, she sniffs out the passions and hearts of men

Sed lacerantes omnia tetri
dentes faucibus eminent,
semper dispare blacterat
pectore linguae,
efflans tabificam Stygem.
Sunt et pectus ei et manus,
quales ventre famelico
simia levis instabiles agitat.
Stat dorsum callo praeduro et morsibus ustum;
demum de femore in pedem
lascivus caper ambulat.
Cum caelum peteret Ambitio procax,
fama est patre tonitruo
monstrum invitis superis divis
progenitum et terris disrupta nube repulsum.
Hinc gelidis flammis aeternum pectore flagrat
pernixque omnem pervolat orbem.
Nunc arces, aditus, atria principum,
nunc et publica compita,
nunc mapalia et humilis glebas
observat celeri ambitu:
sed gymnasia pallidae
intrat penitus falsa Minervae.
Ex frugi atque pio impium
letumque malis comitum reddit,
fraudem iudiciis serit
frontemque notat scelere tristem.
Ipsum non Herebi fores
obiectae valeant procul
arcere: subit, perstat, inhaeret;
quin et semideos quoque
atrox hic furor occupat.
Heu Livor, quid non mortalia pectora cogis?

everywhere. But repulsive fangs stick out from her jaws, which rip everything to shreds; she chatters forever with the deformed mass of her tongue, exhaling the putrid Styx. Both her chest and hands are always in motion like those of a monkey whose stomach is empty. Her back is covered with a thick hide, smarting with bites. Finally, from her thighs to her feet she trundles about more like a lascivious goat than anything else. When willful Ambition sought the heavens, it is said that this monster, against the will of the gods above, was spawned by the Thundering Father and sent back to the earth through a rent in the clouds. For this reason there forever blazes on her breast chilling flames, and swiftly she flies through the whole world. Now the citadels, gates and halls of princes she views on her swift journey, now also the public crossroads, now huts and humble gardens. But she enters most deeply into the sham schoolrooms of pale Minerva where she changes a worthy and pious man into someone wicked, who is made happy by the misfortunes of his friends. She sows deceit in legal proceedings and brands its sad brow with crime. The gates of Erebus, shut to Envy, are not strong enough to keep her away; she enters, loiters about, and sticks close. Nay, her cruel madness even seizes the demigods. Alas, Envy, what evils do you not force mortal hearts to commit?[11] Yet he who moves through the pub-

Sed pestem hanc fugiet face
pre se ardenti fora qui lustret
vel qui sola rideat umbra.
At quid tristis prodit Hyempsal?

: II :

Hyempsal et Polymites

Hy. Velim furentis aethere obvolvi Nothos
vastisque convalles hiatibus hiscere
fragoreque ingenti superba rupium
circumruere culmina et ab imis sedibus
alte procellis concuti totum mare
in ultimam pestem luemque gentium,
quandoquidem in hominum genere tam male liberos
iam tum parentes impii oderunt suos.
Quis adeo fortis est, quis est tam ferreus
qui non ut ego scelus in Micissa fulminet?
En mihi furore pectus accensum labat.
Po. Quisque facinus suum male admissum ferat
aegre et moleste, nil per alienum vigil.
Hy. Externa ab iniuria oritur vehemens dolor.
Po. Tuum esse iam incipiet malum quo non bene
tecum sit, et quicunque, secum dissidens,
animo suo illuctatur, haud quaquam ocium
prestabit aliis. Esse te regem scias.
Hy. Servum scio atque ipsum quidem regnum est miser-
rum. Illi et mali hoc inest, ut omnia cum queas
tum et tibi nihil satis queas aeque ut velis.

lic squares bearing a blazing torch before him, or who laughs to himself in the shadows, will flee this plague.[12] [*Hiempsal approaches*] But why is Hiempsal coming forth with such grim looks?

: II :

Hiempsal and Polymites

Hiempsal. I wish the raging southern winds would whirl in the sky and the valleys would gape wide with tremendous chasms, that with a huge crash the high mountain peaks would collapse and from its deepest bottom the whole sea would be whipped from on high by storms, to the point of bringing the final plague and affliction upon the nations, seeing that in the human race, from that moment,[13] there have been impious parents who so wickedly hated their own sons. Who is so courageous, so steely, that he would not, like me, rage against the crime of Micipsa? See, my heart is trembling with fury!

Polymites. Each man should bear with pain and distress the sins that he has wickedly committed, and not concern himself with those of others.

Hiempsal. Yet deep distress arises when another injures you.

Polymites. The evil will now start to be yours, and through it you will not be at peace with yourself. Whoever struggles with his own soul, discordant within himself, will by no means give peace to others. Know that you are a king.

Hiempsal. I know I am a slave, and that kingship itself is wretched. This evil too is inherent to it: that you can do everything, and at the same time you can do nothing satisfactory to yourself, nothing that equals what you want.

Po. Iuvat in hominum vita minus velle ac minus
eniti in omni re usque quam possis tibi:
quo fit ut et inde plura possis quam velis.
Hy. At regium est grandia minus nolle ac queas.
O impium dirumque productum ex ea
dura impiaque stirpe Getula! O ferum,
cui filii tam sint odio ut hunc sordidum
adiecerit regni coheredem sui!
Eum ne Iugurtham patre incerto editum
dolisque regiam male acturum suis?
Et quem ille tu ne, tu ne regem, tu parem
regnique filiisque consortem tuis?
Sceleste!
Po. Nemo solus imperium gerit.
Hy. Quisquis alieno arbitrio aget rem, serviet.
Po. Profecto consiliis bonis nisi ultro rex
paruerit, aegre abinde parebit malis.
Hy. Quisquis malos timet, profecto omnes timet.
Homines vel oderunt vel optant quod neque-
unt; male qui et oderit, studet semper male.
Regique regem qui dabit, regnum abstrahet.
Po. Frater ne fratrem non colet?
Hy. Colet? Ubi nam
tutus erit amor, odisse cum possis homo
et nostra mens a rebus omnis pendeat?
Po. Amabere ut voles.
Hy. Volam ut tempus feret.
Po. Modo ne hoc agas invitus et regum omnium
eris ipse foelicissimus.
Hy. Id optent licet.

Polymites. In human life it helps to wish for less and to strive for less in everything as far as possible: as a result you can achieve more than you wish.

Hiempsal. But it is kingly to not wish for fewer great deeds than you are able to achieve. O the unholy and dread offspring of the hard and unholy stock of the Gaetuli![14] O the cruel man, who hates his own sons so much that he thrust this low fellow upon us as coheir of his kingdom! Will this man Jugurtha, sired by an unknown father, not govern the realm badly through deceit and trickery? [*He addresses the shade of his father.*] Aren't you—yes you!—the one who chose this man to be king, to be an equal in kingship, to be the consort of your own sons? You villain!

Polymites. No one wields the power of command by himself.

Hiempsal. Whoever will act at the bidding of another will be a slave.

Polymites. Surely, unless a king obeys good counsel willingly, he will of necessity obey bad counsel unwillingly.

Hiempsal. Whoever fears bad men surely fears all men. Men either hate or wish for what they cannot have; wrong hatreds always accompany wrong desires. He who gives a king to a king takes his kingdom away.

Polymites. Will a brother not devote himself to a brother?

Hiempsal. Devote himself? Where will love ever be secure when, as a man, you can conceive hatreds, and all our thoughts depend upon events?[15]

Polymites. You will be loved as you wish to be.

Hiempsal. I shall wish as the times direct.

Polymites. So long as you don't do this without wishing it, you will be the happiest of kings.

Hiempsal. It's right that kings should desire this. [*Hiempsal departs*]

Chorus et Polymites

Ch. Quo nam hinc agitur aut abit Hyempsal? Quid furit?
Po. Quo eum volentem fata praecipitant sua.
Ch. Fatum est id homini nosse fatis cedere?
Po. Fatum ferendo vincitur.
Ch. Quicquid feras,
premit atque fatum posse ferre fortiter
fatum est.
Po. Enim hominum nemo foelix unquam erit
invitus. At Livor quod aspectu foret
truculentus ac foedus, quod horrendus nimis,
a matre primum medio in oceani scoplo
expositus aspero et minaci rupibus,
circumstrepentis aquae fragore fervido
alitur; abinde cadavere advectus petit
terras et extemplo mali accepti memor
totum per orbem persequitur odiis deam.
Exterrita illa metu, abdidit sese procul
spelunca opaca intra nemus Ericthonium.
Subinde nostram regiam Ambitio haec parens
ut subiit, heu, Livor inimicus appulit
turbatque prosternitque cuncta funditus.

Chorus

Non est invidia quis minus invido
dignus: nam miser est quilibet invidus,
obiecte simulac invidet aree.
Inprimisque sibi est ille nocentior
qui livore alium findere nititur,
aeternum siquidem tristibus uritur
curis sollicito pectore languidus:
sic auctor propriis obteritur malis.

Chorus and Polymites

Chorus. Where is Hiempsal being driven from here, where is he going? Why is he enraged?

Polymites. His fates are sending him headlong where he wills.

Chorus. Is it fated for a man to know he should yield to fate?

Polymites. Fate is overcome by enduring it.

Chorus. Whatever you endure weighs you down, and it is fated that you can bravely endure fate.

Polymites. In fact, no man will ever be happy without choosing to be. But Envy, because he[16] was so truculent and loathsome in his appearance, because he was so awful, was first abandoned by his mother on a rock in the middle of the sea, harsh and threatening for its cliffs, and was brought up with the sound of the waves crashing and boiling around him. Then, carried by a corpse, he made for the shoreline and, remembering at once the evil he had suffered, pursued the goddess through the whole world in hate. Terrified, his mother hid herself far away within a dark cave in an Ericthonian grove. Then as soon as this mother, Ambition, came to our royal palace, alas! hostile Envy landed, disturbing and knocking everything down to its very foundations.

Chorus

No one is less enviable than the envious man: for whoever is affected by envy is miserable; he envies empty space as soon as he comes upon it. Most of all, he harms himself the more who tries to shatter another through envy, since he burns forever with severe anxieties, languishing with worry; thus he who caused them is crushed by his own evils. Therefore, learn,

Vos Numidae igitur discite puberes
virtutis studio quaerere gloriam.
Virtus praesidium est nobile et unicum,
virtus imperium non violabile.
Vindicte et satis est, si prius invidens
multo praedoluit quam male missili
contorto potuit laedere quempiam.
Ecce Iugurtham quoties periclis
vidimus missum probitate et armis!
Ipse fortunam invidiamque parto
nomine vicit.
Caeteros quantum superabat acri
gloria, tantum et meritis studebat
omnibus charus fore liberali
pectore et ore.
Strenuus ferro, genio sagaci
plenus et rebus bene consulendis
aptus, ac spes et nova Masinissae
gloria gentis,
usque virtutis cupidus magis quam
laudis; hic unus didicit ferendo
imperi leges, simul esse quantus
debeat armis.
Ergo virtutem cole, prompta pubes;
te tibi exorna et decus et decorum.
et genus, laudemque tibi ipsa soli
posce, iuventus.
Nam sibi quisquis sciet imperare,
ille proh quantum et sibi quam perenne
regnum habet, semper nihil occupata
mente triumphat.
Non eum tum fors furiosa vexat,
non et irati superi lacessunt.

young men of Numidia,[17] to seek glory through zeal for virtue. Virtue is a noble and unique safeguard, and its realm is inviolable. There is vengeance enough if the envious man suffers by far the most pain before he can injure anyone else with a poorly thrown projectile. Behold, how many times have we seen Jugurtha sent into dangers because of his integrity and skill in arms! He has overcome fortune and envy and won renown. As much as he excelled the others with dazzling glory, so much did he strive through merit to be loved by all for his generous heart and tongue. Valiant with the sword, full of wisdom and well fitted for giving advice, he was the hope and the new glory of Masinissa's line, more desirous of virtue than of praise; this one man learned the laws of command by enduring them,[18] and at the same time learned how much he should owe to arms. Therefore foster virtue, eager youth; ennoble yourselves with honor and distinction, and seek praise and high descent for yourselves through virtue alone.[19] For whoever will learn how to command himself, how great and how enduring is the kingdom he will possess for himself! With a mind free of worry, he triumphs always. Then raging Fortune does not vex him nor

Gaudet aeternum, celebri invidentes
luce fatigat.

: III :

Adherbal et Hyempsal

Ad. Non tanta, quantam qui intulerit, iniuria est,
sed tanta, quantam quis sibi illatam estimat.
Hy. Modicum est nihil, quod a dolore est maximo.
Ad. Dolebis in dies minus, cum plus sapis.
Hy. Homini sat est nosse agere rem ex sententia.
Ad. Quaeque institueris rite, facile est exequi.
Hy. Consilia probet eventus. Interim hac mea
fruor voluptate ac libidinem expleo:
medio ne consessu quasi et parentem eum
dignabimur nostro, ne sordidum in domum
nostram hunc calonem pene conventitium.
Operae precium abiisse sit eum tristius
a sede quam, velut arrogans est, abfuit.
Confingat ut vult modo Iugurtha atque ut solet.
Hoc ipse letor quando sub risu impio
undare sensi lachrymas moestas suo.
Sed cum molestus esse cuiquam ceperis,
opprimito, moles interim in te ne ruat.
Ad. Immo et, molestus esse cuiquam ut coeperis
desinito, ne tuum in caput molem struas.
Qui e fronte risu tedium abstersit sua,
cum consulit sibi, tum et infestis simul
importat ut doleant; et usque principem
beneficiis clarum esse pulchre condecet.

the wrathful gods above provoke him. He rejoices forever, wearing down the envious with his glorious splendor.

: III :

Adherbal and Hiempsal

Adherbal. The amount of an injury is not judged by the one who inflicts it but by the one who suffers it.

Hiempsal. Nothing is slight which involves the greatest pain.

Adherbal. You will grieve less each day as you grow wiser.

Hiempsal. It is enough for a man to know how to act according to his convictions.

Adherbal. It is easy to execute whatever you have planned aright.

Hiempsal. Let the outcome justify the plan. In the meantime, I enjoy this pleasure of mine and satisfy my desire: shall we dignify him with the middle seat as though he were a parent, shall we receive into our house that dirty camp follower, encountered almost by chance? It would be worth it if he has departed hence with more ill humor than he showed in his arrogance when vacating his seat. Let Jugurtha put on a face in whatever way he wants and is used to doing. I rejoice when I see his tears of sorrow well up beneath his unholy smile. But when you undertake to vex someone, crush him, so that in the meantime the building doesn't collapse on you.

Adherbal. No: when you undertake to vex someone, stop doing it, so you don't construct a building to fall on your head. A man who wipes disgust from his brow with a smile does himself a favor and at the same time brings sorrow to his enemies; and it is a fine and fitting thing for a prince to be famous for his beneficence.

Hy. Beneficio ne tu satis hominem tuo,
qui prebet ingratum inde se, devincies?
En gratum hominem amarique dignum qui, inmemor
doni a Micissa patre collati sibi,
decreta, quibus est tractus in regnum, rogo
vix funerum extincto, esse per se turpiter
rescissa studeat impudens, et impudens
qui exordium regni eruendi patriis
sanctisque vertendis capiat a legibus:
regni luem excidiumque nimirum parat.
Cavendum, Adherbal, tibi necem is ferox parat.
Ad. Fastum quidem obsequio propere vinces tuo.
Hy. Quin fastus obsequio procacius intumet,
et insolentem qui haud cohercet, illicit.
Sed familiae nostros Penates ac deos
probe in dies opem esse laturos scio.
Ad. Spem esse meriti filiam vulgo ferunt,
sperasse et adeo bona bene merendo licet.
Hy. Apud inmerentem bene mereri dum voles
demerueris.
Ad. Rem egisse pro officio sat est.

Adherbal, Hyempsal et Phitonissa

Ad. Et quid soluto crine, nudo pectore
scissaque Phitonissa veste cursitat?
Quid se furore concitat? Quid igneos
obvolvit oculos atque murmurans tumet?
En ut repente, quasi obviis exterrita
umbris grave infestis, propere haerens loco
vim ponit irarum atque conatus fremens.
Phi. Euhoe!

Hiempsal. Will your kindness to a man be enough to bind a man who then shows he is ungrateful? Look, *this* is your grateful man worthy of being loved: it is this shameless fellow who, forgetful of the gift bestowed on him by our father Micipsa—whose funeral pyre is scarcely gone out—disgracefully strives to rescind the decrees by which he was taken into the kingship; it is this shameless fellow who would begin the process of destroying the kingdom by subverting its ancestral and sacred laws. He is surely preparing for the extinction and ruin of the kingdom. Beware, Adherbal, this wild man is planning your death!

Adherbal. You will quickly conquer his pride by your deference.

Hiempsal. Rather, pride swells up even more impudently with deference, and the insolent man who is not reined in is ensnared by it. But I know that our Penates and family gods are rightly going to bring us aid, day by day.

Adherbal. People say that hope is the daughter of merit, and one can have good hope if it is well merited.

Hiempsal. So long as you wish to win merit from one who is without it, you diminish your own.

Adherbal. It's enough to have done one's duty.

Adherbal, Hiempsal and Phitonissa[20]

[*Phitonissa rushes in wildly*]

Adherbal. Why does Phitonissa run about, her hair disheveled, her breast exposed, and her gown torn? Why is she inflamed by frenzy? Why does she roll her fiery eyes all around and swell up as she mutters? [*She stands still*] But look, suddenly, as though terrified by meeting hostile shades, she hastily stops and puts her anger and agitation aside, groaning.

Phitonissa. O woe!

Hy. Ut inter clamitandum obmutuit
truculenta, ut introrsus renitens faucibus
verba negat, ut se se premens totis simul
exaestuans membrisque nervisque attremit,
ut torpet, ut modo pone subvertit solo
obliqua lumina, modo subrepta altius
cervice torvos erigit vultus. Papae!
Phi. Io Libes misere, Libes misere, libes
matresque nurusque misere, complete, io,
complete sylvas atque montes planctibus!
Te, te quidem te cerno Tyrmidam impiam:
tu male latentem clave adultera necas,
et te tridentem, una resecta cuspide,
male in duas findi hinc et inde dissides
partis video. Tu Cirtha profugum, he he, tuo
profugum, tuo haud gremio satis servas diu!
Stat ales Evandri atque rostro et unguibus
libycos male exturbat gravi nidos lue.
Heu, Zama, purpureis madescis imbribus!
Vaccea pubes, tertio haud rides die!
Igne tibi, Tala, facis tenebras ultimas!
Capsa, aureos tum reddis ungues aliti
et tibi, Mulucha, non cocleis laetus tuis
noctem iubare fuscat alacrem Titan suo!
Et tu ipse, quem surrepta servat litera,
ne crede, ne crede veteri atavorum hospiti!
Plura vetat hac in parte Phoebus proloqui,
sed fata summum denique exuperant Iovem.
Ad. O plena numine, cui futura Phytius
ordine aperit, si precibus ullis flecteris,
nostros aperte iam edoce casus, precor!
Quo liceat evitasse per te aut fortiter
subiisse, praevisum imminens quicquid mali est.

Hiempsal. Look how the truculent girl goes mute in the midst of her howling, as though, struggling within herself, the words stick in her throat; look how she clutches herself convulsively, trembling in all her limbs and sinews, so that at one moment she goes limp, at another she looks down at the ground with twisted eyes, at still another her neck jerks upward and she raises up her twisted face. O woe!

Phitonissa. O wretched women of Libya, wretched Libyan women, wretched Libyan mothers and brides, fill, O fill the forests and the mountains with your laments! It is you—yes you!—I see, unholy Tyrmida:[21] you kill the one who was badly hidden with a false key, and you, trident, I see with one of your points lopped off, the rest badly split into two quarreling parts, a part here and one there. You, Cirta,[22] do not for long protect the exile—alas, the exile!—in your bosom. There stands the bird of Evander,[23] and with its beak and claws it causes the Libyan nests grave damage and destruction. Alas, Zama,[24] you are soaked by showers of blood! You smile not beyond the third day, Vaccean youth![25] You make final darkness for yourself, Thala,[26] with fire! Then, Capsa,[27] you yield your golden claws to the bird, and for you, O Mulucha, unhappy with your snails,[28] Titan obscures the eager night with his glow! And you, you, whom a stolen letter saved, put no faith, put no faith in the ancient host of your forefathers![29] Phoebus forbids me to reveal more about this, but the Fates in the end overcome highest Jupiter.

Adherbal. O woman filled with divinity, you to whom Apollo reveals future events in their succession, if you can be moved by any of our prayers, I beg you now to explain to us in clear terms our destiny! With your help let us either escape or bravely endure whatever impending evil you foresee.

Phi. Euhoe, nefandus Livor infernas agit
res pessime, ingrediens eburna vortices
Stygios sub afflatu usque concretos dedit
in marmor; Alectoque atque ipse mutuis
utrinque Gorgoneis venenis obsiti
sese efferunt in rabiem, et interior stupet
Tartarea sedes ac tumultu contremit,
stridoreque ululatuque latrans Cerberus
cedit metu. Quin rex et infernus metu
una tyranno colla subclinat novo
novumque sontibus additum est poenae genus.
Sibi quisque tormentum alterius optet magis:
euhoe libes matresque nurusque heu libes!

Chorus

Hominem quisquis condere primus
statuit, vultus oraque divum
contemplatus faciem finxit
arte manuque prope divinam,
tum crinem nitido surpuit aureum
Phoebo: nobile, nobile furtum!
Hunc ubi sensit radiis tenebras
pellere et flammis coquere aestuosis
arce velut celsa, lucem sub fronte locavit
fervoremque procul subter praecordia adegit.
Hoc opus quidam superi ut moveri,
ut frui vita simul intuentur,
forsan, ut fama est, operi invidentes,
ne novus terris deus et colonus
viveret, morbos varios dedere.
Urunt etenim frigora et aestus
siccisque sitis faucibus haeret
ventremque fames improba mordet,

Phitonissa. Alas, wicked Envy wreaks havoc in hell, entering by the ivory gates, and with his breath turns the Stygian whirlpools to stone. And Alecto and Envy madden each other, each attacking the other with the poison of the Gorgons.[30] Inside, the realm of Tartarus is amazed and trembles with the tumult; even Cerberus, barking, hissing, growling, draws back in fear. Nay, even the infernal king bends his neck in fear to this new tyrant, and a new kind of punishment has been added for guilty souls. Each one would rather have the other's torment: O woe, Libyan mothers and brides, alas!

Chorus

Whoever first decided to fashion man considered the countenances of the gods and created his face, nearly divine, with skilful hand. Then from shining Phoebus he stole his golden hair—a noble, noble theft! When he realized that his creation expelled the darkness with its rays and burned with seething flames as on a lofty citadel, he put the eyes under his brow and thrust the heat away into his breast. Certain gods, seeing how this creature was moving and enjoying life, perhaps (as the story goes) were envious of it, and to prevent a new god and colonist from living upon the earth, they gave the creature various ills. Thus cold and heat torment man, and thirst sticks to his dry mouth and cruel hunger gnaws at his belly, while both fever and

sternit et hunc febrisque dolorque.
Hinc sollicito pectore factus
odit amat ve
et sic aestu rapitur rerum
ut continuo verbere turbo.
At laboranti hic opifex misertus,
aegrum si quando torrent incendia pectus,
extingui dedit alveo
in Pegaseo.
Sed nos miseri mente proterva
in scelus acti labimur ultro.
Hinc erumnis premimur crebris,
hinc est nobis vita molesta,
hinc est aliquid semper ubi nos
acti poeniteat mali
atque et nobis semper in horas
novus incumbat trepidis casus.
Tu ne fortunam poteris, Hyempsal,
his tuam tristem tibi non dedisse
moribus? Scis ne ut novus ignis igne,
sic et ex flamma petulantis irae
iam lacessitos animos et ira
surgere contra?
Impetum frena male mentis actae.
Disce ne nolis tibi quaeque possis.
Vinces alios, te modo vincas.
Tibi eris qualem statues ipse.

sorrow lay him low. Thus he has been made with an anxious heart that hates or loves, and so he is swept along by the tumult of events, spun round continually like a top. But the craftsman[31] took pity on his troubled creation, and whenever fires raged in man's afflicted breast, he permitted them to be extinguished in the pool of Pegasus.[32] But, wretches that we are, our reckless thoughts drive us to wickedness and we fall of our own free will. Hence we are oppressed by constant sorrows; hence life is hateful to us; hence there is always a reason for repenting of our wicked deeds, and always a new peril threatens our fearful selves each hour. Will you be able to deny, Hiempsal, that this harsh ill fortune has been yours because of your bad character? Don't you know that, as new fire is kindled from fire, so from the flame of insolent anger, anger rises up against minds that are already inflamed? Rein in the violent thrust of your evil motives. Learn not to want for yourself everything you can have.

You will conquer others only so far as you conquer yourself. You will be the kind of man you yourself decide to be.

: IV :

Jugurtha

Iuppiter ab alto cuncta prospectans polo,
vosque veteris Manes Masinisse pii,
quibus parentandum bonis a me reor
studiis et ad laudem quoque aemulo gradu,
vosque patrii obtestor dii et deae libes:
non sponte me haec animo sed invitum mihi
contra impios regnique consortes datos
sumpsisse odia. Sed evenit id usu quidem:
ut sole pix quae liquitur, eadem ab aestibus
itemque itemque usta evitrescat horrida,
sic et virorum saepius animi exciti
iniuriis, inviti inhorrescunt he heu.
Aude invidum domesticumque hostem tuum
hostem putare, piumque ducito fore
tuae referre dignitati quicquid impiis et improbis merentibus inferas.
Semper ne perferemus hoc: ut qui modis
nos omnibus laedere per invidiam parent,
non sui aliquando iure poeniteat nefas?
Nunquam ne te tot atque tantis obrutum
iniuriis, Iugurtha, te ostendes virum?
Nunquam ne te posse aliquid in petulantium
protervitatem proferes? Livor scelus.
Aude, anime, superis non vetantibus diis,
eumque presta te virum, qualem solet
armatus hostis metuere. An te forsitan
ignobili editum parente scilicet
fastidiunt proceres? Sumus cuncti a Iove.
Sed mea perinde me satis virtus fovet

: IV :

Jugurtha

Jupiter, gazing out upon all things from the height of heaven, and you, sacred shades of old Masinissa, to whom I believe I should pay due reverence through honorable pursuits and the emulous quest for glory, and you ancestral gods and goddesses of Libya, I call you to witness that, not of my own volition but against it, I have formed a hatred of these unholy men who were given me as associates in kingship. But, indeed, it often happens that, just as pitch is melted by the sun and after repeated heatings turns hard and rough, so also the human spirit, provoked too often by injustice, unwillingly begins to bristle, alas. Dare to reckon that the hateful stranger you have in your home is your enemy, and consider that it will be a holy act, one owed to your dignity, whatever punishment you deservedly inflict upon impious and worthless persons. Shall we always endure it that those who in their ill will set out in every way to harm us are never made justly to regret their crime? Will you never, Jugurtha, show yourself a man—you who have been buried under so many injuries? Will you never give proof that you can resist the recklessness of these insolent men? Envy is criminal. Be daring, my soul, the gods above do not forbid it, and show that you are the kind of man an enemy fears, armed though he may be! Perhaps these princes look down on you because you were born of common stock? We are all from Jove.

satisque, quisquis ille sit, sibi met genus
dignum parat, quem victor orbis comprobet
populus. Mea haec laus atque nobilitas mea est.
Non id meum est sed patris, Hyempsal, dedecus,
si dedecus talem edidisse filium,
qualem Micissa, si rogetur, liberum
quam quos habet multo editum malit sibi.
At vero ego patre proinde non certo satos
arbitror eos, qui tam impares se pristinis
nostrae familiae moribus nunc praebeant.
Uter Masinissae est avo similis magis,
illi ne qui superbia atque ignavia
degunt iuventam, an et Iugurtha? Qui quidem
his artibus quibus imperium avus nactus est,
pridem integrum libycum merebar unicus?
Meam ego meo labore partam gloriam
nostrae ad familiae contuli certum decus.
Illi hunc perisse optant virum cuius micat
splendore domus: omnis et honos titulis nitet.
Verum, ut aiunt, quod agas agito pro viribus.
Iuvabit interim simulasse id artibus.

Polymites et Ammon

Po. Regni labes est principum discordia.
Amm. Cum principes ipsi mali sint, id boni
optent.
Po. Bene usquam nulla successit bonis
res, quae ocium perturbet inde publicum.
Amm. Si dura tempora fuerint et principes
ipsi mali rempublicam gerant male,
quis audeat praestare se civem bonum?
Po. Quisquis bonum se se esse civem quam videri malit, ad bene agendum habet semper bona

But just as my virtue nurtures me enough and more, so a people who has conquered the world will endorse a man who makes for himself a worthy lineage, whoever he is. My merits and nobility are mine alone. My shame is not mine, but that of my father, O Hiempsal, if shame it is to have produced the sort of son that Micipsa, if asked, would have much preferred to his legitimate sons. But frankly I believe that their own parentage is uncertain who now show themselves so inferior to the pristine character of our family. Who is more like our grandfather Masinissa: those who spend their youth in arrogance and sloth, or Jugurtha, who now alone deserves all Libya, having the same abilities that our grandfather used to acquire his empire? I have added the glory achieved through my own efforts to the manifest luster of our family. They want the man to die whose splendor illuminates their house and whose distinction reflects upon all their own honor. But, as they say, do what you are doing to the limits of your strength. Meanwhile, it will be useful to mask what I will do with stratagems. [*Jugurtha departs*]

Polymites and Ammon

Polymites. The discord of princes is the ruin of kingdoms.[33]

Ammon. When princes themselves are evil, good men may wish for that outcome.

Polymites. Nothing ever turns out well for good men when the public peace is disturbed.

Ammon. If times are hard and bad princes govern the state badly, who would dare play the part of a good citizen?

Polymites. Whoever prefers to be, and not just seem,[34] a good citizen always has good occasions to act well. The decent and hon-

is ipse tempora, et homo frugi, quisquis est,
sibi unico haud duros putet eos principes,
quos et populus omnis ferat.

Amm. Suo in malo
nemo quidem luget aliorum lachrymis.
Quaeque mala sunt muta atque mox fient bona.

Po. Erunt bona ipsos quaeque delectant bonos.
Hoc ego nihil placere placatis scio
civibus et intimis dolere probos animis: regulos gaza atque sedibus ocyus
sectis temere et abisse diversos locis.

Amm. Qui dissident animis, eadem aegre queunt
umbra tegi.

Po. Ni aliquo tenentur invicem
animi usque vinculo, haud coherent insimul.
Tum si Iugurtham, si satis novi virum,
tandem is vereor nequid ferus acerbi paret:
stat frons ei vultusque pallentes gravi
cura igneoque furore suffuse genae.
Latet quid alta mente subvolvat mali,
neque temere illud est quod impexam comam
secum ipse iam tum inmurmurans quassat suam.

Amm. Animo ubi sunt alto viri usquam praediti,
semper animis secum alta versant ac parant.
Sperasseque et de fortibus viris bene
multo magis quam metuere satis condecet.
Proinde privati domum curent suam,
rempublicam reges suo curent gradu.

Chorus

Fata ne rerum inconstansque dea
an magis hominum segnis ratio
ita mortalibus ocia turbat?

est man, whoever he is, will not think that princes are hard on him alone whom all the people must endure.

Ammon. No one, to be sure, weeps with another's tears in his own misfortune. Change whatever is bad, and soon it will turn into good.

Polymites. Whatever things delight good men will be good. But this, I know, does not please peace-loving citizens and causes good men mental suffering—namely, that petty kings quickly divide their treasures and palaces and rashly go off, each to his own place.

Ammon. Men who disagree find it hard to share the same roof.

Polymites. Unless they are kept together by some bond of spirit, they can hardly stick together. Then too, if I know Jugurtha, if I know the man at all, I fear that, with his aggressive character, he is planning something dreadful. His brow and face are pale with grave anxiety, and his cheeks are flushed with fury. The evil deed he's hatching deep in his heart lies hidden, and it is not without reason that he keeps muttering to himself and shaking his unkempt hair.

Ammon. When men are endowed with genius, they are always turning deep thoughts over in their hearts and thinking ahead. In the case of courageous men, it is much more proper, surely, to have hoped for the best rather than to fear them. On this account private citizens should tend to their own homes and kings should tend to the state in accordance with their rank.

Chorus

Is it the Fates and the inconstant goddess[35] or the lazy reasoning of men that thus disturbs the repose of mortals? This royal

Utrum haec Libyae regia et armis
et opum luxu nobilis aula,
hanc usque diem clara per orbem,
ultro et fato et sorte suapte
an hominum vi ruet ab imo?
Orta ne levis haec odii flamma
inter proceres, inter fratres,
irae tantos exciit ignes?
An hinc sumpta superi causa
instituerunt penitus Libyae
invisam sibi perdere gentem?
Te altitonantis, te, Iuno, Iovis
soror et coniunx, cui res Libyae
cordi aeternum credimus esse,
te et Getulie Mavors, veteris
Masinissae simul invoco alumnum:
bene et o omnes diique deaeque
quaeque parantur vertite scelera,
impendentem tollite diram
fortunam, neu tam adeo sinite
conscelerari pia delubra,
ignes, aras vestraque tecta
Furiis, ferro, caede cruenta
inter se se turpe furentum.
Vosque expertes rerum iuvenes,
desinite virum laedere fortem,
namque ex surdo pelagi fluctu
vis erumpet saeva procellae.
Et tu Libyae, Iugurtha, decus,
te et virtutem et fortia facta
ad consilium protinus adde,
ut quo clypeo pectoris olim
regnum et laudem clarus inisti,

palace of Libya, noble in arms and opulence, famous throughout the globe unto this day, will it fall into ruin by the will of fate and its own destiny, or from below, through the violence of men? Does this little flame of hate that has arisen among lords, among brothers, provoke such conflagrations of wrath? Or have the gods, taking this as their reason, decided to destroy the Libyan race utterly as hateful to themselves? You, Juno, you, sister and wife of high-thundering Jove, to whom the affairs of Libya, we believe, are an ever-present concern, and you, Getulian Mars, dear to old Masinissa, I call upon you together, and O all you gods and goddesses, turn to good whatever crimes are being plotted and take away the dreadful fortune that hangs over us! Do not allow your holy shrines, fires, altars and temples to be defiled by the Furies, sword and bloody slaughter of those who rage shamefully amongst themselves! And you youths who lack experience of affairs, stop doing harm to that valorous man, or from the silent flux of the sea a savage storm shall erupt. And you, Jugurtha, pride of Libya, join now your courage and brave deeds to wise counsel, so that your endurance will preserve your people and their glory unharmed, using as

hoc ipso etiam et gentem et famam
illaesam tibi patiens serves.
Gravia in castris Marteque saevo
passum atque hostem ferre furentem
suetum, levibus levium offensis
iuvenum dedecet acre moveri.
Aspera primum nosse subire est
regia virtus, regia virtus.
Satus Alcmena caelum didicit
petere et gravia et multa ferendo.
Quin et Iuppiter ipse tacendo
quam terribili fulmine quasso
grandia solus longe exequitur.
Perfer igitur pectore duro,
perfer dum mox monitu divum
secum indoleant impia facta
iuvenes. Nihil est certius usquam,
nihil adnexum magis est rebus
quam ut poeniteat quemque admissi.
Perfer, siquidem deerit nusquam
ne quem lateat quanto stomacho
etiam possis ipse moveri.

: V :

Polymites, Chorus, et Nuncius

Po. Metus an dolor vexet magis mortalium
animos apud me non quidem constat satis.
Ita me vel invitum novae deum minae
exterritum ante ora positae longe premunt.

shield the same moral qualities that once distinguished you as you embarked upon kingship and glory. It is shameful for one who has borne the hard life of the camps and cruel Mars and is used to the rage of enemies to become embittered by the frivolous offenses of frivolous youths. To know how to endure adversity is a royal virtue—a royal virtue! The seed of Alcmena[36] learned how to climb to heaven by enduring many hard labors. Indeed, what great deeds does Jupiter himself, alone and from far off, achieve when without utterance he shakes his terrifying thunderbolt. Endure, then, with firm resolve! Endure, since soon at the gods' command the youths will repent of their unholy deeds. Nothing ever is more certain, nothing more inherent in the nature of things, than that every man should repent of his guilty deeds. Endure, since it will never be hidden from anyone how angry even you can become.

: V :

Polymites, Chorus and Messenger

Polymites. Whether fear or sorrow torments the souls of mortals more is not evident to me. So these new threats from the gods, placed for a long time before my eyes, oppress and terrify me in spite of myself.

Ch. O Polymites, o et interpres deum,
quid est quod apportas novi?
Po. Libyae luem,
siqua est malis adhibenda portentis fides.
Ch. Virtute consilioque praestans ac potens,
similis tibi vir frontem ubi suam gravem
portendit, arduas adesse res liquet.
Po. O patria, patria, sic ne sacrarum aedium
insigne culmen turbine avulsum ruit?
Ex ultimo aenei colossi vertice
lateque fuseque albicantes ignium
arsere flammae. Fertur et formiceis
populis vagis horrere pulvinar deum.
Ruptisque vinclis, taurus excaepto fugax
cervice ferro cessit ex ara petens
cruore sparsos regios iuvenes suo.
Quin etiam Hyempsal ipse, prodiens domo
pollice sub illiso moleste limiti,
faciem in suam pronus propere lapsus gemit.
Incendiariaque avis alta a porticu
volitans patrum simulacra polluit aurea.
Nu. Accursito ut vatem deumque interpretem
hunc certiorem Polymitem de novis
mirisque rebus ordine faciam celer.
Po. Meliora superi!
Nu. Res inauditas fero.
Po. Malo malum congruit.
Nu. At emori expedit,
o Polymites.
Po. Quid ita?
Nu. Tanta nos mala
coram obsident.
Po. Imo et quidem vel maxime

Chorus. O Polymites, O interpreter of the gods, what news do you bring us?

Polymites. The ruin of Libya, if any trust is to be placed in evil portents.

Chorus. When a man like you, outstanding in virtue and wisdom, makes augury of an ominous brow, it's clear that adversity is at hand.

Polymites. O my country, my country, is it thus that the famous pinnacles of your sacred temples fall, knocked loose by a whirlwind? From the crown of the bronze colossus there bursts forth fires, blazing white, visible afar off. It is said also that the couch of the gods bristled with swarms of ants. A bull with an axe through its neck broke its chains and fled the altar, chasing the royal youths who were splashed with its blood. Nay, Hiempsal himself too, leaving his house, stubbed his toe painfully on the threshold[37] and instantly fell flat on his face and groaned. The firebird, flying from a lofty portico, has polluted the golden statues of our ancestors. [*A messenger arrives*]

Messenger. I hasten to inform the seer and interpreter of the gods, Polymites, speedily of new and extraordinary events.

Polymites. May the gods grant better omens!

Messenger. I bring news about unheard-of things.

Polymites. Bad goes with bad.

Messenger. Better to die, O Polymites.

Polymites. Why?

Messenger. So many evils besiege us close by.

Polymites. Rather, it's better to survive now most of all, so that by enduring evil you may at last become the more used to conquering it.

superesse nunc expedit, ut inde vincere
malum ferendo denique assuescas magis.
Nu. O te virum fortem, ipse si factis tibi
aeque atque dictis es!
Po. Etenim ex dictis probe
egisse discimus. At quid apportas novi?
Nu. Iras deum: nam busta patrum regia
sanctaque sepulcra sponte aperta ex ultimis
imisque sedibus usque tertii Iovis
dedere gemitum ac iurgio altercarier
circum theatra larvulas visas ferunt.
En et sacelli veteris obversas fores
lemures tenere laremque regium deum
crepitu strepentique sonitu triclinia
cuncta labefactare atque mixtim sedibus
ultro citro mutatis Penates propalam
migrasse, multaque alia tetra atque horrida
et visa et audita optimi patres ferunt.
Po. Vos quaeso me, o proceres, labans ne corruam
tenete: ruo, ruo. Quippe spiritus fugit,
totumque nervi animique deficiunt. Humi
consternor et oculi et genua fluunt simul:
tantus dolor metus ve me rerum tenet.
Nu. Hinc illud est, o Polymites, quod solet
dici: viros doctos, ut es tu, fortiter
de rebus asperis ferendis dicere,
nescisse tamen adversa, sicut caeteri
homines solent, non ferre tandem molliter.
Verum quid est quod pro re agendum censeas?
Po. Votis deos mox esse placandos reor,
lustranda passim templa, iustitium urbibus
ubilibet indicendum; et inde ego hinc simul

Messenger. O you brave man—if your deeds are equal to your words!

Polymites. Indeed it is from words that we learn how to act well. But what news do you bring?

Messenger. The wrath of the gods! The royal graves of our fathers and the holy sepulchers have opened of their own accord, and up from the final and lowest seats of the third Jove[38] they sent up a groan, and they say ghosts have been seen wrangling by the theatres. Look! Specters occupy the open doors of an ancient shrine, and the royal household god with a banging and crashing sound knocks down all the couches. In broad day the Penates have left their abode and fled in confusion; many other foul and horrid sights and sounds are reported by our venerable elders.

Polymites. O nobles, please, I'm tottering, hold me up! I fall, I fall! [*He collapses*] Surely my spirit is fleeing, and my sinews and soul failing utterly! I am felled to the ground; my eyes flow with tears and my knees grow weak: such is the pain and fear of events that possesses me.

Messenger. It is for this reason, Polymites, it is customary to say that learned men like you speak bravely about enduring difficulties, but in the end, like the rest of mankind, do not know how to avoid cowardice amid adversity. But what do you think we should do?

Polymites. I think we must placate the gods with prayers immediately. The temples should be purified everywhere, and the administration of justice should be suspended in every city. Now

secedo, me quo linteis sacris parem.
Vos et sequimini. Supplices movent deos!

Discordia et Perfidia

Di. Confecta pulchre res mihi ex sententia est.
Nam me Invidia mater Herebo accitam ultimo
complexa dudum et suavio libans suo:
'O,' inquit, 'omne, o unicum decus meum,
Discordia, modo prebeas te ipsam mihi
facilem atque morigeram! Opus est ad id rei
quam dignitatis gratia meae paro.
Genus hoc enim Numidiae et tumidum et ferox
et insolens odi. Id quidem cum caeteras
ob res tum eo quod Ambitio dea, quam unice
perisse cupio, a se recepta splendidis
colitur honoribus, aureo praestans gradu.
Proinde decretum est apud me funditus
delere gentem. Fuerit officium tuum
matri obsequi praesertim in hac causa mea,
qua, si sit opus, equidem et mori, ut tandem meo
satis furori fiat, audens expetam.'
Haec ubi parens me mea precatur lachrymans,
per Styga, per infernas paludes, per grave
pallentis atrae noctis horrendum caput
iuravi et obstrinxi volens pro viribus
me prorsus acturam, mea ut noscat parens
quid ego sibi a me iure deberi putem,
quidve artibus meis in hominum denique
possim luem Discordia. Ergo ex abdito
Orco mihi socios truces ad horridum
coexequendum facinus eductos agens
exercui ac passim pallantes late agros
tectaque furore et pessima opplevi lue.

I depart to dress myself in the sacred linens. Follow me! Suppliants move the gods! [*They depart; Discord arrives from Orcus*]

Discord and Perfidy

Discord. The plan has been executed beautifully, just as I wished. For my mother Envy, having summoned me from the depths of Erebus, embraced me just now, and kissing me says, "O Discord, my whole pride and joy, show yourself now to be propitious and obliging toward me! I need your help in a plan I'm hatching that touches my honor. For I hate the pride, ferocity and insolence of this Numidian race. Among other reasons, I hate them because the goddess Ambition, whom above all others I would like to see dead, has been welcomed by them and is worshipped with splendid honors, as preeminent on the golden stairway. So I have decreed that the race should be wiped out utterly. Your duty will be, above all, to obey your mother in this affair of mine, for which, if need be, I would dare seek out even death, so that at last I may satiate my wrath." When my mother implored these things of me tearfully, I swore by the Styx, by the lakes of hell, and by the grave, dreadful head of bloodless, dark night. I swore and bound myself willingly that I would do this to the best of my ability, so that my mother would know what I reckoned I rightly owed her, or what destruction I, Discord, could wreak upon mankind with my arts. Thus from the hidden recesses of Orcus I have marched out ferocious companions in order to execute this horrible crime, and I have deployed them as they wander, pillaging hither and yon, filling the fields and houses far and wide with terror and the worst kind of destruction. [*Discord sees Perfidy coming*] But behold Perfidy,

Sed ecce Perfidia uti prona est ad scelus!
Viden quibus se se dolis, qua fronte, quo
vultu atque gestu penitus ostentat piam?
En iri obindutam aurea ferro igneque
malo et veneno subter armatam deam,
quae quidem hominum sensim per astum ambit greges.

Pe. Quae facto opus fuere belle exegimus.
Nam res eo ducta est loci ut satellites
noctu Iugurthae in Hyempsalis domum dolis
irruperint illicque diversi ocyus
regem frequentes quaeritant, internecant.
Alii oscitantis dormientisque obvios
omnes et impetu et mucrone competunt,
mactant et inversos tenus sternunt solo.
Scrutari et alii abdita, alii diffringere
clausa loca non cessant; domusque omnis simul
cadentium gemitu et fragore et aspero
plagis tumultu exterrita intus volvitur.
Tandem repertum Hyempsalem opprimunt, caput
ferro amputant. Res hunc igitur acta in modum est.
Ego nunc et ad comites revertor ut exequar
ex instituto reliqua, ut hinc et plenius
vestram libidinem expleam. Adducam mihi
et Inopiam et Furtum et Rapinam concitas,
quarum opera huic calamitas genti magis
magisque dura sit.

Di. Ergo matura.

Pe. Obsequor.

Di. Ego vero ad Invidiam parentem pervolo.

Phenissa, Phytonissa, Matronae, Nuncii duo

Phe. Ite io, matronae, et sacrum et opacum in nemus
io demus hunc celebrem simul Baccho diem!

poised for wickedness! Do you see the tricks, the expressions and gestures she uses to make a parade of her faithfulness? Lo, the goddess goes about dressed outwardly in gold, but underneath she is armed with a sword, fire and evil poison; she cleverly circles around the flocks of men without attracting their notice.

Perfidy. We have accomplished beautifully what we had to do. For the plot has been brought to the point that henchmen of Jugurtha, having through deceit broken into the house of Hiempsal by night, from there quickly spread out in packs to find the king, spreading slaughter. Others, meeting with yawning and sleeping men, fall upon them all with drawn swords and kill them, throwing their bodies face down on the ground. Others search ceaselessly for secret boltholes, while others break into locked places. The whole house is terrified, enveloped in the groaning of the fallen, the clash of swords and bitter tumult. At last they find Hiempsal and kill him, cutting off his head with a sword. In this way the plan has been realized. Now I am rejoining my companions to follow through on the rest of the plan, so as more fully to satisfy your lust. I shall bring with me Poverty, Theft, and Rapine once I rouse them; with their help the calamity should cause ever more suffering for this people.

Discord. Then make haste.

Perfidy. I obey.

Discord. For my part, I fly to my mother Envy. [*They depart*]

A Phoenician Woman, Phitonissa, Matrons, and two Messengers

Phoenician Woman. Come matrons, io![39] into the holy, shady grove, io! and let us together consecrate this day to Bacchus! Io!

Io Bacche, formose io matrone io!
Tu flamen aereae Tonantis coniugi,
matri deum tu, Galle, plaudito Cybeli.
Vos et pudicae virgines mecum lybes
patrios deos placate votis thureque,
quatite io thyrsos, quatite pulchro deo.
Simul io matrone, io Bacche inclite!
Phy. Io Libes, Libes, io parens, parens,
Ditique Manibusque litandum tibi!
Ma. Ferale Phytonissae abigite omen, dei.
Phe. Quid penditis, matronae? Agite Baccho diem
sacrum, agite festum, io agite Bacho diem!
Phy. Io Libes, io Libes, misere Libes,
ululatibus luctuque complenda est dies.
Phe. Me miseram! Id omen horridum quemnam petit?
Nu. Qui nuncium, prout fertur, apportat malum,
is, commodus etiam si eat, molestus est.
Quid inde agam nescio. Ne vero non feram
nati ad parentem immane discrimen sui,
ut, siquid opis habet, peroccurrat malis?
Ma. Et quid is Hyempsalis haesitans venit puer?
Nu. Tibi filium gravi in periclo nuncio,
o mater, esse. Nanque noctu vi aedium
fractis foribus intro satellites globis
quaque irruentes vulnere et caede et lue
totam penitus Hyempsalis vexant domum.
Stant lubrici undantesque scalarum omnium
cruore fuso alte gradus ac undique
strepitu atque fremitu tecta et una omnis domus
tremit et suum strage intus atra congemit.
At sibi suis non prorsus iratis diis:

Bacchus, io! beautiful matrons, io! You, Gallus, priest of the heavenly wife of the Thunderer, of the mother of the gods, give you praise to Cybele![40] And you, modest maidens of Libya, placate with me our ancestral gods with prayers and incense. Shake, io, your thyrsi,[41] shake them for the beautiful god. And, io! matrons, io! glorious Bacchus!

Phitonissa. Io! Libyan women, Libyan women, io! mother, mother, we must sacrifice to Dis and to the shades of the dead!

Matrons. Dispel the deadly omen of Phitonissa, O god!

Phoenician Woman. Why do you hesitate, matrons? Celebrate the day for Bacchus! Celebrate this sacred feast, io! celebrate the day for Bacchus!

Phitonissa. Io! Libyan women, io! Libyan women, wretched women of Libya, the day should be filled with wailing and grief.

Phoenician Woman. Woe is me! At whom does that dreadful omen aim? [*Messenger arrives.*]

Messenger. It is said that whoever brings bad news, even if his coming is useful, is unwelcome. So I don't know what to do. Should I tell the mother of her son's disaster, so that, if she has the strength, she may ride out these misfortunes?

Matrons. And why does Hiempsal's slave boy come with such hesitation?

Messenger. I report to you that your son, O mother, is in grave danger. For at night a group of henchmen broke down the doors of Hiempsal's house by force, and rushing into it in a mob, ravaged the whole house with blood and slaughter and destruction! The steps of every stairway are slippery, wet with the oceans of blood that have been shed, and on every side the whole house is atremble with uproar and commotion, bewailing its losses in the black slaughter within. Yet the gods were not entirely filled with wrath, for Hiempsal escaped the heaps of

cadentium ex cumulis Hyempsal diffugit.
Tu, mater, his praesentibus rebus metu
luctuque secluso tibique consule.
Ma. Oe miseram matrem! Sed eccum et alterum
Hyempsalis properantem et anxium intimum.
Nu. O tempora, o mores! Ita ne frater necem
fratri parat? Ubi nam, ubi erit, o cives, fides?
Ubi pietas apud homines tandem sita,
hanc si integram non iura servant sanguinis?
Tibi, o miserrima omnium mater, tuos
unde aut inibis aut acerbos finies
luctus?
Ma. Quid et tu denique apportas mali?
Nu. Iugurtha herum ferro he extinxit meum.
Ma. He he he! Adeste, accurrite, he succedite,
lapsamque prae dolore et exanguem solo
stratam parentem tollite hanc in regiam
funestam et infaustam domum. Vos, o probi
cives, bonis fatis, bonis et moribus,
iam bene valete, et quid nefandum ac pestilens
malum invidia possit per haec agnoscite.

the slaughtered men. You, mother—this being the state of affairs—put away your fear and grief and think of yourself.

Matrons. Alas, miserable mother! [*A second messenger approaches*] But, look: a second associate of Hiempsal hastens anxiously toward us.

Messenger. O what times! O what moral standards! Is this the way that brother plots the death of brother? Where, O citizens, where will loyalty be found, where among men shall we ever find piety, if the laws of blood kinship do not preserve it inviolate? O most wretched of mothers, where will your bitter grief begin or end?

Matrons. And what evil tidings do *you* bring?

Messenger. Alas, Jugurtha has killed my master with his sword. [*She collapses*]

Matrons. Woe, woe, woe! Come here quickly and help! Take his mother: she's collapsed from grief and has fallen senseless to the ground; carry her into the royal palace, that house of mourning and misfortune. [*They carry her away*] You, respectable citizens, with your good fortune and character, now farewell, and learn from these events how wicked and pestilent an evil Envy can be.

MARCELLINI VERARDI CAESENATIS

FERNANDUS SERVATUS

Caroli Verardi Caesenatis pontificii cubicularii in Fernandum Servatum ad reverendissimum patrem Petrum Medozam archiepiscopum Toletanum, Hispaniarum primatem ac Sanctae Romanae Ecclesiae cardinalem praefatio

1 Cum accepissem, praesul optime, Fernandum invictissimum Hispaniarum regem, dum Barcinone conventus ageret ac iura populis daret, a vesano nescio quo ferro petitum vitae discrimen adiisse, tam atroci nuntio percussus, coepi non sine admiratione mecum ipse cogitare quonam modo divina providentia cuncta gubernante fieri potuisset, ut vir tantae virtutis ac probitatis in tam dirum luctuosumque casum incideret. Ac me multa cum animo meo agitantem ratio ipsa in hanc potissimum sententiam duxit, ut existimarem humani generis hostes, deo permittente, nefarium illud facinus esse molitos. Legeram namque saepe in sacris litteris daemonum invidiam potius in viros probos quam facinorosos saevire suasque nocendi artes exercere consuevisse, quippe quod hos iam pro suis satellitibus ac ministris habeat, illos vero sui (ut ita dixerim) Tartarei regni acerrimos infestissimosque hostes experiatur.

2 Itaque cum Fernandus nihil ageret, nihil moliretur, nihil postremo dies noctesque cogitaret nisi quae ad verae fidei amplificationem et summi dei cultum pertinerent, mihi non modo vero simillimum, sed et certissimum visum est daemonum consilio et instigatione factum esse, ut vesanus ille regem ferro necare conatus sit. Quippe cum mens eius nullis artibus aut dolis, non illecebris

MARCELLINO VERARDI OF CESENA

FERDINAND PRESERVED

Preface of Carlo Verardi of Cesena, of the Pontifical Chamber, to the Ferdinand Preserved, addressed to the Most Reverend Father Pedro Mendoza, Archbishop of Toledo, Primate of Spain, and Cardinal of the Holy Roman Church

When I learned, best of prelates, that Ferdinand, the invincible king of the Spanish, during an assembly at Barcelona where he was dispensing laws to his people, had been attacked by an unknown madman, whose sword had endangered the king's very life, I was deeply shaken by this shocking news and began to wonder how it could possibly happen, Divine Providence governing all things, that a man of such great virtue and rectitude could fall into so grievous and dire a misadventure. And as I turned the various possibilities over in my mind, reason itself led me to conclude that, with God's permission, the enemies of the human race had plotted that wicked deed. Indeed, I have often read in the Bible how the malice of demons usually rages much more against upright men than against the wicked, that it is against the good that they aim their destructive arts. This is naturally the case because demonic malice already has control of the wicked, who act as its satellites and ministers, but it has found the upright to be the bitterest and most hostile enemies of the infernal kingdom. 1

Thus, since Ferdinand did nothing else, planned nothing else, and day and night thought of nothing else but what pertained to the aggrandizement of the true Faith and the worship of God on high, it seemed to me not only very likely but certain that this madman had tried to kill the king with his sword thanks to the counsel and instigation of demons. Indeed, since the king's will could be turned from the path of right and of holy purpose by no 2

voluptatum, non terrore, non minis, non denique ullis laboribus aut capitis periculis a recto cursu ac sancto instituto deflecti posset, ea una diabolicae fraudi ad sua regna tuenda restabat via, ut scilicet de medio tolleretur et sua nece alios principes qui fortasse
3 eius vestigia in posterum essent imitaturi deterreret. Divina vero providentia iccirco id fuisse permissum existimari debet, ut regis virtus enitesceret et inter adversa illustrior fieret, siquidem ut a sacris doctoribus traditum est, virtus in infirmitate perficitur, sine hoste marcescit. Et prospera etiam sapientum animos nonnunquam transversos agunt a recto; adversa viros explorant atque ad usum virtutis exercent. Et propterea solitus est eleganter dicere Demetrius philosophus nihil sibi infoelicius videri eo cui nihil unquam evenisset adversi. Non tamen daemonum impietas ad necem usque saevire permissa est. Eorum enim potestatem constat dei voluntate quodammodo ligatam esse, neque illis licere pro animi libidine in bonos viros suas nocendi artes exercere, sed eatenus duntaxat quatenus eorum crudelitas et insidiae sint ad exercitia et corroboramenta virtutis, non ad eius interitum. Indignum etiam divinae clementiae visum est ut vir tam sanctus, rex tam iustus, tam pius, tam bene de omni religione Christiana meritus inhonesto mortis genere interiret, et propterea eum ad magnas et praeclaras res gerendas reservans coelesti ope ab impiis manibus liberavit.

4 Haec igitur mihi mente agitanti visa est sane digna materia in qua praeclara quaeque ingenia desudarent. Itaque ut ipse quoque, quoad vires meae ferrent, regiae gloriae non deessem, sumpto calamo totam eam digessi et personis variis quas induxi loquentes distinxi, quo res non solum lecta sed etiam oculis, quorum sensus in nobis acerrimus est, spectata plus haberet et voluptatis et gratiae. Cumque iam mihi, ut Nasonis verbis utar,

devices or deceits, by no voluptuous snares, by neither fear nor threats nor struggles nor even peril to his life, there remained only one way for devilish guile to preserve its rule, and that was to remove him from the scene entirely, and by his death to deter other princes who might in future be inclined to follow in his footsteps. But it should be reckoned that Divine Providence permitted this 3
to happen in order that the king's virtue might shine forth and be rendered the more illustrious by adversity, it being handed down by holy teachers that virtue is perfected by adversity and withers without an enemy. Sometimes prosperity may divert even the minds of the wise from the right path, while adversity puts men to the test and trains them in the practice of virtue. Hence the elegant saying of the philosopher Demetrius that nothing seemed to him more unfortunate than the complete absence of misfortune.[1] Yet the impiety of demons was not allowed to rage to the point of actual killing. It is evident that their power is bound in a certain way by the will of God, and they are not permitted to practice their noxious arts against good men to the extent that they might wish, but only insofar as their cruelty and deceit may act to train and strengthen virtue, not destroy it. It also seemed a thing unworthy of the divine clemency that a king so holy and just and so well-deserving of the Christian religion should die so ignoble a death, and on that account divine aid saved him from the hands of the impious, preserving him for great and famous deeds.

Hence, considering all this, the subject matter seemed to me to 4
call for the exertion of every noble intellect. And so that I myself too, as far as my powers allowed, should not fail the glory of His Majesty, I took up my pen and summarized the whole affair, assigning speaking parts to the various persons involved. Thus one might not simply read of the affair but gaze upon it with the eyes—the sharpest of our senses—making the experience more attractive and pleasurable. And since I may use of myself the words of Ovid,

si quis erat dicendi carminis usus,
deficiat sitque minor factus inerte situ,

fungarque hoc tempore Horatiano more,

vice cotis, acutum
reddere quae ferrum valet, exors ipsa secandi,

materiam ipsam Marcellino nepoti et alumno meo, qui poesi mirifice delectatur, versu describendam poeticisque coloribus, salva rerum dignitate ac veritate, pingendam exornandamque tradidi. Quod is plane assecutus videtur. Nam ita res inter utrumque temperata est ut cum veritate ac religione maximopere consentiret et a poesi — cuius auctore Lactantio officium est 'ut ea quae vere gesta sunt, in alias species obliquis figurationibus cum decore aliquo conversa traducat' — non penitus abhorreret.

5 Cum autem hic adessent regii oratores, Berardinus Carvaial Pacensis et Iohannes Medina Astoricensis praesules, quorum uterque cum summa bonitate ac prudentia singularem in omni scientiarum genere doctrinam coniunxit, eorum acerrimo iudicio opusculum ipsum iam ad calcem perductum subiiciendum putavi. Quibus argumentum et carmen laudantibus, hortantibusque ut pro honore et gloria inclyti regis res in lucem deduceretur, eam, ut comoediae seu tragoediae solent, iisdem suffragantibus agi recenserique curavi. Potest enim haec nostra, ut *Amphitruonem* suum Plautus appellat, tragicocomoedia nuncupari, quod personarum dignitas et regiae maiestatis impia illa violatio ad tragoediam, iucundus vero exitus rerum ad comoediam pertinere videantur. Tanto autem favore et attentione ab ipso pontifice maximo pluribusque cardinalibus ac praesulibus (ut inferiores taceam) spectata est, ut facile appareret eos omnes, vel sola fama virtutum Fernandi regis illectos, omnia quae ad eius laudem dicerentur aut fierent

whatever skill I had in speaking song
is failing, and diminished by idleness and neglect[2]

and at the present time serve the function, in the manner of Horace

of the whetstone, able to make sharp
the sword's edge, itself unable to cut,[3]

I handed the material over to my nephew and protégé Marcellino, who takes marvelous pleasure in poetry, so that he might turn it into verse, painting and embellishing it, while at the same time preserving its nobility and truth. This he has plainly achieved. For he has balanced with considerable success the claims of truth and religion with those of poetry, whose business, according to Lactantius, is "to take true events and convert them beautifully into other representations using oblique figural patterns."[4]

Since the royal ambassadors, Bernardino Carvajal, Bishop of 5
Badajoz, and Johannes Ruiz de Medina, Bishop of Astorga,[5] were here [in Rome], both of whom united great goodness and wisdom with extraordinary learning in all branches of learning, I decided to submit to their penetrating judgment the little work which by now had been completed. They praised the argument and the poem, and encouraged us to publish it to the honor and glory of the famous king. So I took pains to have it passed in review, as tragedies and comedies usually are, and to have it acted with their support. For this work of ours can be called a "tragicomedy," as Plautus calls his *Amphitruo*,[6] because the rank of the characters and the impious attack on His Majesty point to tragedy, while the happy ending belongs to comedy. The play was viewed with great favor and close attention by the pope, numerous cardinals and leading prelates (to say nothing of the lower clergy), and it was readily apparent how they all, drawn in by the fame alone of Ferdinand's virtues, listened and watched intently all that was said or

studiose audire et cernere atque, ut acerbo eius casu ingemuissent, ita sanitate reddita plurima voluptate laetitiaque affici.

6 Hoc igitur opusculum, quod *Fernandi Servati* titulo praenotavi ut regio nomine insigni tum gratius in studiosorum manus deveniret, cui potissimum dicarem, nullus te, venerande pontifex, magis idoneus occurrebat, siquidem haec, quae ad laudem veramque gloriam istorum Christianissimorum principum, quos tu summa fide et observantia colis, spectant, et in quibus is tibi locus, qui et dignitatem et qua apud illos vales gratiam decebat, assignatus est, iucundo nimirum animo laetoque vultu excipies, et tua auctoritate, qua polles plurimum, facile ab invidorum morsibus tueri poteris. Quod ut facias, reverendissime pater, te etiam atque etiam rogo.

Ad pontificem maximum prologus

O pater, o pastor, mundi fidissime custos,
qui portas summi reseras et claudis Olympi,
ne pigeat nobis aures praestare benignas
et placidos vultus ut libera corda timore
Fernandi eximium nomen laudesque loquantur,
infera quem ferro dum turba necare pararet,
servavit superi clementia summa Tonantis,

done to his praise; they groaned at his bitter misfortune and were overjoyed when he was restored to health.

I have therefore entitled this little work *Ferdinand Preserved*, so 6
that it might come into the hands of learned men with greater favor under that famous royal name. And I decided that no more suitable dedicatee could be found than yourself, Most Reverend Archbishop, because these matters redound to the praise and true glory of those most Christian princes, to whom you devote yourself with complete sincerity and respect; because you have yourself gladly accepted the role you were assigned in the play, a role that befits your rank and the favor you enjoy with the king and queen; and because your powerful authority can protect the play from the criticism of the envious. And that is what I entreat you to do, Most Reverend Father, again and again.

CHARACTERS

Pluto, *god of the Underworld*
Alecto, Megaera, Tisiphone — *the Furies*
Cardinal Pedro Mendoza
Ferdinand II, *king of Spain*
Isabella, *queen of Spain*
St. James[7]
Ruffus,[8] *the assassin*
Nurse
Chorus

Prologue to the Pope

O father, O shepherd, most faithful guardian of the world, who locks and unlocks the gates of high Olympus, let us willingly present friendly ears and calm faces, so that, with hearts free from fear, Ferdinand's exceptional reputation and praises may be expressed. When a hellish throng prepared to kill him with the sword, the high mercy of the Thunderer above preserved him, so that, under

eius ut auspiciis, rerum te sceptra tenente,
immensum Christi volitent vexilla per orbem.

Pluto ad Furias

O spes Tartareae sedis regnique profundi,
Eumenides, quondam (memini) mecum ipse querebar
et subitus tumidas concoepi saepius iras,
concutiens caput horrendum, quod saepe viderem
nescio quos nostris popularibus indere mentem
ut nos desererent, iactantes ditia et ampla
dona piis tribui, sceleratis infera regna.
Sed tamen ista levi fuerant hortamina damno;
vix quota pars praestare fidem nam vocibus horum
noverat, assuetis pergens confidere rebus!
At nunc res agitur maior: nam tota laborant
regna nisi, audaces, vestra succurritis arte.
Hesperiae rex ille potens (nam vera fatebor,
sit licet hostis atrox nobisque inimica retractet
strenuus arma diu) properat confinia nostra
imperio domitare suo, nostrosque clientes
insequitur veteri denudans arva colono,
non aliter quam si victor foret iste secundus
Amphitryoniades, cui nunc Stheneleia proles
imperet haec duro monitu Iunonis iniquae.
Quid memorem quotiens nostra de gente triumphos
rettulerit, quotiens spoliis remearit honustus,
innumera iuvenum comitatus utrinque caterva?
Quis nescit quotiens hostili sanguini campos

His auspices and Your universal scepter, the banners of Christ might fly throughout the illimitable globe.

: I :

Pluto, Alecto, Megaera, Tisiphone

Pluto addresses the Furies. O hope of Tartarus and of the kingdom deep below, O Eumenides, I remember in times past complaining to myself and swelling with throbbing pulses of anger, shaking my frightening head, because I would often see some man or other trying to persuade our popular following to desert us, boasting of the rich gifts that would be given to the pious and the infernal kingdom that awaited the wicked. But those exhortations had as yet done little harm, for how small was the proportion who had learned to trust those voices, while most continued to rely on their usual resources! But now a greater threat has arisen, for all our kingdoms are in distress, unless, bold ones, you aid us with your arts. That powerful king of the West—for I shall speak the truth, even if he is a terrifying enemy and has been strenuously resisting us in arms for a long time—that king hastens to dominate our borders with his own empire and persecutes our own clients, stripping the fields of their ancient settlers, no otherwise than if he had become a hero, a second Hercules, a man whom now the offspring of Sthenelus[9] should be commanding in accordance with the harsh injunction of unjust Juno. Why should I recall the many times this king has earned triumphs over our people, how many times he has returned home laden with spoils, thronged on every side by innumerable troops of young men? Who does not know how many times he has soaked our fields with the blood of

sparserit atque amnes mutare coegerit undas
et se mirari solito non ire colore?
Nec contentus adhuc nuper Magmede repulso
sede sua, veteres proscindens undique leges,
Baudelique meo foedissima sub iuga misso,
Granatam domuit, victorque intravit in urbem,
improbus, et populum dictis parere coegit.
Optima nonne mihi dudum pars cesserat orbis?
Africa nonne mei fuerat latissima iuris?
Nonne Asiam nostris dederam parere ministris
Europaeque bonam partem? Lateque vagabar
et totum nostro molibar subdere mundum
servitio, vestra confisus fraude dolisque.
At nunc Fernando contraria signa ferente,
pro dolor! Europa iandudum cessimus omni.
Nec dubium quin hic Nabatheum subiuget orbem
Eoasque domos, proprio nisi forte labore
nunc mihi fertis opem, qua vobis bella movere
innumerasque datur gentis ad proelia ferre
et pacem turbare gravisque ciere tumultus.
Este precor memores, o summa potentia Ditis,
pacificas quotiens urbes ad bella vocatis
concordesque domos, quotiens discerpere mater
lymphata per vos properat sua pignora mente.
Ergo agite, o nigri spes et tutela Baratri!
Per Stygias undas, stagna intemerata, rogamus:
artibus innumeris foecundum vertite pectus
nostraque quae pereunt defendite regna, sorores.
Consilio parili vos hic decernite, quaeso,
qua regis furor hic possit ratione teneri.
Sic nos securo repetemus pectore sedes
Tartareas caecasque domos noctemque profundam.

his enemies, how he has compelled our rivers to change their stream, marveling to see them flow with a new color? Still unsatisfied after driving Mohammed from his territory, shattering ancient laws on every side, and sending my Boabdil[10] under the yoke of foul disgrace, he has subdued Granada and entered the city victorious, the scoundrel, and forced the people to obey his dictates. Had not the best part of the globe long been ceded to me? Wasn't broad Africa once under my law? Had I not determined that Asia should obey our ministers, and a great part of Europe? I was roaming widely and plotting to subject the whole world to our dominion, having put my trust in your deceit and your stratagems. But now with Ferdinand bearing the standard against us (O the pain of it!), for a long time now we have given up all Europe. There is, indeed, no doubt that this man will subjugate the Arabian world and the eastern dwelling places, unless perchance, with great effort on your part, you bring me those resources wherewith you cause wars and drive countless peoples into battle, disturb the peace and stir up grievous tumults. I pray that you be mindful, O highest power of Dis, how many times you provoked peaceful cities and harmonious homes into war, how many times with frenzied mind a mother rushed to tear her own children to pieces on your account. Therefore, come, O black hopes and guardians of the infernal regions! Through the Stygian waters, the inviolable waters of Hell, we call upon you: ponder within your fecund breasts your countless wiles, and defend our kingdoms, sisters, which are perishing. Please decide here with equal counsel on a course of action whereby the fury of this king may here be held in check. Thus may we return again with carefree heart to the realms of Tartarus, our lightless homes, our deep night.

Alecto

Dux Herebi, venerande pater, cui turba silentum
tristis et immensi famulantur regna Baratri,
quanquam sollicita non vanos mente timores
concipis et merito tantum compescere regem
moliris nostro minitantem vincula regno,
at desiste tamen gravibus tua pectora curis
sollicitare: metu tristi molimine nostro
liber eris. Nihil est gemitu quod pectora lasses.
Concutiam diro foecundam crimine mentem
qua valeo mortale genus confundere et orbem.
Mutato faciam soli tibi serviat ille
consilio solique manus tibi tradat et arma.
Ergo age securus per me, ad tua Tartara migra,
teque sinu carae moestum solare maritae.

Megera

O soror Alecto, gravibus redimita colubris,
reddere sollicitam mentem cui Fata dederunt
et stimulis homines deflectere tramite recto,
horrisona tu voce quidem nunc multa tyranno
Tartareae sedis promittis et impia facta.
Sed quae certa tuae tandem sententia menti
sederit; expedias breviter paucisque resolve.
Nam nos ambiguo sensu varioque tenemur,
quo pacto liceat tantum subvertere regem
qui stabili ratione pedes defixerit ambos.

Alecto

O sociae, num vos, quidnam mea pectora possint
horrida, quid valeant lambentes membra Cerastae,
praeterit? An nostrum penitus torpere putatis

Alecto. Leader of Erebus, venerable father, on whom the sad throng of the silent dead and the kingdoms of measureless Hell dance attendance, the fears you conjure up in your agitated mind are not vain ones, and it is right that you strive to rein in this great king who threatens the chains of our kingdom. But stop tormenting your heart with these grave concerns: through our machinations you will be freed from this dismal fear. There is no reason why you should weary your heart with sorrow. I shall stir up my fertile mind to a wicked crime, that mind which is able to confound the human race and the world. Altering his resolve, I shall cause that man to serve you alone and deliver over his arms and forces to you alone. Therefore rest assured on my account, and return to your Tartarean realms; on the breast of your dear wife[11] seek comfort for your melancholy. [*Pluto exits*]

Megaera. O sister Alecto, wreathed in deadly serpents, to whom the Fates have given the power to produce anxiety and by their stings to divert men from the proper path, it is with a terrifying voice, indeed, that you promise many impious deeds to the tyrant of the realm of Tartarus. But that fixed intention of your mind will in the end subside; you must extricate us quickly and find a solution forthwith. For we are thought to be wavering and uncertain in our resolve, and for this reason let us be content with toppling this king, who has planted both feet on stable principles.

Alecto. O my partners, surely it has not escaped your notice what my dreadful heart is capable of, and how great is the power of these limb-licking snake tongues? Do you think the heart deep

pectus? An oblitae quot pestes quotque minaces
mente geram Furias? Cur me Nox atra sinistro
fuderit in tenebras partu rabiemque cruentam
ipse parens Herebus dederit mentemque malignam?
Num totiens dabitur nostro subvertere gentis
concordes fremitu insano, regesque superbos
arte mea potero crudelia ad arma vocare,
nec fas unius fuerit mihi vertere mentem?
Sed, vos germanae, mihi credite: numina testor
inferni patris magni Phlegetontis et undas,
iam faciam pateat, quidnam mea pectora et Hydrae
verbera quid valeant, rabiesque infusa per omne
corpus et undantes spumis furialibus irae.
Huic ego confundam mentem caligine caeca,
et variis tentabo modis, animumque labantem
armata impellam dextra serpentibus atris.
Desistat subito faciam melioribus actis,
deserat et superi sublimia signa Tonantis.
Hinc nostrum cupiet praecedere fervidus agmen
viribus et nostris invadere castra suorum.
Restituet nostro Plutoni quicquid ademit,
Christicolumque omnis late populabitur agros,
instaurans veteres leges, monimenta verendi
Magmedis, quae nunc misere prostrata videmus;
denique, quicquid habet numerosa potentia mundi,
hoc duce (nec fallor) Stygia ditione premetur.

Megera

Non equidem inficior multum, germana, colubras
posse tuas scimusque etiam te crine venena
fundere concusso; scimus tibi pectora late
innumeris perfusa odiis quibus undique saeva
bella movere potes subitosque ciere tumultus.

within me is slow to act? Have you forgotten how many plagues, how many menacing Furies I can deploy? Why did blackest Night give birth to me ominously in the shadows, why did my father Erebus give me a rage for blood and a malicious will? Has it been granted me so often to undermine with insane commotions whole peoples living in concord, shall I be able to summon proud kings to cruel arms through my arts, and yet not have the right to change the mind of a single man? But believe me, sisters, I call to witness the spirit of the Infernal Father and the waters of great Phlegethon that I shall now reveal the power of my breasts and of the Hydra's blows, and madness shall spread through his entire body with waves of furious, foaming wrath. I shall spread confusion in the man's mind with blinding fog, and I shall test him in various ways, striking his tottering mind, my right hand armed with black snakes. I shall cause him at once to abandon his better deeds and to desert the lofty banners of the heavenly Thunderer. Thus he will long fervently to march at the head of our ranks and with our forces to invade the camps of his own men. He shall restore to our Pluto what he has taken from him, and shall devastate far and wide all the lands of the Christ-worshippers, renewing the old laws and the traditions of awesome Mohammed that at present we see to be wretchedly cast down. Finally, whatever power of harmony the world retains will be oppressed by the writ of Hell (and in this I am not deceived) under his leadership.

Megaera. For my part, sister, I do not deny that your snakes are powerful, and we know also that when you shake your locks you pour forth poisons. We know your heart is suffused with numberless hatreds which let you provoke cruel wars on every side and stir up sudden tumults. On your account Pirithoos

Per te Pirithous fugisset Thesea; per te
dilectum fratrem vitasset Castora Pollux
et Piladem infidum quondam vocitasset Orestes;
denique sola tenes scelerum tu quicquid ubique est.
Sed tamen heu frustra, soror, haec molimina dira
mente tibi concepta reor. Sunt irrita crede
consilia. O quotiens comitatu instructa profano
multiplicique dolo circumque nocentibus hydris
hunc hominem volui pervertere ab ordine recto.
Nec valui, quanquam multos ad talia facta
impuleram prius arte mea multosque coegi
in proprios saevire patres vetuique parentes
parcere pignoribus. Quotiens mihi nata parentis
coniugium infandum petiit? Quotiensque furentis
gestare in superos crudelia tela coegi?
Et tamen hunc precibus blandave libidine nunquam,
non precio dirisque minis nulloque periclo,
non solitis stimulis, tacita non fraude movere,
non trepidante metu potui, non artibus ullis.
Sed ne te nimium longo sermone moremur,
crede mihi, citius rapidissima flumina cursum
sistere cernemus solemque micare tenebris
et Phoeben splendere die non ordine recto
quam quis consilio valeat vel fraude profana
hunc hominem a superis convertere ad impia facta.
Quare age, Tisiphone, si quid tibi mente resedit
quo nobis firmare queas fluitantia corda,
anguibus in tergum solito de more reiectis,
prome tuam rabidis tumefactam vocibus iram.

Tisiphone

Non ego Tartareo credar concepta baratro,
ni scierint quodcunque nefas committere nostra

would have fled from Theseus;[12] Pollux shunned his beloved brother Castor;[13] and Orestes would long ago have called Pylades a false friend;[14] in short, you alone control whatever evil exists in the world. Yet nevertheless, sister, alas! I believe these dreadful plans you have conceived are vain; believe me, your plans are useless. O, how often have I assembled my unholy band and with multiple deceits and surrounded by deadly Hydras have I wanted to pervert this man from the path of rectitude. But I never could, despite my previous artfulness in driving many to such acts, in forcing many to use violence against their own fathers, and in forbidding parents from sparing their own children. How many times, because of me, has a daughter sought an accursed mating with a parent? And how many times have I forced enraged men to wield cruel weapons against the gods? Yet still I have not been able to budge this one man by prayers or coaxing lust, nor with bribes nor dire threats nor danger, nor with my usual stimulants, silent deception and fear — no stratagems at all have been successful. But lest we delay overlong in lengthy talk, believe me, we shall see the swiftest rivers stop in their course, the sun gleaming in the darkness and Phoebus running backward across the sky sooner than anyone shall be able by schemes or impious fraud to turn this man away from the gods and toward unholy deeds. So come then, Tisiphone, if you have any idea how to stiffen our inconstant hearts, throw your snakes down your back in the usual way and pour forth your wrath, swollen with their furious hissing.

Tisiphone. No one would believe me to be the offspring of Tartarean Hell if my heart knew not how to commit every kind of

pectora, ni scierit caput hoc confundere coelum,
si iubeant dominus Phlegetontis et infera turba.
Nunc opus aggredior maius quam vertere mentem.
Postquam nil fraudes prosunt, nil dira venena,
nil stimuli tristesque minae, nil blanda voluptas,
non opus est verbis, video, sed sanguine et armis.
Me vocat iste labor. Nihil est quod verbera nostra
non valeant agitare. Mihi est immanius Hydris
ingenium et rapidis fluviorum incertius undis,
acrius Harpyis, multo violentius Haustris.
Hoc onus ergo mihi, totamque relinquite curam.
Iam scio quid Furias deceat, quid pectora nostra.
Per me nunc orbis gemitu reboabit et axis
Hesperius; per me regalia tecta madebunt
sanguine; nunc referam tanto de rege triumphum
vulnere inaudito capite et cervice recisa.

Alecto

O soror, o nostri suprema potentia regis,
funereas, germana, manus nunc porrige nobis.
Oscula iunge, precor. Picei per numina Ditis
pallida iuramus: nihil est quo regna tueri
nostra queas melius. Sic, sic rex iste protervus
non alia ratione potest aut arte domari.
Per te nunc (fateor) solam, germana, repertum est
ars mea quod nunquam potuit nec torva Megera.
Ergo vale, et solers iamdudum perfice coeptum.

Tisiphone sola

Concute, Tisiphone, foecundum concute pectus;
anguiferum commisce caput; reminiscere quantum
saeva pares facinus tendens in Fata deosque
spicula, convolvens Furiali cuncta paratu.

wickedness, if this head knew not how to confound heaven above at the command of the lord of Phlegethon and his infernal throngs. Now I undertake a task greater than changing a man's mind. Since our deceptions are of no avail, nor our dreadful poisons, nor our grim spurs and threats, nor our coaxing pleasures, I see there is need, not for words, but for blood and arms. That is the task that summons me. There is nothing that my whips cannot stir up. My mind is more bestial than the Hydra, more unpredictable than the rivers' rapid flow, more bitter than a Harpy, and more violent by far than the desert wind. This then shall be my burden; abandon all your anxiety. Now I know what course of action will suit the Furies and my heart. At my behest the western orb will now resound with the groaning of its axis; because of me royal palaces will be drenched in blood. Now I shall celebrate a triumph over a great king, thanks to a prodigious wound to his head and a slit throat.

Alecto. O sister, O greatest power of our king, now stretch forth your deadly hands to us, sister. Seal your promise, I pray, with a kiss. We vow it by the pale divinities of pitch-black Dis: there is nothing you can do that will better protect our realm. Yes, yes! There is no other way, no other scheme, that will bring that impudent king to heel! Through you alone now, sister—I confess it—there has been found what never could have been accomplished by my art nor by grim Megaera. Therefore, fare you well, and bring your deep-laid plan skillfully to a conclusion! [*Alecto and Megaera exit*]

Tisiphone. [*Alone*] Tisiphone, stir up, stir up your fecund heart; add to it the power of your snaky head, and remember how great a deed you are plotting as you direct their cruel tongues at the Fates and the gods, while they writhe around all things in

Non opus ignavo nunc est nec inerte ministro,
sed quo non usquam fuerit crudelior alter,
qui sit et humano consuetus sanguine foedas
semper habere manus, qui gestet pectora plena
criminibus diris, qui blando fallere risu
norit et illecebris occultam intexere fraudem.
Obvius ergo mihi, dum sic furibunda pererro.
Quis dabitur? Quisnam? Cui nunc serpentibus atris
pectora confundam stimulemque furore profano,
et quem regalem deducam ad principis aulam,
sanguinis ut cupidus flagransque cupidine regni
regem obtruncatum solio deturbet ab alto?

Eadem Ruffum conspicata

Sed quem tam dirum video liventibus ire
huc oculis variisque genis et sponte furentem
sanguineaque acie properantem? An Ruffus, iniquae
progenies vesana Stygos? Iam verba tenebo
ut bene percipiam quo mentem dirigat omnem.

Ruffus secum

Siccine tranquillam mentem vitamque quietam
esse mihi patiar? Cur dudum a sanguine fuso
cessavere manus? Non haec clementia nobis
convenit; ha, nimium marcescunt membra quiete.
Ocia nunc abeant! Agito crudelia mente,
veh, quibus occurram. Satiabo sanguine ferrum;
mortibus innumeris ditabo Tartara nigra.
Si scelus hic deerit, tentabo sidera coeli
aut violabo diem superis vel bella movebo

furious preparation. You need now no low nor lazy accomplice, but the cruelest man who has ever lived, a man used to dipping his foul hands in human blood, who boasts a heart full of dire crimes, who knows how to deceive with a flattering smile and to weave invisible deceptions into his charms. Well, then, I shall meet him while I wander all about in a rage. Who will be given me? Who, pray, will he be? Whose heart shall I ruin with my black serpents and sting with unholy madness? Whom shall I bring inside the prince's royal court, so that, thirsty for blood and burning with desire for rule, he may butcher the king and cast him down from his lofty throne? [*Ruffus approaches*]

: II :

Tisiphone, Ruffus

Tisiphone. [*Seeing Ruffus*] But what terrifying man with livid eyes and mottled cheeks do I see coming toward me, spontaneously afire with rage, hastening with a bloody stare? Isn't it Ruffus, the mad offspring of unjust Styx? I shall just listen now to his words to understand the direction of his thoughts.

Ruffus. [*To himself*] Should I be letting myself live quietly this way with a calm mind? Why has my hand stopped shedding blood for so long? This virtue of clemency doesn't suit me—ah, my limbs are getting weak from too much peace and quiet. Begone now, times of quiet! Let's think up some cruel deeds I can go out and do, blast it! My sword will drink blood, I'll enrich black Tartarus with numberless dead. If there is no opportunity for crime here, I shall assault the stars of heaven. Either I'll profane the day there or tirelessly provoke wars on the gods

impiger et Ditis furibundus iura tuebor:
haec me facta decent, non vitam ducere inertem.
Nam mihi cur rabiem dederit violenta Megera?
Cur me Tisiphone nutriverit ubere diro?
Tertia monstrarit cognatum haurire cruorem?
Cur proprios letho manus haec robusta parentes,
cur natos dederit, cur fratres curve sorores,
si pia facta iuvant recto deducta tenore?
Cur tamen heu nobis, cur non se tanta facultas
obiicit ut valeam mores ostendere nostros?
Dispereo misere, solitum nisi dextra cruorem
hauriat et virus conceptum pectore fundam.

Tisiphone secum

Aptior haud nobis poterat se offerre minister!
Hic (fateor) longe superat me nempe magistram!
Possidet hic quicquid scelerum possedimus omnes.
Ibo igitur propius coeptumque augebo furorem.

Eadem ad Ruffum

O decus armipotens, o spes, o dulcis alumne,
dic mihi, dic agedum: quid te turpissima dudum
ocia, Ruffe, tenent? Cur sic inglorius annos
exigis et florem vitae consumis inertem,
heu! Tandem cognosce, precor, quid teque tuamque
nunc deceat rabiem. Ne spernas verba, rogamus,
si te prima meo tenerum de matre cadentem
sedula suscepi gremio, si membra refovi
saepe sinu rigido quom fletibus ora rigares,
si tibi materna porreximus ubera voce,
per me si ferrum nosti satiare cruore
undanti et populis crudele intendere lethum.

above and, raging, uphold the rights of Dis. Those are the deeds that suit me, not leading this life of inaction. For why otherwise would violent Megaera have given me such madness? Why would Tisiphone have nourished me at her dreadful breast? Why would Alecto have taught me to shed the blood of my kinsmen? Why did this strong hand put to death my own parents, children, brothers, or sisters if holy deeds conducted rightly were of any advantage? Why, alas, is a great opportunity not put in my way to let me display my depravity? I shall despair in misery if I may not shed the blood I am used to shedding with my right hand, if I may not discharge the venom spawned in my heart.

Tisiphone. [*To herself*] Hardly could a more suitable accomplice offer himself to us! Surely this man, I confess, far surpasses me, his teacher! Whatever wickedness the three of us possess, this man possesses! I shall therefore draw nearer and intensify his incipient rage. [*To Ruffus*] O my glorious man of arms, O my hope, O my sweet nursling, come tell me, do tell me, Ruffus, why shameful inactivity has so long kept you in thrall? Why do you thus pile up years without glory? Why do you waste the flower of your youth in torpor, alas? I pray that you will now at last realize the actions that befit you and your bestial rage. Do not spurn my words, I implore you, if ever I was the first to take you carefully into my bosom as you came weak from your mother's womb, if ever I warmed your limbs, as I often did, in my stern lap when the tears bathed your cheeks, if ever I offered you my breasts with a mother's voice, if ever you learned through me to satiate your sword with streams of blood and to

Heu, nescis, nescis quidnam tua fata pararint,
quid fortuna tibi, quid sidera, quidque deorum
numina, si in melius rabidam convertere mentem,
nec tibi segnitie libeat corrumpere vitam.
Hesperiae (mihi crede) plagae dominabere toti,
si parere velis solitasque resumere vires.

Ruffus

O quae ceruleos gestas pro crinibus angues,
per te perque tuum caput inviolabile nunquam
desistam, genetrix longe veneranda, rogare
ut mihi nunc monstrare velis quid fata pararint,
quid fortuna mihi. Doceas ubi praemia tanta;
fare age, cara parens, monstra dum pectora fervent,
dum manus in promptu dumque impius ardor inhaeret.
Eia, age iam precibus cari flectaris alumni.
Sic tibi perpetuo liceat per regna silentum
Tartaream in turbam rigido saevire flagello.

Tisiphone

Postquam magnanimum pectus tibi, Ruffe, paratum
effrenesque animos tantis assurgere prompte
conspicio rebus, dabitur, mihi crede, minister
optime, quod summis precibus contendis habere.
Nunc monstrabo viam qua teque tuumque furorem
augusto liceat iam iam satiare cruore.
Quod decus inde feres quantamque merebere laudem!
Quippe, mihi videor clarum diadema videre
temporibus radiare tuis. Sed viribus uti
nunc opus et validae nequaquam parcere dextrae.

threaten whole populations with cruel death. Alas, you know not, you know not what your fates have in store for you, what your fortune, what the stars, what the spirits of the gods have prepared for you if you turn your rabid mind to a better goal and do not waste your life in sloth. You shall have dominion—believe me!—over all the Western shores, if you would only prepare yourself and take up again your accustomed acts of violence.

Ruffus. O you who brandish greenish-blue snakes in place of hair, by you and your imperishable head may I never cease, awesome mother, to ask that you would show me what my fates, what my fortune have prepared for me. Teach me where to find such great rewards; tell me, dear parent; show me while my heart is aboil, my hand at the ready, while this unholy ardor clings to me. Come, let your prayers prevail now upon your dear nursling. Thus may it be allowed you forever throughout the kingdom of the silent to flog the Tartarean hordes with your pitiless lash.

Tisiphone. Ruffus, since I see your great-souled heart is prepared and your wild spirit ready to rise to mighty deeds, believe me, best of accomplices, that it shall be given you to have that for which you strive with your utmost prayers. Now I shall show you the way by which you may presently satisfy with royal blood yourself and your rage. What honor you shall carry off from this deed, what praise you shall merit! Indeed, it seems to me I see a noble crown shining on your brow. But now you must use violence and spare not at all the strength of your right hand.

Ruffus

Iam, me iam nimium longo sermone moraris;
expedias tandem quae sit, quae tanta facultas,
quo pacto valeam facinus committere tantum.
Crede mihi, genetrix: nihil est tam turpe quod ardens
dextra reformidet cultro munita furenti,
dummodo me possim solio trabeaque superbum
reddere et augusta caput hoc ornare corona.

Tisiphone

Advertas igitur; paucis te, Ruffe, docebo.
Iam scio novisti Fernandum, Martis alumnum,
qui communis amor lati nunc dicitur orbis,
pro dolor! et nostras totiens qui fundere gentis
approperans, semper remeat victricibus armis,
clara triumphali redimitus tempora lauro,
quem supplex oriens audito nomine tantum
occiduusque dies posita feritate veretur.
Hic est qui regnum certa tibi sorte dicatum
possidet et magna munitus utrinque caterva
praeradiat, solio fruiturque quod ipsa pararant
provida Fata tibi. Sed te quid, Ruffe, quid ultra
detinet imbellem? Cur non in regia tecta
sponte furis? Cur non recipis violenter adempta?
Si vir es, en, tempus nunc est quo vota sequaris
expectata diu. Trepidis nunc iura superbus
dat populis, tantae securus fraudis et astus.
Ipse per insidias tacita sub veste latentem
illuc fer gladium quem tergo regis adhaesus
exere et audaci iandudum perfice dextra;
horrida terrifico maculentur rostra cruore.
Ipsa frequens adero; nunquam te, Ruffe, relinquam:

Ruffus. You are already delaying me now with your overlong speeches; explain finally what it is, what this great opportunity is, how I may be able to commit so great a crime. Believe me, mother, a passionate right hand, armed with furious knife, shall shrink from no shame so long as I have the chance to make myself haughty with a throne and royal purple, and embellish this head with a majestic crown!

Tisiphone. Then pay attention, Ruffus; I shall explain it to you in a few words. Now I know you have heard of Ferdinand, the nursling of Mars, who at present is loved by the whole wide world—O the pain of it!—and who, whenever he rushes up to rout our peoples, always returns victorious in arms, his noble brow encircled by the triumphal laurel. This is he of whom the suppliant East and the West alike stand in awe, laying aside their ferocity at the mere sound of his name. This is he who holds the kingdom assigned to you by sure destiny, who outshines all others, protected by great troops on either side, and who enjoys the throne which the provident Fates themselves had readied for you. But what is keeping you any longer from taking up arms, Ruffus? Why aren't you bursting into spontaneous rage against the royal halls? Why aren't you taking back with violence what has been stolen from you? If you are a man, look! now is the time to go after what you have so long wished for. That proud fellow at present is giving laws to timid people, secure against deceit and cunning on such a scale. Take a sword to that place, hiding it treacherously under your silent cloak; then come up close behind the king, unsheathe it, and at last do the deed with your daring right hand; the platform will be stained horribly with awful gore! I shall be close beside you; I shall never leave you, Ruffus: [*holding up her right hand*] this will

haec erit illa manus quae certum dirigat ictum.
Nunc curare tuum est tanto ne dextera coepto
neve animus titubet. Fac altum vulnus ad ossa,
si qua potes, penetret. Studiis popularibus ipsa
sis gratus faciam magnumque sequare favorem.
Omnibus immittam viridi serpente furorem
pervertamque hominum mentis caligine caeca.
Tota salutabit subitum te Hispania regem.
Ergo age; tolle moras. Dum se tibi commoda praebent
tempora, dum faciles venti, tu carbasa pande.

Ruffus

Non opus est verbis nec tanto, diva, rogatu.
Nanque ego, ni longe superem documenta Megerae,
ni capiti imponam madidum diadema cruore,
Sisyphium facito subeat mea vita laborem.

Tisiphone sola

Quas mihi debebunt laudes qualesque triumphos
Tartara, si tantum regem prostrarit alumnus
noster et intrepidus hostilia colla secarit,
Hesperio sellam denudans rege curulem,
qui solus nostros popularis impete magno
perdere tentabat totumque fugare per orbem,
nec superum fulcire fidem propriumque cruorem
fundere cessabat semperque resurgere maior
squallida consuerat longi post vulnera belli!
At nunc quis tantos proceres tantasque phalanges
pro superis ductare volet per aperta pericla?
Haud ducibus cunctis sedet haec sententia cordi.
Bella sibi nunc quisque gerit solumque laborat
imperium proferre suum cessatque tueri
quod commune videt. Marcescunt pectora turpi

be the hand that directs the unerring thrust. It will be your task now not to waver, either in hand or in thought, from this great undertaking. Make the wound penetrate deep into his bones, if you can. I shall see to it that the deed wins you the gratitude of the popular party, and you will acquire great favor. I shall send the fury of the green serpent upon them all and shall pervert the minds of men with a blinding fog. All Spain will straightway hail you as king. Therefore, go; delay no further. While the suitable moment presents itself, while winds are fair, spread your sails!

Ruffus. There's no need for words, goddess, nor for such urgent pleas. For if I don't far surpass the example of Megaera, if I don't place a crown upon my head, wet with blood, make my life suffer a Sisyphean labor. [*He departs*]

Tisiphone. [*Alone*] What praise, what triumphs Tartarus shall owe me if my foster child shall lay low so great a king, fearlessly slitting his hostile neck, stripping the curule chair of its Western king—the only man who used to aim with great force to destroy our peoples and put them to flight throughout the globe, who never would cease to prop up the faith of the gods above and pour out his own blood, and who always would rise up again greater than before after suffering the filthy wounds of long war! But now, who will want to lead the great princes and armies as Heaven's champion through open dangers? Holy resolve is hardly fixed in the heart of all war leaders. Now each ruler wages war on his own behalf and works only to extend his own empire and no longer protects the common good. Their

segnitie potius quam quis succurrat amicis.
Nunc sola ambitio regnat; calcatur honestum
sub pedibus; cumulantur opes discrimine nullo.
Nusquam Fabritius, nusquam mens sancta Camilli.
Hic solus (fateor) communia bella gerebat
non sibi sed fidei, clypeo munitus et hasta
semper et assuetis nunquam defessus in armis.
Quare hic, si nostri percussus vulnere Ruffi
sanguineam pulsabit humum, quis deinde vetabit
auspice me totum Plutoni tradier orbem
Magmedisque mei late monimenta vagari?
Quis digna me laude feret, quae sola sororum
nunc fuerim commenta viam, qua nostra iuventur
imperia, heu, tantam iandudum passa procellam?
Ulterius sed certa vetant me Fata morari
iam video prohibentque frui regione serena.
Hinc Acherontaeas descendere cogor ad umbras
Tartareique Iovis tenebrosa revisere regna.

Regina audito regis vulnere exanimata egreditur cum nutrice.

Me miseram, pavidas quam tristis perculit aures
nuntius! Heu pereo quotiens audita recordor!
Pro superi, subito potius mihi terra dehiscat

courage grows faint with shameful lethargy rather than each one succoring his friends. Now only ambition rules; honor is trampled underfoot; they pile up wealth indiscriminately. Fabricius[15] is nowhere to be seen; nowhere to be found is the holy resolve of Camillus.[16] This man alone (I confess it) was waging wars on everyone's behalf, not for himself but for the Faith, always equipped with shield and spear and tireless in his accustomed arms. Wherefore, if this man, wounded by our Ruffus, shall fall with a thud on the bloody ground, who then will forbid the whole world from being turned over to Pluto under my auspices, and trophies to my Mohammed from being carried far and wide? Who will lift me up with worthy praise? I alone of my sisters have now devised this way in which our realms may find aid—realms, alas, that for a long time now have suffered terrific storms. But I see the unbending Fates forbid me further delay and prohibit me further enjoyment of the serene regions of earth. Henceforward I am compelled to descend to the shades of Acheron and to revisit the dark kingdom of Tartarean Jove.

: III :

Queen Isabella, Nurse, St. James, Ferdinand,
Cardinal Peter Mendoza, Chorus, in Barcelona.

The Queen, shocked by news of the king's wound,
comes out with her nurse.

Queen. Wretch that I am, how sad the news that has stricken my frightened ears! Alas, I die whenever I call to mind what I've heard! By the gods above, may the earth open wide to receive me, may lightning strike me down among the eternal shades

vel me perpetuas demittat fulmen ad umbras
quam quisquam nostri violarit corpora regis!

Nutrix

Parce, precor, lachrimis et fletibus ora rigare.
Qui scis an verus fuerit de vulnere regis
nuntius, an potius mendaci venerit ore?
Vix equidem credo quenquam, regina, fuisse
tam dirum et tota penitus ratione carentem
ut violare tuum tentaverit ense maritum,
qui placidus semper tractabat cuncta benigno
imperio, qui tantus erat moderator honesti
iustitiaeque simul, per quem iam saecla redibant
aurea, qui tanta populos in pace regebat,
praemia digna bonis qui solus reddere norat
et fraeno cohibere malos, quo principe tandem
tuta videbatur nimium sibi machina mundi!

Regina

Heu, mirum hoc minime, nutrix mihi cara, videtur,
tempore praecipue nostro, quo regnat Erymnis
infera, quo nusquam maiestas regia tuta est.
Haec animum tamen afflictae spes unica reddit,
quod perhibent vulnus divina sorte retentum,
ne penitus cari resecaret colla mariti.

Eiusdem oratio pro salute regis

O pater omnipotens, o summi rector Olympi,
cuius opus mortale genus coelumque profundum
planitiesque immensa maris spatiosaque tellus—
hoc caput o libeat mundo servare cadenti
quod fuerat totiens alienae causa salutis!
Profuerit proprii capitis tot aperta pericla,

rather than that some man should outrage the body of our king!

Nurse. Please, restrain the tears that are streaming down your face! Do you even know whether the news of the king's wound is true? Perhaps it came from a lying tongue. For my part I scarcely believe that there would have been anyone, queen, so desperate and utterly irrational that he would try to murder your husband with a sword. The king was such a peaceful man who always handled every affair with kindly power and who was such a great ruler, tempering honor with justice! Thanks to him, golden ages were already returning and he ruled his peoples in great peace. He alone knew how to render worthy rewards to the good and to rein in evil men. Under this prince, in short, the very fabric of the world seemed exceedingly safe!

Queen. Alas, my dear nurse, this incident doesn't seem surprising to me at all, especially in these times of ours when a Fury rules the lower world; when royal majesty is never safe. This one hope gives me courage in my affliction: that they say the wound was providentially contained, so that my dear husband's head was not completely cut off. [*The queen petitions for the safety of the king.*] O Almighty Father, O ruler of highest Olympus, who made the human race and high heaven and the measureless surface of the sea and the wide spaces of earth: O please keep his life safe for this reeling world of ours—that life which so many times was the cause of another's salvation! To benefit our holy Faith he underwent so many manifest dangers to his own

tot sumptus, divine pater, variosque labores
pro sancta subiisse fide, tot milia vinclis
exoluisse hominum diro famulantia regi.
Impia profuerit Maurorum castra fugasse
insignesque sacris templis posuisse triumphos
et Magmedaeas totiens fudisse cohortes.
Tu quoque, quo foelix patrono Hispania fertur,
huc ades et meritum regem, divine Iacobe,
aethereo committe patri, relevetur acerbum
vulnus et ignavo reddatur poena nocenti.
Nec liceat regnare malis virtute iacente
sub pedibus diris. Quis enim fas esse putarit
vexarique pios contraque vigere nocentis?

Eadem viso divo Iacobo

Sed quis tam subitus percussit lumina fulgor,
humanam superans aciem? Sint omnia fausta!
Sit foelix quodcunque paras, pater optime divum!

Divi Iacobi ad reginam consolatio

Desine iam lachrimis, castissima femina, tristes
commaculare oculos. Cessent iam vota precesque
sollicitare deum; deponas corde timorem.
Vox tua iandudum placidas pervenit ad aures
aetherei patris. Qui cum spectaret ab alto
horrendum facinus quod barbara dextra parabat,
huc me festinum supero demisit Olympo,
qui caeleste manu laenirem vulnera regis
immeritaque virum prohiberem morte perire.
Duxerat indignum coeli pater ille supernus,
si regem tanto superum qui flagrat amore,
cui fidei commissus apex, qui regna Tonantis
assidue proferre studet per mille pericla,

life, so much expense, Divine Father, and varied labors; he loosed from their chains so many thousands of men enthralled to the dreadful king. He helped put to flight the ungodly camps of the Moors and placed triumphant standards on their sacred temples, and so many times routed the troops of the Mohammedans. You also, under whom, as her patron, Spain remains prosperous, come hither, St. James, and entreat our heavenly Father that this deserving king might have his painful wound healed and that punishment be meted out to his cowardly assailant. Let evil men not be allowed to rule, with virtue cast under their dreadful feet. For who would think it right for the pious to be afflicted while the guilty grow in strength? [*The queen sees a vision of St. James.*] But what flash of light is this that strikes so suddenly, its radiance blinding human sight? May these be good omens! May whatever it is you are going to do, best father of the gods,[17] be propitious.

St. James. Most upright of women, stop reddening your sad eyes with tears now. Cease entreating God with your holy vows and prayers; drive fear from your heart. Your voice has for some time now reached the indulgent ears of the heavenly Father. When He saw from on high the horrific crime the man was plotting to commit with his brutal hand, He sent me hither quickly from lofty Olympus that I should with heavenly hand mitigate the king's wound and prevent him from dying an undeserved death. That sublime Father of Heaven deemed it a thing unworthy if a single, base traitor might murder in ignoble fashion a king who burns with such great love of the gods above, to whom was entrusted the crown of faith, who devoted himself zealously to advancing the Thunderer's kingdom through a

proditor unus iners ignava morte necaret.
Non tamen haec regem credas mala talia passum
criminis ob poenas aut laesi numinis iram,
sed pater omnipotens voluit sic principis huius
explorare animum. Nam virtus inclyta sese
rebus in adversis melius probat inque periclis.
Corrumpunt mentem sapientum animosque fatigant
prospera; nutritur generoso vita labore.
Pace diuturna marcescunt fortia corda
sordescuntque situ, nisi portas cuspide pulset
miles et hostili minitetur vulnera ferro.
Gaude igitur matrona dei dignissima donis:
vir tuus evasit servatus grandibus actis,
imperioque Asiae. Veniet iam sub iuga supplex
Africa, et immensus divinis legibus orbis
sub vestro imperio discet parere subactus.

Regina sola

Quas tibi nunc grates referam, quae munera tandem
coniuge pro incolumi, pro toto denique regno,
maiestas veneranda dei, quae lumine recto
cuncta videns subiecta polo mortalia facta,
praemia digna bonis, poenamque nocentibus addis?
Sed quid lenta moror? Cur non adolentur odores
ignibus accensis? Cur non in templa facesso
tot rea votorum? Salvo quae multa marito
debemus! Sed quid crepuerunt ostia regis?

Eadem conspecto rege

O decus! O carae spes et generosa voluptas
coniugis! O vitae requies! O dulce levamen!
Pectore quis rabido, coniunx, quis mente profana,

thousand perils. Nevertheless, you should not believe that the king suffered such evils as these as punishments for crime or on account of the wrath of an injured divinity. Rather, the Almighty Father wished in this way to test the prince's mettle. For renowned virtue better proves itself in adversity and danger. Prosperity corrupts the minds of the wise and wearies their hearts. Life is nourished by noble effort. Strong hearts grow weak from prolonged peace and become squalid from disuse, if there is no soldier hammering on the doors with his spear and threatening to inflict wounds with hostile sword. Therefore, most worthy wife, rejoice in the gifts of God: Your husband has escaped safely, preserved for mighty deeds and empire over Asia. Now Africa like a suppliant will come under the yoke, and the measureless globe, subdued beneath your empire, will learn to obey the law divine.

Queen. [*Alone*] What thanks should I return to you now? What gifts should I give, pray, for the safety of my husband, and finally for the entire kingdom, O venerable majesty of God? Seeing in your righteous light all mortal deeds lying beneath the pole, you confer worthy rewards on the good and punishment upon the guilty. But why am I slow; why delay? Why is not incense rising up from burnt offerings? Why am I, who have made so many vows, not carrying them out in the churches? Many vows indeed I owe in return for a husband saved! But why are the king's doors rattling? [*She sees the king.*] O my glory, O hope and noble pleasure of a loving wife! O my comfort in life, O my sweet solace! O husband, who was the mad and im-

quis penitus ratione carens tibi fata pararat
impia? Num Scyron fuit hic, num Sparthacus atrox?

Rex

Dic, rogo, dic, coniunx, nunquid de vulnere nostro
auribus hausisti? Scin quantum colla periclum
vitarint nuper superum servata favore?
Scin quanto clypeo pro me divina Iacobi
numina nunc steterint? Scin vulnera sana repente
ipsius auxilio minimum movisse dolorem?

Regina

Ordine nunc recto mihi cuncta relata fuerunt.
Verum age, dic, coniunx, num debita quaeso nocentem
poena manet patiturque ferox adamantina vincla?
An sibi consuluit pedibusque fugaque rapaci?

Rex

Servatur vinctus tenebroso carcere et atro;
impia iam gravibus premitur religata catenis
dextera, iamque pedes plectuntur compede grandi.

Regina

Iure quidem. At quonam monitu, qua mente nefandum
crimen id insano concepit pectore? Scistin?

Rex

Nescio: nam vulnus lecto me affixerat altum.
Sed Mendoza—mei requies non parva doloris—
quem non ista latent, poterit tibi cuncta referre.

pious lunatic who plotted an unholy fate for you? Was the man some sort of Sciron,[18] some deadly Spartacus?[19]

King. Tell me, please, wife: have you heard anything about my being wounded? Are you aware of the great danger my neck avoided just now, saved by the favor of the gods? Do you know how the divine spirit of St James stood and shielded me at this time? Have you heard that my wound was instantly healed through his aid and caused me only the smallest pain?

Queen. Everything has now been told me in its correct order. But come, my husband, tell me, please, surely condign punishment awaits the guilty party? And is this savage man bound in adamantine chains? Or has he looked to his own safety and taken to his heels?

King. He's being kept chained in a dark and gloomy dungeon; his impious right hand is already bound and bitten hard by heavy chains, and his feet are already clamped in great shackles.

Queen. And rightfully so! But what advice did he have, what was going through his mind when he conceived this unspeakable crime in his insane heart? Do you know?

King. I don't: you see, the deep wound confined me to my bed. But Mendoza—who was no small comfort in my pain—is aware of the facts; he will be able to tell you everything. [*Mendoza steps forward*]

Petrus Mendoza Cardinalis

Quid nisi mira nimis referam credendaque tarde?
Nam quotiens proceres vestri scitantur ab illo,
quaenam causa foret sceleris tantique paratus,
respondet tanquam penitus ratione careret.
Nec dubium: ratione caret prenditque catenas
mordicus et populo spectanti triste minatu,
res monstrosa quidem. Capiti stant lumina tetra;
terribilis facies premitur pallore nefando,
intuiturque solum semper non lumine recto;
lingua venena gerit; livent rubigine dentes;
deformis macies apparet corpore toto.
Nusquam risus adest; suspiria semper abundant,
horrendumque caput redimitur crinibus atris.
Inficit aspectu quicquid conspexit acerbo.

Rex

Quid, nisi suppetias nobis divina tulissent
numina, quam facile cecidissent colla recisa
vulnere terribili! Quanta est (en, cerne) cicatrix!
Nunc igitur vere patuit quam mutua cura
sit nostri superis. Nunc sunt, nunc magna gerenda,
ne tanti immemores meriti donique vocemur!
Iam ducibus nobis totum veneranda per orbem
aetherei patris volitabunt signa, per Afros
perque Asiae campos. Imponam gentibus illis
divinas leges. Ibis, regina, per urbes
innumeras gentisque truces documenta docebis
mitia. Magnanimos quotiens mirabere reges
imperio parere tuo feritate subacta!
Haec sunt, quae dudum flagranti mente revolvo,
nunc peragenda magis. Dum non praesentia desint

Mendoza. What can I say that isn't too shocking and hard to believe? For as often as your nobles questioned him as to the purpose of his crime and his great plot, he responded like someone entirely bereft of reason. There's no doubt that he's mad: he takes his chains in his teeth and utters dire threats to the people watching him. It's monstrous. His vile eyes stand out from his head; his horrible face is imprinted with an unspeakable pallor; he always stares at the ground with a twisted eye. He has a poisonous tongue, his teeth are stained with tartar, his whole body is disfigured and gaunt. He never smiles but is always overflowing with sighs; his repulsive head is matted with foul hair. Whatever he looks at, he poisons with his acid looks.[20]

King. How easily my neck might have been cut with a terrible wound and felled if the divine spirits had not come to our aid! Look at the size of the scar! Now it has been truly made clear how this care of the gods above for ourselves ought to be reciprocal. Now great deeds must be performed, lest we be called forgetful of their gifts and how much we owe them! Now, with us taking the lead, the awesome banners of the Heavenly Father shall fly throughout the globe, through the fields of Africa and Asia. I shall impose the laws of heaven upon those nations. You, queen, shall go through cities innumerable and shall instruct the fierce nations in the teachings of gentleness. How many times will you marvel at great-souled kings, their ferocity laid aside, obeying your imperial command! These are the plans I have long been turning over in my ardent mind; now, all the more, they must be achieved! So long as the divine powers now present do not desert us, I have resolved to shirk no effort.

numina, constitui nullos vitare labores.
Tu vero interea, dum nos pia tela paramus
magnanimasque acies animosaque classica Martis,
in tua tecta redi, conceptaque solvere vota
cura sit atque aris meritos imponere honores.
Mente dein grata Pario de marmore surgant,
fac, servatori sublimia templa Iacobo,
qui me teque simul servavit corpore in uno.

Chorus

Exuperat solidum virtus interrita ferrum;
non timet insanos hominum bene tuta furores,
non Siculos ignes, rapidi non fulminis iram
et viget in duris gaudetque per aspera ferri;
pectore magnanimo contemnit inertia facta.
Saepe quidem adversis agitatur casibus atque
fluctuat, at nunquam didicit succumbere victa.
Nil fraudes, nil vincla nocent, nil dira venena,
nil pelagus, nil Scylla rapax, nil saeva Charybdis.
Nullus in hanc (moneo) crudelia tela movere
audeat; amittet vires et robora dextrae;
huic omnis debetur honos; haec denique sola
immortale decus meruit nomenque perenne.
Haec nos conciliat superis; haec scandere coelum
aethereasque docet sedes. Super astra volare
nos facit et nunquam sentit communia fata.
Discite nunc igitur, reges, aeterna mereri
nomina et excelso contingere vertice coelum,
Fernando monstrante viam cum coniuge clara,
perque omnis resonet 'foelix Hispania!' terras.

Fernandi Servati *finis*

Meanwhile, while we ready our holy weapons, our brave battle lines and the spirited trumpets of Mars, you return to your home, and let it be your care to fulfill the vows we have made and to place due honors upon the altars. Then, with grateful mind, cause a lofty temple of Parian marble to be erected to our preserver, St. James, the one who has protected me and you at the same time, since we are one in body.

Chorus. Fearless virtue overcomes a hard iron sword; being well protected, virtue has no fear of raging madmen. It does not fear the fires of Sicily nor a wrathful thunderbolt; it thrives amid hardship and rejoices to endure adversity. With a courageous heart it disdains base deeds. Often, indeed, it is troubled by misfortune and is shaken, but it has never learned to succumb to defeat. Deceptions, chains, deadly poisons, the sea, fierce Scylla and cruel Charybdis[21] do virtue no harm. No one should dare (I warn you) take up merciless arms against it; he will lose his power and the strength of his right hand. To virtue, all honor is due; it alone, finally, has merited immortal glory and its fame will never end. It reconciles us to the gods; it teaches us how we may rise up to heaven and the ethereal regions. It causes us to fly above the stars, and it never experiences the fate of common things. Now, therefore, you kings, learn to win eternal fame and to touch heaven at its lofty summit. With Ferdinand pointing the way, along with his noble wife, the words "Fortunate is Spain!" shall resound throughout all the lands.

The End of Ferdinand Preserved

Eiusdem in Ruffum regiae maiestatis violatorem invectiva

Quis tantum infoelix dederat tibi Ruffe furorem
armaratque truces ense furente manus?
Quis caecam indiderat mentem? Quis talia monstra
suaserat? O Stygii dira propago lacus,
quod tibi conferri possit facinusque scelusque,
quod maius monstrum Phoebus in orbe notet?
Tu Schyrona gravem superas et Bebryca dirum;
Busiris minor est impietate tua.
Huic sceleri cedunt violenti facta Procustis,
et Schinis Istmiacis poena timenda viris.
Bistonii ingenium superasti immane tyranni
carnibus humanis qui satiabat equos.
Iam tibi Tantalidae vincuntur, perfide, fratres,
turbarunt nitidos qui dape Solis equos.
Spartacus et Chrisus servilia signa ferentes
dicentur mites Enomausque simul.
Non Marius, non Sulla ferox, nec Cinna cruentus
conferri poterunt, impie Ruffe, tibi.
O scelus indignum, quod nulla piacula solvant
quodque patet supero displicuisse patri!
Oblitus recti, commiscens sacra profanis,
oblitus quidnam fasque piumque petant,
tune caput sacrum gladio resecare parabas
quod vitam innumeris praebuit ante viris?
Tune ducem tantum violare, insane, putaras,
qui gerit assidue Martia bella Deo,
qui veneranda ferens victricia signa Tonantis
impia barbarici contudit arma ducis,
qui Mauro Hesperia foelici Marte fugato
inde domum victor clara trophoea tulit,

The Same Author's Invective against Ruffus, the Assailant of His Royal Majesty

Unhappy Ruffus, who was it who had implanted in you such fury, and who had armed your pitiless hands with raging sword? Who blinded you? Who had persuaded you to carry out such monstrous deeds? O dreadful offspring of the Stygian lake, what greater crime and act of wickedness could be laid to your charge, what more monstrous act could the sun god observe in all the globe? You surpass troublesome Sciron and dreadful Bebryx; the impiety of Busiris is less than yours.[22] The deeds of violent Procrustes give place to yours, and your punishment would have to be feared even by men like Sinis of Corinth.[23] You have surpassed the brutal disposition of that tyrant of the Bistones who fed his horses with human flesh.[24] Now the two brothers descended from Tantalus who disturbed the bright horses of the Sun at their meal are beaten by you, traitor.[25] Spartacus and Crixus, bearing the signs of their enslavement, and Oenomaus[26] too, may be called mild in comparison. Not Marius, not savage Sulla, not bloody Cinna[27] could be compared to you, unholy Ruffus. O ignoble crime, which no rites of expiation can remove and which, it is clear, offended the Heavenly Father! Forgetful of righteousness, mixing sacred with profane, forgetful of that which goodness and piety seek, were you not trying to cut off with a sword the sacred head which had granted life to countless men in times past? Did you think you could outrage, madman, so great a commander, who ceaselessly conducts Mars' wars for God's sake, who bears the awesome, victorious banners of the Thunderer and blunts the impious arms of the barbarian general, who has caused the Moor to flee the happy Western lands through warfare and returned home thence victorious, bearing famous trophies, who, desirous of cleansing his

quique suos cupiens purgatos reddere fines
  Iudaicum Hispano reppulit axe genus?
O caput insanum, quod nulla cucurbita purget,
  o cui vipereo pectora felle virent,
solvere tun, demens, adamantina vincla furebas,
  queis superi Hispanos implicuere duces,
quos stabili iunxit divina potentia cesto?
  Haud furor hos hominis dissociare potest.
Ergo in Fernandum non haec, sed in aetheris alti
  numina direxti tela nefanda, miser;
haec genus humanum crudelis dextra petebat,
  orbis in hoc quoniam statque caditque salus.
Sed superi, qui cuncta vident mortalia iusto
  lumine quique regunt ordine quaeque suo,
vocibus Helisabes flexi precibusque pudicis
  e manibus diris eripuere ducem,
divinumque caput servant ingentibus actis,
  teque gravi dedunt, vipera saeva, cruci.
Si sapis ergo, tuo gratare, Hispania, regi,
  turicremos spargens flore et odore focos.
Sancta sacerdotes exornent templa corollis;
  maxima sanguineam victima plangat humum,
omnibus et superis concordi voce rogatis,
  'sit tibi, rex tantus, laeta' precare 'diu'!
Sed tamen, heu, facias ut perfidus ille furensque
  det poenam, qualem commeruisse vides.
Crede mihi, nulla est, nulla inclementia: fas sit
  innocuo regi non timuisse malos.

Finis

borders, has driven the Jewish race from Spanish skies? O mad brain, which no bloodletting can purge, O breast made strong by viperous bile, were you not, demented man, raving when you tried to loosen the adamantine chains by which the gods above have linked our Spanish leaders, whom divine power has joined together with a firm Venusian band?[28] The fury of a single man could hardly break them apart. Thus you have directed, wretch, your wicked weapons, not against Ferdinand, but against the divine powers of heaven above. This cruel hand was attacking human kind, since the salvation of the world stands and falls with Him. But the gods above, who see all mortal things in the light of justice and who rule each thing in accordance with their own ordering, were prevailed upon by the cries and chaste prayers of Isabella, snatched the leader from dreadful hands and preserved his divine life for great deeds—and they have turned you over, savage viper, to torture and death. Therefore if you are wise, Spain, felicitate your king, and sprinkle fragrant incense upon your hearths. Let priests adorn the holy temples with flowery wreaths; let the largest of sacrificial animals fall loudly upon the bloody ground, and calling upon all the heavenly spirits above with one harmonious voice, pray "may you long flourish, great king!" But nevertheless, alas, may you see to it that this treacherous madman be given the punishment you see he has deserved. Believe me, there is no lack of clemency in this: it is right and holy that a blameless king should not have to fear the wicked.

The End

Note on the Texts and Translations

The Latin text of Mussato's *Ecerinis* is based on Luigi Padrin's critical edition of 1900, which readers may consult for an *apparatus criticus* as well as for classical sources and parallels. Padrin also prints an early commentary (before 1317) by the Paduan grammarians Guizzardo of Bologna and Castellano da Bassano and a later *argumentum* by Iacobinus Iadre *physicus*. The act and scene divisions used in the English version, however, are taken from Manlio Dazzi's translation (1964). Padrin suggested a number of emendations, mostly *metri gratia*, which are listed in the Notes to the Texts, but these have not for the most part been accepted by subsequent scholarship. The text offered by Chevalier's excellent edition of 2000 has been collated with Padrin, and two improved readings from his text have been recorded in the Notes to the Texts.

The Latin text of Antonio Loschi's *Achilles* is based on the critical edition of Vittorio Zaccaria (1981) included in *Il teatro umanistico veneto: la tragedia* (1981); it is used by kind permission of Longo Editore.

The Latin text of Gregorio Correr's *Procne* is based on the critical edition of Aldo Onorato (1994) and is used by kind permission of Professor Vincenzo Fera and the Centro interdipartimentale di studi umanistici, Messina (the successor to the Centro di studi umanistici).

The Latin text of Leonardo Dati's *Hiempsal* is based on the critical edition of Aldo Onorato (2000) and is used by kind permission of Professor Vincenzo Fera and the Centro interdipartimentale di studi umanistici, Messina.

The Latin text of Marcellino Verardi's *Ferdinand Preserved* was edited for this volume by James Hankins, General Editor of the I Tatti Library, and Dr. Ornella Rossi. The only modern edition is that of Sir Henry Thomas, which appeared in volume 32 of the *Revue hispanique* (1914). The latter is essentially a rather faulty transcription of the 1493 *editio princeps*. There are no known manuscripts of the play. The present edition is based on a fresh collation of the *princeps* (which may be viewed online at http://www.juntadeandalucia.es/cultura/bibliotecavirtualandalucia). The incunable's orthography has been preserved, but punctuation and capitalization have been modernized. Divergences from Thomas' edition, other than the merely orthographic, are given in the Notes to the Texts. Included with Marcellino's *tragicomoedia* is a preface composed by his uncle, Carlo Verardi, who apparently worked up into a dramatic sketch the story of Ferdinand's injury and recovery, which was later handed over to his nephew for versification. The work is followed in all printings by an invective, *In Ruffum regiae maiestatis violatorem,* which has also been included here.

In preparing my own translations of these texts, I have consulted the English versions of the *Ecerinis* by Robert W. Carrubba et al. and of the *Ecerinis, Achilles, Procne,* and *Hiempsal* by Joseph R. Berrigan (see Bibliography). Despite the serious inadequacies of these versions, I have sometimes adapted their renderings when I found them felicitous. In compiling the Notes to the Translations, I am deeply indebted to the work of annotation undertaken by previous editors, especially Padrin, Chevalier, Zaccaria, Casarsa, and Onorato. The *apparatus fontium* of Chevalier, Zaccaria, and Onorato give detailed analyses of verbal debts and parallels to ancient sources, especially Seneca, which I have not repeated here. In the first four plays, the stage directions, added in the English translation within square brackets and in italics, are those of the present editor. In the *Ferdinand Preserved,* the stage directions are based in part on those found in the *editio princeps.*

The Notes to the Texts were prepared by James Hankins (JH) and Ornella Rossi (OR).

Notes to the Texts

ECERINIS

178. tale producat] procreet penitus *Chevalier*

283. *Padrin proposes emending* hoc digni patre *to* hoc patre digni

353. *Padrin proposes emending to* sub lege certa. Haec praepotens sed quis movet?

394. *Padrin proposes emending to* quot polluere hi caedibus mundum suis

413. *Padrin proposes* pretium *for* praemium.

495. *Padrin proposes* ac *or* atque *for* et, *but* atque *is preferable.*

508. *Padrin proposes emending to* calcaribus tunc concitatum urgens equum

611. ensem tenus] ense inruens *conjectured by Padrin*

ACHILLES

78. victus: *possibly to be emended to* vinctus *on the model of Seneca,* Troades *624:* torpetque vinctus frigido sanguis gelu: *see Zaccaria, 67, 38n.*

105. regio: *corrected to* regia *in Da Schio's edition, and metrically preferable (compare Seneca,* Hercules Furens, *717:* adversa Ditis regia, *and Ovid,* Heroides *2.72:* nigri regia caeca dei*), but Zaccaria prefers* regio *as the reading of the MSS.*

108. *Above* hoc certum *Zaccaria reports an interlinear gloss,* sed bene, *which he suggests may be a variant.*

187. *Possibly* trahent *should be read (JH).*

214. *Zaccaria prefers the* chao *of the 1636 edition but retains the* chaos *of the manuscripts in his text.*

302. *The seventeenth-century editor Felice Osio emended* ciet *to* ciens, *which seems better syntactically but has no authority in the MSS.*

623. fictus: *possibly* fretus, *as Zaccaria suggests.*

831. *sc.* abrepta. *As Zaccaria notes, Loschi may borrow* abrapta *from, e.g., Seneca,* Troades, *1003, where it appears as a variant for* abrepta *in one branch of the tradition.*

PROCNE

286. iaceat *emended to* iaceas *by JH.*

407. violente: *sc.* violenter

411–13. *The sentence perhaps reads more naturally as a rhetorical question than as an exclamation (JH).*

470. *The verbal form* evixit *is unattested in classical Latin and may be a coinage, as Casarsa notes.*

486. Bacchi: *sc.* Bacchi furorem.

624. *sc.* invertit. *The form* inversat *is found in patristic Latin.*

688. *Probably* hac *should be read for* haec *(JH). For* invertit *see the preceding note.*

712. *The passage should be punctuated:* morabor, crimini *(OR).*

732. me ira *should perhaps be read for* pietas; *compare Seneca,* Medea *939–44 (OR).*

909–10. *The passage should be punctuated:* fuerat, avi / animos *(OR).*

988. *See the Notes to the Translations* ad loc. *(JH)*

HIEMPSAL

290–92. *The sentence* medio ne [*sc.* medione] . . . conventitium *should be interrogative.*

418. iram *should perhaps be read for* ira *(OR).*

587. *We should probably read* limini *here for Onorato's* limiti, *on the analogy of Pliny 7.53.181,* iam egrediens incusso pollice limini cubiculi, *an action which in Pliny as in Dati is a portent of death (JH).*

FERDINAND PRESERVED

Pr 2. cursu] cursa *Thomas*

Pr 3. crudelitas et] et *omitted by Thomas*

Pr 4. quoque] quaque *Thomas*

Pr 4. dicendi] ducendi *Ovid*

Pr 4. deficiat] deficit *Ovid*

Pr 4. sitque] estque *Ovid*

11. memini *emended by JH*: nemini *ed., Thomas*

36. Magmede: *sc. Maumet(h)e*

61. nostracque *Thomas (sic)*

103. faciem *Thomas*

111. nostram *Thomas*

116. Magmedis] Vagmedis *Thomas*

161. Me] Ve *Thomas*

183. convolvens] conuduens *Thomas*

304. Magerae *ed., Thomas*

334. iuventur] iuuentus *Thomas*

359. Erymnis: *sc. Erinys*

377. Maginedaeas *Thomas*

411. *Line omitted by Thomas*

Inv 13. Tandalidae *ed., Thomas*

Inv 15. Chrisus: *sc. Crixus*

Notes to the Translations

ECERINIS

1. Adeleita degli Alberti da Mangona, from a family of Tuscan counts, married to Ezzelino II in 1184, died 1214; she had the reputation of being a sorceress.

2. The Blessed Luca Belludi (ca. 1200–1286), a Franciscan priest, was a disciple and companion of St. Anthony of Padua.

3. Ansedisio de Guidottis, appointed *podestà* in Padua by Ezzelino.

4. The word *devota* might also mean "accursed," but the sense of "lovingly attached" seems more appropriate here; a play on words is possible.

5. The description of the palace recalls the fortress of Pelops described in Seneca's *Thyestes*, ll. 641–47, a play to which Mussato was particularly indebted (see Introduction).

6. Ezzelino II da Romano (d. 1235), father of the famous tyrant Ezzelino da Romano. When he entered a monastery in 1223 (thus acquiring the epithet *il Monaco*, "the Monk"), he left his possessions to his two sons: Alberico received the castles and villages in the territory of Vicenza, and his older brother, Ezzelino III da Romano (1194–1259), controlled the March of Treviso.

7. Compare Seneca, *Phaedra*, l. 1035ff.

8. The line is taken almost entirely from Seneca, *Troades*, l. 28.

9. The Morning Star is one of the names for Lucifer, or the Devil in the Christian tradition.

10. The three Furies and Pluto's queen in the underworld, respectively. Mussato analyzes their activity in terms of the four Aristotelian causes: Alecto is the first or material cause, Tisiphone the formal cause, Megaera the efficient cause, and Persephone the final.

11. As noted by Dazzi (1964), l. 144, the word alludes (*inficit* suggests taking on the colors of a party) to the conflicts between the Guelf and

Ghibelline factions, referred to again at l. 164 (*partes*). Ezzelino, allied to Frederick II, was one of the chief protagonists in the Ghibelline victory at the Battle of Cortenuova in 1257 and was named imperial viceroy for the March of Treviso.

12. I.e., the wheel of Fortune.

13. The March of Treviso in the Middle Ages comprised the territories of Padua, Vicenza, Verona, and Treviso itself.

14. The history of Verona detailed here by the Messenger concerns events that occurred between 1204 and 1208 and provides the political background to the main action of the play. Ezzelino II, *podestà* since 1200, had established amicable relations with the family of the Montecchi (Shakespeare's Montagues); the opposing party in Verona was led by Richard, Count of San Bonifacio, to whom Azzo VI d'Este (1170–1212) allied himself. In 1206 the Montecchi were driven out and appealed to Ezzelino, who found an able supporter in Torello Salinguerra, a competitor of Azzo d'Este for the rule of Ferrara. The entire March of Treviso was now arrayed in two hostile factions: on one side the houses of Este and San Bonifacio, and on the other Ezzelino and Salinguerra, supported by the inhabitants of Bassano and the commune of Treviso. Confusion ruled. In Ferrara alone, a chronicler says, rival parties had expelled one another ten times before 1220.

15. A piazza just inside the main gate of Verona; now Piazza Bra.

16. Ezzelino III da Romano, *podestà* of Verona from 1226.

17. *Bistonis stabuli* refers to Diomedes, the king of Thrace, whose man-eating horses it was the seventh labor of Hercules to capture; compare Seneca, *Hercules furens*, ll. 227–28. Procrustes was legendary outlaw of Eleusis, who used to lay travelers on a bed, and if they were too long for it cut off their limbs, but if the bed was longer stretch them to make their length equal. He was killed by the hero Theseus.

18. The people (*popolo, populus*) at the time when Mussato was writing composed the middle ranks of society, often in Italian societies politically organized against the nobles. The force of Mussato's words here is that *even* the middle classes, not just the urban rabble, have been made subject

to the tyrant—words perhaps more applicable to Cangrande della Scala than to Ezzelino da Romano (see Introduction).

19. The Furies.

20. Ruler of the underworld in Roman religion, often identified with Pluto; here identical with the Devil or Lucifer in the Christian tradition.

21. Lucifer was often identified with the morning star, i.e., Venus, rising in the East, on the basis of Isaiah 14:12–20.

22. Typhoeus was a terrible monster with a hundred serpents' heads, fiery eyes, and a horrid voice that Zeus attacked with thunderbolts, set on fire, and flung into Tartarus. Enceladus was a giant who attacked Zeus but was killed by Athena, who threw the giant's body under Mt. Aetna.

23. Alluding to Julius Caesar's famous opening line of his *Gallic War*, where he says that "all Gaul is divided in three parts."

24. Originally loyal to Ezzelino, Monaldo de' Limizoni, called Linguadevacca ("Cow's tongue") took part in a plot against Ezzelino and was beheaded in 1239 by Ziramonte, acting on Ezzelino's orders; presumably he was one of the deserters disclosed by the stratagem of Ezzelino and his brother mentioned in line 320.

25. St. Paul, apostle to the Gentiles, named Saul before his conversion. See Acts 9:1–31.

26. Alexander the Great.

27. The marquis Uberto Pellavicino, *podestà* of Cremona.

28. Buoso di Dovara was another former ally of Ezzelino who turned against him.

29. Martino della Torre (d. 1263), one of the leaders of the Guelf league in Milan, along with Oberto Pallavicino. In 1259, after a broad Ghibelline offensive the year before in Lombardy and the Veneto, Ezzelino unsuccessfully assaulted Milan itself. He was wounded by an arrow at the Battle of Cassano d'Adda, retreated, but was captured and died in captivity.

30. The Bridge of Cassano.

31. Either his mother or a devil predicted that Ezzelino would die at *Assano*, which, on the advice of his astrologers, Ezzelino interpreted as a reference to the city of *Bassano* near where he was born. *Cassano* refers to the battle at the Adda River.

32. The Castello di San Zeno in Montagnana near Padua, built by the Este and made into a stronghold by Ezzelino III da Romano after capturing it in 1242.

33. Azzo VII d'Este, "il Novello" (ca. 1205–1264).

34. In actuality, Alberico da Romano (1196–1260), sometimes called Alberico II, had two wives: the first was Beatrice, with whom he had one daughter, Adeleita, and five sons, Ezzelino (killed in battle in 1243), Alberico, Romano, Ugolino, and Giovanni; the second was Margherita, with whom he sired three daughters, Griselda, Tornalisce, and Amabilia.

ACHILLES

1. Helen, taken from her husband, Menelaus, by Paris.

2. The blood of Iphigenia, who was sacrificed at Aulis by her father, Agamemnon, to ensure the passage of the Greek fleet to Troy.

3. The Xanthus (or Scamander) and the Simois were rivers close to Troy.

4. The walls of Troy were built for Laomedon by Neptune and Apollo; Apollo was said to be able to move stones by the mere sound of his lyre. See Ovid, *Metamorphoses* 11.194–204 and *Heroides* 16.180.

5. As the Greeks were gathering for the Trojan War, Achilles' mother, the Nereid Thetis, knowing that her son would die at Troy, hid him at Scyros and dressed him as a girl. When Calchas told the Greeks that Troy could not be taken without Achilles, Odysseus (Ulysses) found him and persuaded him to join the expedition.

6. The "Phoebus-bearing maiden" could also be identified with the Sibyl, the priestess of Apollo.

7. Paris. After the apple of Discord was given to him on Mt. Ida, where he was tending his flocks, Paris was asked to award it to the most beautiful of three goddesses: Juno, Minerva, or Venus. Bribed with the promise of Helen, he awarded it to Venus.

8. The Wain (sometimes known in Great Britain as Charles' Wain), here in a poetic plural (*plaustra*), is today called the Big Dipper and is part of the Ursa Major constellation.

9. Identified as Troilus in a marginal note found in one of the MSS; see the notes to Zaccaria's edition, 67.

10. Zaccaria reports that in one manuscript the marginal note *yronice* stands next to *iacete segnes* (the same note is repeated at lines 125 and 494).

11. Tantalus, Sisyphus, Ixion, and Tityus were all punished for their crimes against the gods. Tantalus, after stealing the food of the gods and giving it to mortals, was forced to stand in water up to his chin with fruit-laden trees over his head; when he tried to drink, the water receded, and when he reached for the fruit, the wind blew the tree away. Sisyphus eternally rolled a rock up a hill, from the top of which it always rolled down again. Ixion, the first to murder one of his kin, was attached to a revolving wheel. Tityus, as a punishment for assaulting Leto, was placed in Hades where two vultures tore at his liver.

12. The Furies or Erinyes: Alecto, Megaera, and Tisiphone.

13. Cerberus.

14. Echoing Vergil, *Aeneid* 6.126–31. After suggesting earlier (87–108) that there is no life after death and punishments after death are an empty tale—a philosophical view reminiscent of Epicurus—Paris now enunciates what appears to be a more orthodox Christian view of the afterlife.

15. See note 4, above.

16. A marginal note in one manuscript reads *Propter metus,* "owing to fears." Hecuba, out of contempt for Paris' courage, suggests a shameful but easy route to achieve her revenge.

17. Daughter of Zeus and Hera, the handmaiden of the gods for whom she pours out nectar, Hebe was associated with perpetual youth. She was represented as married to Heracles (Hercules) after his ascent to heaven.

18. Loved by the sea-god Glaucus, Scylla was turned into a monster by her rival, Circe. Scylla seized and devoured the mariners who sailed close to her cave, situated according to tradition in the Straits of Messina, with the whirlpool of Charybdis opposite it.

19. The hero Perseus, son of Jupiter and Danaë, half sister of Athena.

20. Diana, who was born on the wandering island of Delos, which remained fixed so Leto could give birth to Apollo and her; see Vergil, *Aeneid* 3.73ff.

21. See Homer, *Iliad* 21.

22. Eos, the goddess of the dawn. She was thought to shed tears in the form of dew when Achilles killed her son Memnon, who, as leader of the Ethiopians, fought on the Trojan side.

23. Zaccaria, 69, proposes reading *liber* as equivalent to *carens*. Telephus was impious because he opposed his fellow Greeks and aided the Trojans; see next note.

24. On their way to Troy, the Greeks landed in Mysia, the king of which, Telephus, was wounded by Achilles. Having been told by the Delphic oracle that the man who had wounded him would also heal him, he went to Troy in search of Achilles.

25. The translation follows Felice Osio's conjecture; see Notes to the Texts.

26. For *sublimi* as "panting" see Horace, *Odes* 1.15.31.

27. Aeacus was the father of Peleus (Achilles' father).

28. I.e., if Mars gave Achilles his beloved Venus to be his, Achilles,' wife, and if Juno left her husband (but also her brother) Jupiter for his bed, if Paris gave up Helen, his prize for adjudging Venus the winner in the Judgment of Paris, he would still prefer Polyxena for his wife.

29. The reference is to the famous "Parthian shot," a military tactic used by ancient Iranian archers who pretended to retreat, then turned and released arrows at the enemy, whose guard was down.

30. In lines 401ff. is a catalog of the various transformations of the gods, especially Jove. For love of Danaë he visited her in a shower of gold, from which union Perseus was born (see l. 235). For Leda he changed into a swan, and their union produced Castor and Pollux as well as Helen and Clytemnestra. In order to win Europa, Jove became a bull so beautiful that she climbed on its back and was whisked away to Crete. For love of Callisto, one of Diana's nymphs, Zeus took on the semblance of the goddess herself. Callisto was punished for her unchastity by being changed into a she-bear, but she and her son Arcas were transformed into the constellations Ursa Major and Minor. Concealed in a cloud, Jove seduced Io, the daughter of Inachus, king of Argos. For love of Alcmena, Jove disguised himself as Amphitryon, to whom Alcmena was betrothed. Jove ordered the sun not to rise for two days to extend his nuptial night with her, a union that produced Hercules. Semele was loved by Jove, and at the instigation of the jealous Juno prayed Jove to visit her in all the splendor of the god. This he did, and she was consumed by his lightning. After Theseus had abandoned Ariadne at Naxos, Dionysus (or Bacchus) wedded her and carried her to heaven. A similar passage about the loves of Jupiter is found in Seneca's *Phaedra*, ll. 299–316.

31. Hesperus, the planet Venus or the "evening star," is identical with Lucifer, the "morning star," Venus in her matutinal role.

32. Artemis, goddess of the moon.

33. The double night: when Hesperus retained his nocturnal identity for two days; see l. 410 and note. Hercules was famously unmanned by his love for Iole; see Servius' commentary on *Aeneid* 8.291.

34. At the court of Lycomedes, Achilles' mother, Thetis, dressed him in women's clothing to conceal him from Ulysses, who wanted him to join the war on Troy; but Ulysses invented a ruse, which led Achilles to reveal his yearning to handle weapons; see note 5 above.

35. She addresses Hector and Troilus, awaiting passage to Hades on Charon's barge.

36. The Fates were three in number and are represented as old women spinning: Clotho held the distaff, Lachesis drew off the thread, and Atropos cut it short.

37. Pyrrhus (or Neoptolemus) grieves for the death of his father Achilles, just as Hecuba's son Astyanax grieves for Hector. Thetis and Hecuba are now linked in common mourning for their sons.

38. A marginal note in one MS reads: *yronice,* ironically.

39. Cassandra's prophecy, cryptic as always, may be understood as follows. Hecuba will not be able to escape a "Thessalian marriage" for Polyxena, i.e., a marriage with Achilles, in that the ghost of Achilles will appear and demand that she be sacrificed at his tomb, so that the Greek fleet can sail away from Troy. See Dares Phrygius 43. But details in the prophecy imply that Loschi also knew Euripides' *Hecuba,* which was available in Latin in the translation of Leonzio Pilato, done for Boccaccio; see Zaccaria, 71n. "A spouse will drink the blood of a spouse": i.e., Achilles' tomb will drink Polyxena's blood; compare Seneca, *Troades,* l. 1164. Zaccaria, ibid., supposes that the phrase about Hecuba seeking her (Polyxena's) brother refers to an episode in which Hecuba finds Polyxena's brother Polydorus dead by the seashore and goes mad as a result; see Ovid, *Metamorphoses* 13.533–75.

40. Pyrrhus.

41. Perhaps because, as Zaccaria (72n.) suggests, Helen married another son of Priam, Deiphobus, after the death of Paris.

42. Perhaps in reference to the dispersal of the Trojans after the fall of Troy.

43. Amphion, son of Zeus and Antiope, along with his twin brother, Zethus, built the walls of Thebes. Cadmus had earlier founded the city when the Delphic oracle told him to follow a cow that he should meet and found a city where it first lay down. See Ovid, *Metamorphoses* 3.1ff. and Hyginus, *Fabulae,* 275.

44. Zaccaria notes that *scilicet rota* is written above *metuenda* in the most authoritative MS.

45. For "example of wickedness" (*sceleris magister*) compare Lucan 1.326, *Sullam scelerum . . . magistrum.*

46. Diomedes was a Thracian king, a son of Mars, killed as one of Hercules' labors and fed to his man-eating horses.

47. For the interpretation of this difficult sentence see Zaccaria, 72–73, note 151, who notes that the most authoritative MS has the interlinear notes *Concordia* above *diva,* and *tibi* above *sprete.* The rash judge of the bright apple is of course Paris, who offers the goddess in tribute the avenging arrows with which he has killed Achilles. But the offended goddess must in fact be Discordia or Eris, excluded from the marriage of Peleus and Thetis. See note 7.

48. Prometheus, who stole fire from the gods, was chained to a rock in the Caucasus, where his liver was eaten daily by an eagle, only to grow back each night.

49. I.e., Jupiter, Apollo and Neptune, the lords of heaven, the air and the seas.

50. The brother of Ilus, father of Laomedon, in whose reign the walls of Troy were built, great-grandfather of Aeneas.

51. As the moon (personified by Artemis, sister of Phoebus) follows the sun.

52. The sisters of Phaëthon, the Heliades, after his death were so afflicted by grief that they were transformed into poplar trees and their tears into golden amber.

53. Referring to the sacrifice of Iphigenia. See note 61.

54. Apollo's earliest adventure was the killing of the Python, a dragon that guarded Delphi; see Ovid, *Metamorphoses* 1.456ff.

55. The daughter of Tantalus and mother of seven sons and seven daughters. She boasted of her superiority to Leto, a daughter of the Titans, who only had two children. Apollo and Artemis then killed Niobe's children with their arrows. She wept for them until she turned into a column of stone, from which her tears continued to flow.

56. Laomedon, for whom Neptune and Apollo built the walls of Troy; he promised the gods rewards, which he failed to deliver.

57. Neptune, who refused the first offer (the kingdom of heaven, given to Jupiter) and the last (the underworld, given to Pluto) but accepted rule of the sea; see ll. 242 and 447.

58. Husband of Leda and supposed father of Helen and Clytemnestra, the wife of Agamemnon.

59. See notes 5 and 34.

60. Helen.

61. A reference to the notorious episode when the seer Calchas told the Greeks that the only way their fleet would sail on Troy was if they sacrificed Iphigenia, eldest daughter of Agamemnon.

62. Jupiter and Juno.

63. Proserpina, wife of Pluto.

64. Atropos, one of the three Fates or Moirae who control the destiny of individuals; see note 36.

65. Whatever grows needs sun, water, and air. Jove is here identified with the element of air. Zeus is called the lord of the air in Empedocles, but the passage may also reflect Christianization; see Genesis 2:7.

PROCNE

1. A medieval form of the more usual classical name, Philomela.

2. As Onorato (121) notes, much of the argument is based on Boccaccio's *Genealogies of the Gods* 9.8.

3. Although he does not appear in Seneca's *Thyestes*, Correr's main source, or in Ovid's account in *Metamorphoses* 6.412–674, Pistus is a character whose name is derived from the Greek *pistos*, in other words, a "faithful" companion.

4. Literally, "into a bird of that name": Philomena (and Philomela) means "nightingale."

5. The hoopoe is a European woodland bird with a prominent crest, considered unclean in the Bible (Leviticus 11:19 and Deuteronomy 14:18); it was supposed to feed on graves and human feces (see Isidore of Seville, *Etymologies* 12.7.66).

6. The line number of each sample verse is given in parentheses following it.

7. The barbarian tyrant Diomedes, king of the Bistones in Thrace, forerunner of Tereus. See *Achilles*, Notes to the Translations, note 46.

8. I.e., he is willing to undergo punishment even if the fallen angels are forgiven their rebellion against God.

9. I.e., may he be punished like Prometheus; see *Achilles*, Notes to the Translation, note 48.

10. I.e., the crime is likely to be unique in history.

11. Possibly a reference to Genesis 1:6–8 or Psalm 148:1–4.

12. Eurydice was Orpheus' wife. Pursued by Aristaeus, the son of Apollo and Cyrene, she was fatally bitten by a snake. Orpheus descended to Hades and so charmed the infernal powers that he was permitted to bring her back to the upper world again if he did not look back at her on the way. By breaking this agreement he lost her. Correr's account follows Seneca, *Hercules Oetaeus* ll. 1061–78. The dramatic aim is to contrast Orpheus' beautiful loyalty and courage with the reality of Tereus' true character.

13. Tereus is the son of Mars (or Ares), who is invoked at the beginning of the next act.

14. The Rhodope mountain range lies mostly in modern Bulgaria; the Tanais, now known as the Don, is a river in southern Russia that flows into the Sea of Azov; both geographical features were believed to belong to Thrace, a wild region of indeterminate size to the north and east of classical Greece.

15. Bacchus. He squats because the rustic Thracians do not have civilized furniture such as chairs.

16. Haemus and Otris are mountain ranges in northern Thrace; Pangaea is a mountain in Macedonia.

17. Quicksands off the coast of North Africa, a legendary navigational hazard.

18. A river on the Thracian-Macedonian border.

19. A constellation, also called Arctophylax.

20. Compare Petrarch, *Trionfo della Morte* 1.172: "Morte bella parea nel suo bel viso."

21. Compare Vergil, *Aeneid* 2.223–24.

22. Giovanni Ricci's conjecture, *concita Maenas iugis*, is metrically impossible.

23. In her haste to see her one sister, she has almost drowned two persons, Philomena and Pistus; on this reading, "almost" would indicate that she does not feel fully responsible for Pistus' death. Another possibility is that Procne here is thinking about Philomena and Tereus.

24. Reading *iaceas* for *iaceat*.

25. For the sentiments, compare Seneca, *Thyestes* ll. 596–97, 615–68, and Vergil, *Georgics* 3.68–70.

26. The mythical helmsman of the Argo, which carried Jason to Colchis in search of the Golden Fleece. The episode here is based on Seneca, *Medea* ll. 301–79. Here Tiphys is identified as the inventor of oceangoing galleys.

27. *Germana* means a real sister who shares a parent with another sister, whereas *soror* can be used of a sister-in-law or half sister, or even looser relations such as cousins; it can also mean, euphemistically, mistress. Correr is imitating here the ancient fascination with how family relationships are bizarrely altered by acts of incest or rape: Philomena, having been raped by Procne's husband, could now be called Procne's sister-in-law or Tereus' mistress.

28. Procne's mother, Zeuxippe, is not otherwise present in the play or in the sources for the Procne legend.

29. In lines 482–86, Procne begins her transition to a Bacchante, who will wander in holy madness through the woods but will secretly be driven by her "greater madness" to rescue her sister.

30. The chorus is modeled on Seneca's *Oedipus* ll. 403–508.

31. Bacchus (or Dionysius) was born of the mortal woman Semele and the god Zeus; Semele was consumed by fire when Zeus appeared to her in his glory.

32. I.e., boxwood flutes are made for Bacchus' use.

33. "Bacchis" is a woman's name, here possibly standing for "Baccha" or Bacchante.

34. Ogygos was a legendary king of Thebes in Euboea; his name becomes an epithet of Bacchus because Thebes was regarded as particularly devoted to that god: see Ovid, *Heroides* 10.48.

35. Agave. When Dionysus (Bacchus) returned to Thebes from his conquests in the east, King Pentheus denied his divinity, and for his sacrilege was torn to pieces by the worshippers of the god, his mother among them. See Ovid, *Metamorphoses* 3.513–25.

36. The "seed of Calliope," Orpheus, was stoned and torn limb from limb by Thracian Bacchantes because he had scorned the rites of Bacchus; see Ovid, *Metamorphoses* 11.1–66.

37. See Seneca, *Oedipus* ll. 481–83.

38. The largest of the Cyclades, this island is where Ariadne, after being abandoned by Theseus, was found by Dionysus, who married her.

39. An island in the Aegean famed for its wine and marble. The identification of Chios as the island where Bacchus lived with Ariadne comes from Boccaccio, *Genealogy of the Pagan Gods* 11.29, who confuses the account in Ovid, *Metamorphoses* 3.636–37.

40. Bacchus had Ariadne's crown put into the heavens as the constellation Corona Borealis; see Ovid, *Metamorphoses* 8.178–79.

41. Referring to an episode in Ovid where sailors kidnap Bacchus, who makes them jump overboard and turns them into dolphins.

42. Minyas, the king of Orchomenus in Thessaly, had three daughters—Leucippe, Arsippe, and Alcithoe—who resisted the cult of Dionysus, were driven mad, and tore to pieces Hippasos, the son of Leucippe. They were turned into bats.

43. A satyr and inseparable companion of Bacchus.

44. A river of Thrace.

45. Onorato, 192n, believes that the parenthetical phrase may be a stage direction brought awkwardly into Procne's speech, but this hypothesis seems unnecessary.

46. A river on the border of Thrace and Macedonia, now the Struma.

47. I.e., both a foreign war brought by Athens or a civil war within Thrace would be ineffective.

48. Mythical founder of Athens.

49. The Thracian or Getic sea is probably the Euxine or Black Sea, while the Bay of Maeotis has been identified with the Sea of Azov. Marshland, known as the Maeotian marshes, stood where the Don River emptied into the Sea of Azov.

50. The fifty daughters of King Danaus, the Danaides, were secretly instructed by the king to kill their husbands on their wedding night. Only one did not; the other forty-nine were punished in Tartarus by being made to carry water in leaky jugs. The water always leaked out before they could bring it to the baths, in which they were to cleanse themselves of their sin.

51. Three MSS have the interlinear note above *at: pro saltem;* i.e., "understand *but* in the sense of *at least.*"

52. See Note on the Texts.

53. The daughter of Aeëtes, king of Colchis, and the niece of Circe. Abandoned by Jason, Medea kills her own children in vengeance. Much of Correr's Procne is modeled on Seneca's Medea.

54. The Tagus and Hister are, respectively, a river of the Iberian peninsula and the lower course of the Danube.

55. A reference to Jupiter hiding from his father, Saturn, on the Cretan plains at the foot of Mt. Dicte.

56. Some of the various transformations of Jove: for love of Alcmena, Jove disguised himself as Amphitryon, to whom Alcmena was betrothed. Jove ordered the sun not to rise for two days to extend his nuptial night with her, a union that produced Hercules; in order to win Europa, Jove became a bull so beautiful that she climbed on its back and was whisked away to Crete; for Leda he changed into a swan, and their union produced Castor and Pollux as well as Helen and Clytemnestra. See also note 30 to *Achilles*.

57. Three of the MSS have *pro damnatur* ("instead of 'are condemned'") written superscript above *damnat* ("condemns").

58. The sea monster Scylla who guarded the straits of Messina was supposed to have rabid dogs attached to her waist; see Ovid, *Metamorphoses* 13.732.

59. Hyrcanian tigers, from northern Asia Minor, were proverbially ferocious; see, e.g., Vergil, *Aeneid* 4.367.

60. I.e., by comparison with what she actually did.

61. Looking forward to the fifth act, when Tereus learns of Procne's crime.

62. I.e., the human race. On Prometheus as the father of the human race, see Ovid, *Metamorphoses* 1.82–83 and Boccaccio, *Genealogy* 4.44.

63. I.e., of Medea.

64. The plural "children" here would seem to result from too servile an imitation of Seneca, *Thyestes*, l. 917.

65. Casarsa, 174, 151n, and presumably Onorato as well (as one must suppose from his punctuation), believes *effer* cannot be a proleptic imperative and prefers to believe that the final syllable of a present indicative has been dropped. But the proleptic imperative would be a fine piece of theatrical realism, giving Philomena time to come out of the wings bearing the boy's head. It also keeps Procne in control of the action and

Philomena a passive agent, here as elsewhere in contrast with Ovid's presentation of her as an avid accomplice.

66. I.e., the Giants. See Ovid, *Metamorphoses* 1.151ff.

67. A legendary outlaw of Eleusis. See note 17 to the *Ecerinis*.

68. An Egyptian king, son of Poseidon, who slaughtered on the altar of Zeus all foreigners who entered Egypt.

69. The same triumphant cry is found in Seneca's *Medea*, l. 982, from which so much of Procne's character and language is taken.

HIEMPSAL

1. For this sequel to the *certame coronario* of 1441, to which the *Hiempsal* was intended as a contribution, see the Introduction.

2. I.e., Athenian or Attic, Erichthonius being a legendary king of Athens.

3. Prospero Colonna (ca. 1410–1463) was a member of one of the great baronial and ecclesiastical families of Rome and a patron of important humanists such as Poggio Bracciolini, George of Trebizond and Lapo da Castiglionchio.

4. Dati was made bishop of Massa only in 1467, twenty-seven years after the original composition of the play; but the addition of Dati's episcopal title to the rubric was made only in a later stage of the play's textual tradition; see Onorato, 77f.

5. Spirits of the dead who had the special care of the house and household and were worshipped at the domestic hearth; metonymously, for "home."

6. The morning star stands allegorically for the virtue of justice (in reference to a famous passage in Aristotle's *Nicomachean Ethics* 5.1), so Asper is asking Jupiter whether it can be right to punish even just human beings with the scourge of Envy.

7. I.e., man shares with the beasts the problems of the flesh, and adds to these the ills of the spirit.

8. *Bonae artes* is one of the Renaissance synonyms for the humanities, the study of classical literature and philosophy.

9. Cerberus.

10. The Furies or Erinyes, named Alecto, Megaera, and Tisiphone.

11. An obvious echo of Vergil, *Aeneid* 3.56.

12. Allegorically indicating the two greatest remedies against Envy: making the truth public, and laughter in private.

13. I.e., from the moment Micipsa included Jugurtha in the succession to the kingdom.

14. A people of northwest Africa, used poetically for Africans in general.

15. Hiempsal's thought seems to be that love and fear are unstable emotions, responding to circumstances. In the background is Cicero's famous question in the *De officiis,* whether it is better for a ruler to be loved or feared. Polymites takes the Stoic view (here as elsewhere) that the emotions are within our control.

16. In Act I, Envy (*Invidia*) is personified as female in gender; now in Act II it becomes masculine (*Livor*).

17. A Roman province extending west and south of Carthage.

18. A version of the proverbial observation that one must learn to obey before one can command.

19. Dati here alludes to the common theme of humanist treatises on true nobility, that nobility is won through virtue alone and not by descent; men of high descent should make themselves worthy of honor through virtue rather than relying passively on a famous name. The theme has obvious relevance to this play, with its rivalry between Hiempsal, a son unworthy of his descent, and Jugurtha, the son adopted because of his virtue. Thus the fullest statement of the "true nobility" theme is put in the mouth of Jugurtha at the beginning of Act IV.

20. Phitonissa displays some of the characteristics of a Dionysian Bacchante, as Onorato notes; the closely related name Pythonissa is attested in the Greek Fathers of the Church as a name for the Delphic Oracle.

21. The name of the Numidian town where Hiempsal was murdered, modern Thirmida Bure in Libya.

22. When Adherbal fled to this town, Jugurtha laid siege to it; Adherbal surrendered to Jugurtha and was killed.

23. The Roman eagle. The rest of the paragraph foretells in prophetic language the defeat of Jugurtha by the Romans.

24. Site of a battle between Marius and Jugurtha sometime between 107 and 106 BCE. The war with Rome that had begun around 111 was directed by an efficient commander, Q. Metellus, but Jugurtha's skill and personality prolonged the struggle even after he had been driven out of Numidia. Marius was Metellus' successor, who eventually defeated Jugurtha. Zama was also the site of Scipio's famous defeat of Hannibal in 202 BCE.

25. The insurrection of the Numidian town Vaga was suppressed by the Romans after two days.

26. The town where Jugurtha kept his treasure. When the Romans occupied the town, they found the palace set on fire and all the people dead.

27. A town destroyed by the Romans.

28. While Marius was encamped near the river Muluccha, which separated the kingdom of Jugurtha and Bocchus, and was uncertain how to advance, owing to the rugged ground, a certain Ligurian who was fetching water noticed snails crawling on the rocks by the river. As he continued to gather them, he came ever closer to the summit where the Numidians were mustered. Marius followed the trail blazed by the Ligurian collecting snails.

29. Bomilcar (*hospes*) unsuccessfully urged Jugurtha to surrender to the Romans. He then enlisted Nabdalsa's help in plotting against Jugurtha, but his accomplice grew timid. Sensing his own undoing, Bomilcar sent a letter entreating Nabdalsa to remain constant, but the letter was stolen by Nabdalsa's Numidian secretary, who, perceiving the plot, went to Jugurtha (*tu*).

30. There were three Gorgons — Sthenno, Euryale, and Medusa — all represented with hideous faces, glaring eyes, and serpents in their hair. The head of a Gorgon turned to stone anything that met its gaze.

31. *Artifex*, "craftsman," is the word used for Plato's demiurge in Calcidius' Latin translation of Plato's *Timaeus*.

32. I.e., the waters of Hippocrene. This was a fountain sacred to the Muses on Mt. Helicon that was created by a stamp of Pegasus' hoof. Dati means that the study of literature and philosophy is a consolation in the misery of the human condition.

33. A version of the famous quotation from Sallust's *Bellum Jugurthae* 10.6 (there put in the mouth of Micipsa) that "Harmony makes small states great, while discord undermines the mightiest empires." See Introduction, xxxiii–xxxiv.

34. The phrase *esse, non videri*, "to be, not to seem," was proverbial, but it is also found in well-known classical sources, such as Cicero's *De amicitia* 98 ("There are not many who would not rather seem endowed with true virtue than to be so") and Sallust's *Bellum Catilinae* 54.6, who said that Cato the Younger wanted to be good rather than seem so. But this entire scene is dense with proverbial wisdom.

35. I.e., Fortune.

36. Hercules, whose father was Zeus.

37. Or "on a boundary stone"; see Notes to the Texts.

38. Pluto, who received the third part of the world as his lot, after Jove had received the heavens and Neptune the seas.

39. "Io!" according to the *Oxford Latin Dictionary*, s.v., is "a more or less ritual exclamation, uttered under the stress of strong emotion, and invoking a god or divine power." In particular it is used by followers of Bacchus.

40. The "Great Mother," a goddess of the powers of nature. Her castrated priests were called *galli*.

41. Again citing the *Oxford Latin Dictionary*, s.v., a *thyrsus* is "a wand tipped with a fir-cone, tuft of ivy, or vine-leaves . . . carried by worshippers in the rites of Bacchus."

FERDINAND PRESERVED

1. Quoted by Seneca, *De providentia* 3.3.

2. Ovid, *Ex Ponto* 1.5.7–8.

3. Horace, *Ars poetica* 304–5.

4. *Divinae institutiones* 1.11.24; 30.

5. Ambassadors of Ferdinand II, king of Aragon, who participated in the public spectacles at Rome that celebrated the king's victory at Granada on February 5, 1492. Bernardino Lopez de Carvajal (1455–1522) was variously bishop of Astorga, Badajoz, and Cartagena, and was made cardinal by Alexander VI in 1493. He was a distinguished diplomat. Juan Ruiz de Medina (d. 1507), a canon lawyer and diplomat, succeeded Carvajal in the bishoprics of Astorga, Badajoz, and Cartagena, then became Bishop of Seville in 1502.

6. Plautus, *Amphitruo*, Prol. 59–63.

7. One of the apostles of Jesus, his remains are said to be in Santiago de Compostela in Spain. He was (and is) the patron saint of the Spanish royal house.

8. Juan de Cañamares. "Ruffus" (*rufus*, "red") suggests "flame" or "fire," possibly an allusion to hell or to the devil or to the color of his hair.

9. Sthenelus, the son of Perseus, was the father of Eurystheus, who imposed the twelve labors on Hercules. For each one of them Juno sided with Hercules' opponents.

10. Boabdil (*Lat.* Baudeles) is the Spanish name for Emir Muhammed XII. He was the last Islamic ruler of Granada, who surrendered control of the emirate to Ferdinand and Isabella in 1492, thus bringing an end to the Reconquesta of Al Andalus.

11. The goddess Proserpina.

12. A close friend of Theseus, who descended with him to Hades. The allusions to the heroic deeds of Theseus and the labors of Hercules throughout the play are perhaps meant to suggest Ferdinand's heroic qualities.

13. Twin sons of Zeus and Leda identified as the Dioscuri and with the constellation Gemini.

14. The constant friend of Orestes, accompanying him to Mycenae to take vengeance on Orestes' mother, Clytemnestra, and her lover, Aegisthus, after Agamemnon's murder.

15. Gaius Fabricius Luscinus, hero of the war with Pyrrhus in the third century BCE, known for his incorruptibility.

16. Marcus Furius Camillus, the savior and second founder of Rome after the Gallic invasion in 387 BCE. His career is described in books 5 and 6 of Livy.

17. *Divus* is commonly used in Renaissance Latin for "saint," so Queen Isabella here is probably still addressing St James.

18. Sciron (Scyron, Skiron), a robber in Megara who is killed by the Athenian hero Theseus; see Plutarch, *Theseus* 10, and Ovid, *Metamorphoses* 7.443.

19. A Thracian gladiator who led a revolt at Capua in 73 BCE and who quickly became a legend because of his bravery and military skill in defeating Roman armies.

20. The description of Ruffus in chains is based on Ovid's description of Envy in *Metamorphoses* 2.774–78.

21. Loved by the sea-god Glaucus, Scylla was turned into a monster by her rival Circe. Scylla seized and devoured the mariners who sailed close to its cave, situated according to tradition in the Straits of Messina, with the whirlpool of Charybdis opposite it.

22. For Sciron see note 18 above; he was said to make passers-by on the Scironian Way wash his feet and, as they did so, kick them over a cliff where, according to some accounts, they were devoured by a great tortoise. Bebryx was a cruel Gaulish king and the father of the virgin Pyrene (see Silius Italicus 3.423), who was raped by Hercules. Busiris was an Egyptian king, son of Poseidon, who slaughtered on the altar of Zeus all foreigners who entered Egypt.

23. Procrustes was a legendary outlaw of Eleusis. See note 17 to the *Ecerinis*. Sinis was a giant and a son of Poseidon, a bandit (also killed by

Theseus) who tore his victims apart with a pine tree. Procrustes and Sinis are paired in Ovid, *Metamorphoses* 7.438–42, probably Verardus' source here. Sciron, Procrustes, and Sinis were all brigands killed by the hero Theseus, the legendary king of Athens.

24. Diomedes of Thrace, a giant who ruled over the tribe of the Bistones; his four man-eating horses were stolen by Hercules in the eighth of his twelve labors. He figures in Act I of the *Procne*, above.

25. Atreus and Thyestes. When Thyestes received the golden ram that signified the kingship, Atreus banished him, but later pretended a reconciliation. At the banquet held to commemorate this, Atreus served up to his brother Thyestes' children, whereupon the sun turned back on its course in horror.

26. Crixus and Oenomaus were gladiators from Gaul who, together with the better-known Spartacus, were leaders in the slave revolt called the Third Servile War by the Romans (73–71 BCE); an account of this is given in Florus' *Epitome* 2.8 and Orosius 5.24.

27. Seven times consul, Gaius Marius (157–86 BCE) was infamous for the revenge he took on his enemies by perpetrating cruel massacres. Lucius Cornelius Sulla (138–78 BCE) was known for the extermination of his enemies, employing the device of "proscription," a posting of lists of victims who might be killed without trial and their property confiscated. Lucius Cornelius Cinna was a patrician leader of the democratic party who massacred the supporters of his enemy Sulla.

28. Referring to Ferdinand and Isabella's marriage, which created the united kingdom of Spain from the kingdoms of Aragon and Castile, as is indicated by the word *cestos*, referring to the girdle of Venus, forged by Vulcan. Verardi perhaps knew the passage in Boccaccio's *Genealogy of the Gods* 4.22.2, in which the *cestos* is said to be worn by Venus when engaging in legitimate unions. This was a particularly delicate point, as Ferdinand and Isabella, being second cousins, had needed a papal bull in order to legitimately wed.

Bibliography

EDITIONS

Ecerinis

Albertini Mussati Historia Augusta Henrici VII Caesaris et alia quae extant omnia. Edited by Lorenzo Pignoria, Felice Osio, and Niccolò Villani. Venice: ex Typographia Ducali Pinelliana, 1636.

Tragoediae duae Albertini Mussati . . . cum notis Nicolai Villani ut et alia auctoris poemata, epistolae nimirum, elegi, soliloquia, eclogae et fragmenta ac lectiones variantes, collationes et notae marginales. Editio novissima, emendatior, et auctior. In vol. VI, pars 2 (1722) of Joannes Georgius Graevius [and Petrus Burmannus], *Thesaurus antiquitatum et historiarum Italiae*. Leiden: Petrus vander Aa, 1704–1725.

Albertini Mussati Tragoedia Eccerinis appellata. Edited by Felice Osio. In L. A. Muratori, *Rerum italicarum scriptores*, vol. X, pars 2 (1727), cols. 785–800. Milan: ex typographia Societatis Palatinae, 1723–1751.

Albertinus Mussatus. *Ecerinide. Tragedia, con uno studio di Giosué Carducci*. Edited by Luigi Padrin. Bologna: Zanichelli, 1900. Reprinted, Bologna: Forni, 1969. The first critical edition, often reprinted with translations, as noted below.

Albertino Mussato. *Ecérinide; Epître métrique sur la poésie; Songe*. Edition critique, traduction et presentation par Jean-Frédéric Chevalier. Paris: Les Belles Lettres, 2000.

Achilles

In *Albertini Mussati Historia Augusta Henrici VII Caesaris*, pp. 209–46, as above.

Achilles: Prototragoedia Antonii de Luschis ad fidem codicis XIV saeculi in bibliotheca vicetina Bertholiana nuncupata asservati. Edited by Alvise da Schio. Padua: Typis Seminarii, 1843. Reprinted with Berrigan's English translation (1975), as below.

Antonio Loschi. *Achilles*. Edited by Vittorio Zaccaria. In *Il teatro umanistico veneto: la tragedia*, pp. 9–96. Testi e studi umanistici 2–3. Ravenna: Longo Editore, 1981. Critical edition with an Italian translation.

Procne

Progne: Tragoedia, nunc primum edita. Edited by Giovanni Ricci. Venice: Academia Veneta, 1558.

Progne, tragoedia nunc primum edita (auctore Gregorio Corraro, curante Joanne Riccio). Rome: Mascardus, 1639. Reprinted from the 1558 edition.

Progne: Tragoedia. In Gerard Nicolas Heerkens, *Icones*. Utrecht: Wild, 1787. Partial edition, retitled *Tereus;* includes prologue and extensive fragments. Heerkens published the work suppositiously under the name of Lucius Varius [Rufus], the Augustan poet.

Joseph R. Berrigan and G. Tournoy, eds. "Gregorii Corrarii tragoedia, cui titulus Progne." *Humanistica Lovaniensia* 29 (1980): 13–99. Critical edition with English translation.

Gregorio Correr. *Progne*. Edited and translated by Laura Casarsa. In *Il teatro umanistico veneto: la tragedia*, pp. 97–236. Testi e studi umanistici 2–3. Ravenna: Longo Editore, 1981. Critical edition with source apparatus and the translation of Domenichi, as below.

Gregorio Correr. *Progne*. Edited by Aldo Onorato. In Correr's *Opere*, vol. I, pp. 158–218. 2 vols. Messina: Sicania, 1991–1994. Critical edition with Italian translation and commentary.

Hiempsal

Joseph R. Berrigan. "Leonardo Dati: Hiensal tragoedia. A Critical Edition with Translation." *Humanistica Lovaniensia* 2 (1976): 84–145.

Leonardo Dati. *Hyempsal*. Edited by Aldo Onorato. Messina: Centro interdipartimentale di studi umanistici, 2000. Critical edition with Italian translation and commentary.

Ferdinand Preserved

Marcellini Verardi Fernandus Servatus. [Rome: Eucharius Silber, January–March 1493].

Fernandus servatus. [Salamanca: Printer of Nebrissensis, "Gramática," about 1494].

Fernandus servatus: Tragicomoedia Caroli Verardi a Marcellino Verardo versibus descripta; Invectiva in Ruffum regiae maiestatis violatorem. [Valladolid: Pedro Giraldi and Miguel de Planes, about 1497].

Marcellini Verardi Caesenatis Ferdinandus servatus cum Barcinonae, ferro petitus, vitae discrimen adiisset. Eiusdem in Ruffum Regiae Maiestatis violatorem. Edited by Beatus Rhenanus. In *Platini Plati Mediolanensis . . . Libellus de carcere.* Strassbourg: Matthias Schürer, 1513.

Fernandus servatus. Edited by Sir Henry Thomas. In *Revue hispanique* 32 (Paris, 1914): 428–57. With an introduction on pp. 428–35.

TRANSLATIONS

Ecerinis

Into Italian:

Ezzelino. Translated by Luigi Mercantini. Palermo: Mirto, 1868.

Ezzelino: tragedia. Verse translated by Federico Balbi. Venice: Gaspari, 1869.

Eccelinide. Translated by Antonio Dall'Acqua Giusti. In his *Alcuni scritti letterari.* Venice: Antonelli, 1878.

Eccerinis. Translated by Michele Minoia. In his *Della vita e delle opera di Albertino Mussato,* pp. 269–92. Rome: Forzani, 1884.

Anton Giulio Barrili. "Il primo drama italiano." *Nuova Antologia di scienze lettere ed arti,* 3rd ser., 59 (1895): 637–60, and 60 (1895): 113–41. Contains a partial verse translation by Barrili.

L'Ecerinide. Verse translated by Manlio Torquato Dazzi. Città di Castello: S. Lapi, 1914.

Ecerinide: tragedia. Verse translated by Michele Di Zonno. Bari: Martini, 1934. Reprinted in *Il teatro di Michele Di Zonno,* Bari: Levante, 1990.

L'Ecerinis. Translated by Ezio Franceschini. In Ezio Franceschini, *Teatro latino medievale,* pp. 120–37. Milan: Nuova Accademia, 1960.

Ecerinis. Translated by Lidia Motta. In Federico Doglio, *Il teatro tragico italiano: storia e testi del teatro tragico in Italia,* pp. 3–49. [Bologna]: Guanda, [1960].

Ecerinis. Prose translation by Manlio [Torquato] Dazzi. In his *Il Mussato preumanista (1261–1329), l'ambiente e l'opera*, pp. 140–58. Vicenza: Neri Pozza, 1964. Reprinted in *Il teatro italiano, vol. I: Dalle origini al Quattrocento*, edited by Emilio Faccioli (Turin: Einaudi, 1975), pp. 293–333 (with Padrin's Latin text). Reprinted in Silvia Locati, *La rinascita del genere tragico nel Medioevo: l'Ecerinis di Albertino Mussato* (Florence: F. Cesati, 2006), pp. 159–88, with Padrin's Latin text.

Into French:

In *Ecérinide; Epître métrique sur la poésie; Songe* (2000), as above. Translated by Jean-Frédéric Chevalier.

Into German:

Ecerinus. Translated by Rolf Engelsing. In *Albertino Mussato, Der Tyrann, Tragödie*. Berlin: Bruno Hessling, 1967. With Padrin's Latin text.

Hubert Müller. *Früher Humanismus in Oberitalien: Albertino Mussato, Ecerinis*. Frankfurt am Main: Peter Lang, 1987. Contains the *Ecerinis* in Müller's German translation with Padrin's Latin text on pp. 93–197.

Into English:

The Tragedy of Ecerinis. Translated by Robert W. Carrubba, et al. University Park, Pennsylvania: Department of Classics, Pennsylvania State University, 1972. With Padrin's Latin text.

Albertino Mussato. *Ecerinis*. Edited by L. Padrin. Antonio Loschi. *Achilles*. Edited by A. da Schio. Reprint of the Latin Texts. Introduction and translation by Joseph R. Berrigan. Munich: Wilhelm Fink Verlag, 1975. Photo reprint of the Padrin text of 1900 with Berrigan's translation.

Achilles

Into Italian:

As above, in *Il teatro umanistico veneto: la tragedia* (1981), pp. 75–96. Translated by Vittorio Zaccaria.

Into English:

As above, under English translations of the *Ecerinus*, pp. 101–87. Translated by Joseph R. Berrigan.

PROCNE

Into Italian:

[Gregorio Correr.] *Progne, tragedia di messer Lodovico Domenichi.* Translated by Ludovico Domenichi (who claims to have composed the work himself). Florence: Giunti, 1561. Reprinted and edited by Laura Casarsa in *Il teatro umanistico veneto: la tragedia*, pp. 187–236, as above.

Into German:

Die Progne des Gregorio Corraro und ihr Verhältnis zur Antike. Translated by Ulrike de Vries. Heidelberg: J. Groos, 1987.

Into English:

In Berrigan and Tournoy, "Gregorii Correrii Tragoedia," as above. Translated by Joseph R. Berrigan.

HIEMPSAL

Into Italian:

In Dati, *Hyempsal.* Edited by Onorato, as above. Translated by Aldo Onorato.

Into English:

In Berrigan, "Leonardo Dati: *Hiensal tragoedia,*" as above. Translated by Joseph R. Berrigan.

SECONDARY LITERATURE

Boyle, A. J. *Tragic Seneca: An Essay in the Theatrical Tradition.* Liverpool: Liverpool University Press, 1997.

Charlton, H. B. *The Senecan Tradition in Renaissance Tragedy.* Manchester: Manchester University Press, 1946.

Cloetta, Wilhelm. *Beiträge zur Literaturgeschichte des Mittelalters und der Renaissance.* 2 vols. Halle: Max Niemeyer, 1890–1892. Reprint, Leipzig: Zentralantiquariat der Deutschen Demokratischen Republik, 1976.

Graziosi, Maria Teresa. "Tradizione e realtà nel *Fernandus servatus* di Marcellino Verardi." In *Atti e memorie dell'Arcadia* 6 (1973): 55–71.

Jacquot, Jean. *Les tragédies de Sénèque et la théâtre de la Renaissance.* Paris: Centre national de la recherché scientifique, 1964.

Kelly, Henry A. *Ideas and Forms of Tragedy from Aristotle to the Middle Ages*. Berkeley: University of California Press, 1993.

Musumarra, Carmelo. *La poesia tragica italiana nel Rinascimento*. Florence: Olschki, 1972.

Nemola, Paola Andrioli, Giuseppe Antonio Camerino, Gino Rizzo, and Paolo Viti, eds. *Teatro, scena, rappresentazione dal Quattrocento al Settecento: Atti del convegno internazionale di studi, Lecce, 15–17 maggio 1997*. Galatina: Congedo, 2000.

Perosa, Alessandro. *Teatro umanistico*. Milan: Nuova Accademia Editrice, 1965.

Pittalunga, Stefano. *La scena interdetta. Teatro e letteratura fra medioevo e umanesimo*. Napoli: Liguori Editore, 2002.

La Rinascita della tragedia nell'Italia dell'Umanesimo. Atti del IV Convegno di Studio, Viterbo, 15–16–17 giugno 1979, Centro di studi sul teatro medioevale e rinascimentale E.P.T. di Viterbo. Viterbo: Amminstrazione Provinciale di Viterbo, 1980.

Staüble, Antonio. "L'idea di tragedia nell'umanesimo." In Staüble's *Parlar per lettera: Il pedante nella commedia del Cinquecento e altri saggi su teatro rinascimentale*, pp. 205–6. Rome: Bulzoni, 1991.

Witt, Ronald G. *In the Footsteps of the Ancients: The Origins of Humanism from Lovato to Bruni*. Leiden: Brill, 2000.

Index of Citations

General Index

Publication of this volume has been made possible by

The Myron and Sheila Gilmore Publication Fund at I Tatti
The Robert Lehman Endowment Fund
The Jean-François Malle Scholarly Programs and Publications Fund
The Andrew W. Mellon Scholarly Publications Fund
The Craig and Barbara Smyth Fund
for Scholarly Programs and Publications
The Lila Wallace–Reader's Digest Endowment Fund
The Malcolm Wiener Fund for Scholarly Programs and Publications